750

MacArthur's
Victory

MacArthur's
Victory

The War in New Guinea,
1943–1944

HARRY A. GAILEY

PRESIDIO PRESS

BALLANTINE BOOKS • NEW YORK

To my son,
Major Richard D. Gailey

A Presidio Press Book
Published by The Random House Publishing Group

www.presidiopress.com

LIBRARY OF CONGRESS CATALOGING-IN- PUBLICATION DATA
Gailey, Harry A.
MacArthur's victory: the war in New Guinea, 1943–1944 / Harry A. Gailey.
p. cm.
Includes bibliographical references and index.
ISBN 0-345-46386-2
1. World War, 1939–1945—Campaigns—New Guinea. I. Title.
D767.95.G37 2004   940.54′265—dc22   2004040062

Text design by Joseph Rutt

Maps by Philip Schwartzberg, Meridian Mapping, Minneapolis

Manufactured in the United States of America

First Edition: December 2004

2 4 6 8 9 7 5 3 1

CONTENTS

LIST OF MAPS

ABBREVIATIONS

Aircraft
  United States
    A-20 (Havoc), Douglas medium bomber
    B-17 (Flying Fortress), Boeing heavy bomber
    B-24 (Liberator), Consolidated heavy bomber
    B-25 (Mitchell), North American medium bomber
    B-26 (Marauder), Martin medium bomber
    C-47 (Skytrain, Dakota), twin-engine transport
    P-38 (Lightning), Lockheed twin-engine fighter
    P-39 (Aircobra), Bell fighter
    P-40 (Warhawk), Curtiss fighter
    P-47 (Thunderbolt), Republic fighter
    PBY (Catalina), Consolidated patrol bomber
  Japanese
    Oscar, Nakajima army fighter
    Zeke (Zero), navy and army fighter

AKA   Attack cargo ship

APA   Attack transport

APD   Destroyer transport

BAR   Browning automatic rifle

CNO   Chief of naval operations

CP   Command post

D-day   Invasion day

DUKW   "Duck," six-wheeled amphibious vehicle

G-2   Intelligence Office

GHQ   General Headquarters

H-hour   Designated hour for invasion

JCS   Joint Chiefs of Staff

KIA   Killed in action

LCI   Landing craft infantry

LCP   Landing craft personnel

LCT   Landing craft tank

LCVP   Landing craft vehicle and personnel

LST   Landing ship tank

M-4   Sherman medium tank

RAAF   Royal Australian Air Force

SWPA   southwest Pacific area

Ultra   Major code-breaking system

WIA   Wounded in action

MacArthur's
Victory

One

OFFENSIVE PREPARATIONS

General Douglas MacArthur and his U.S. and Australian staffs could congratulate themselves in early January 1943 on having wrested the initiative from the Japanese. In conjunction with the naval and ground forces in the eastern Solomon Islands, the threat to Australia, once so feared, had been removed. Allied air forces, particularly the Fifth Air Force, dominated the skies over Papua New Guinea, and made systematic regular raids on the Japanese strongholds at Rabaul on New Britain. The Japanese attempt to take Port Moresby by crossing the Owen Stanley Mountains along the Kokoda Trail had been halted within sight of the objective. In a bloody six-month advance, the Australians had reversed the situation and driven the Japanese back along the trail toward the north coast of Papua. Another attempt to take Port Moresby was foiled in August by the Australians at Milne Bay. MacArthur committed the green troops of the 32nd Division in an attempt to quickly capture the Japanese stronghold of Buna. Without adequate artillery or naval support, the U.S. troops, augmented by Australians, fought a bloody and at times seemingly fruitless campaign against fanatical Japanese resistance in the swamps around Buna. Ultimately they would succeed. The last major defensive position in the Buna region fell on January 22.[1]

At the same time, the Australians drove the remnants of the Kokoda invasion force into enclaves at Sanananda and Gona. These were systematically reduced, with massive losses to the Japanese. In total the Japanese lost approximately 12,000 men from an original 18,000 committed to the invasion. The victory was also costly for the Allies. The Australians had suffered 2,037 killed and 3,533 wounded. The U.S. losses amounted to 847 killed and 1,918 wounded.[2] These figures are misleading since tropical disease took such a toll that a large percentage of Allied troops engaged were rendered unfit for immediate duty. Nevertheless, despite tactical mistakes, MacArthur was in possession of valuable bases on the north coast. Oro Bay would become a major area for mounting later operations. The airfields, particularly that at Dobodura, would be invaluable to the Allies' continued dominance of the air. However, MacArthur was still plagued by many of the problems he had wrestled with since assuming command of the Southwest Pacific Theater in April 1942.

The first and most pressing problem continued to be the need to increase the number of troops available for future operations. Secondarily, he needed to be assured of the requisite supplies, particularly landing craft, if he were to launch any amphibious operations against Japanese positions at Lae, Salamaua, Wewak, and Hollandia. In late August, MacArthur returned to the question of the need for more troops and ships. He wrote Army Chief of Staff George C. Marshall that without additional naval and ground forces, there would arise "a situation similar to those that have successfully overwhelmed our forces in the Pacific since the beginning of the war."[3] The continuing pleas of Australian Prime Minister John Curtin and MacArthur for more troops were silenced on

September 16 by President Franklin D. Roosevelt, who in a communication to MacArthur agreed with the Combined Chiefs of Staff that his present armed forces were "sufficient to defeat the present Japanese force in New Guinea and to provide the security of Australia against an invasion."[4] The Southwest Pacific Theater would remain subordinate to all others.

Much to MacArthur's chagrin, the Southwest Pacific Theater was from the first viewed by Washington and the Joint Chiefs as tertiary to the European and South Pacific Theaters. MacArthur had imagined before his arrival in Australia in March 1942 that a large number of combat troops would be waiting for him and that reinforcements and supplies that would enable him to immediately take the offensive would be quickly forthcoming. He discovered that not only did he not have any prospects for an immediate substantive augmentation to his forces, but also that his appointment as supreme commander was being held up by opposition from Admiral Ernest King, chief of naval operations, who maintained that command should go to a naval officer. This would set the tone for the difficult relations with the Navy that would persist throughout the war.

Even after his command had been approved, MacArthur encountered continuous opposition in Washington to his requests for more troops. After a series of communications with Marshall over a period of months, he was bluntly informed that few troops could be spared from the European buildup. His and Curtin's requests for a return of all Australian divisions then in Europe and North Africa were met at first with excuses. British Prime Minister Winston Churchill feared that the removal of Australian units from North Africa would seriously damage an already weakened front.[5] Ultimately most of the Australian divisions were released, but at first only the 7th Division and one brigade of the 6th were returned. As a belated recognition to Australia's vulnerability, two U.S. Army divisions were sent. The 41st and 32nd Divisions, ill prepared for warfare in New Guinea, had arrived by May. The protracted battle for Buna reduced the effectiveness of the 32nd so much that in January 1943 it was ordered back to Australia, where the bulk of reinforcements received in early 1943 would be used to replace those lost. The 41st Division, although having suffered during the latter stages of the Buna campaign, was kept in the vicinity of Buna. Elements of this division were used to pursue the remnants of the Japanese garrisons up the coastline. Two Australian divisions that had been used on the Kokoda Trail were also available in the Sanananda region and at Milne Bay. They, too, had suffered heavy battle casualties, and a large portion of these troops also suffered from malaria. There was also a small contingent of Australians, the Kanga Force, based at Wau in the interior from Lae. Most of the other Australian units then in training would not be immediately available for offensive action since the Australian government insisted on retaining a large defensive force in Australia.[6]

In March 1943, at the time of the Pacific Military Conference in Washington, D.C., which was attempting to devise a Pacific strategy, MacArthur's force had been augmented by the 1st Marine Division, which was refitting after its bloody battle in Guadalcanal. However, he was informed that this unit would not be permanently assigned and was needed for the contemplated island campaigns in the central Pacific. Of the total of 374,000 U.S. troops in the Pacific, more than half were on garrison duty and were to be utilized in the planned-for campaigns in the central Solomons. The answer from Marshall, brought back by Major General Richard Sutherland, MacArthur's representative to the Washington conference, was that, given the situation elsewhere, MacArthur would simply have to make do.[7]

MacArthur's problems with the Navy existed at a number of different levels. At the highest was the opposition of Admiral King to MacArthur's appointment. (Later, King would be the most active opponent to MacArthur's strategy of liberating the Philippines.) As chief of naval operations, King was committed to building the big blue-water Navy based on Hawaii under Admiral Chester A. Nimitz's command. The goal of this fleet would be to defeat the Japanese navy and support the seizure of island stepping-stones in the central Pacific. This strategy was in dramatic opposition to MacArthur's plans.[8] Thus it was obvious that the Navy would not approve the transfer of any significant number of capital ships from Nimitz's command to MacArthur's. Even when it became necessary for major fleet units to support actions in the southwest Pacific, these were only loaned and were never totally assigned to MacArthur.

MacArthur had real as well as imagined problems with the U.S. naval commanders. When he arrived in Australia, he inherited commanders not of his choosing. One of these was Vice Admiral Herbert Leary, who had only token forces made up of a few submarines, smaller U.S. craft, and the tiny Australian fleet. It was obvious that MacArthur did not appreciate Leary's problems, which were compounded by King's insistence that he communicate directly with Nimitz without immediate reference to MacArthur. The situation was not improved when Leary was replaced in September 1942 by Vice Admiral Arthur Carpender, who suffered from the same problems of lack of ships and a divided command structure. Personalities obviously played a part in the tension between MacArthur and Carpender, but there were significant differences in the way they felt the small naval force should be used. For the Navy in the latter months of 1942, the most important campaign was Guadalcanal, and MacArthur was ordered to share his meager air and naval units with Vice Admiral Robert Ghormley. MacArthur's main naval contingent, the Australian cruisers *Australia, Canberra,* and *Hobart,* were shifted to the Solomons and took part in a series of important naval operations there, including the disastrous battle of Savo Island, in which the *Australia* was sunk. Nimitz even wanted the submarines based in Australia placed under his control for the Guadalcanal campaign. MacArthur protested vehemently to the Joint Chiefs but to no avail. The submarines were transferred.[9] The main elements of "MacArthur's navy" were not returned to his command until after the major actions on Guadalcanal had been completed.

The Buna campaign was fought almost entirely without naval support. The ostensible reasons were the lack of good charts showing the reefs and the proximity of Japanese airpower. The supply of men and matériel to the Buna-Gona region was provided mainly by small craft run by a Dutch maritime company. General Sir Thomas Blamey, commander of the Allied ground forces, requested a number of times that the Navy dispatch at least a destroyer whose guns could support the infantry attacks. His dissatisfaction with the Navy mirrored MacArthur's when he pointed to the dire situation facing the ground troops in November 1942. He noted, "The attitude of the Navy in regard to the destroyers appears to avoid risk at a time when all services should give a maximum of cooperation to defeat the enemy."[10] After considerable delay Carpender reported to MacArthur that his naval experts had vetoed sending any capital ships into the area until more was known of the reefs. Thus the men of the 32nd Division had to attack the entrenched Japanese without artillery or naval gun support. A contrast in commanders can be seen in the actions of Vice Admiral William Halsey, Ghormley's successor, who concluded that his major task at Guadalcanal was to support the ground troops and committed all his resources to that end. One observer later reported that if only a token naval force had been available for the assaults at Buna, the Japanese could have been driven out within a few weeks instead of months.[11]

MacArthur's navy was not improved by the designation of this small naval force as the Seventh Fleet on March 15, 1943. The mainstay of the fleet was the two remaining Australian cruisers and one U.S. light cruiser. By contrast, Halsey's Third Fleet consisted of five carriers, six battleships, and thirteen cruisers.[12] An example of

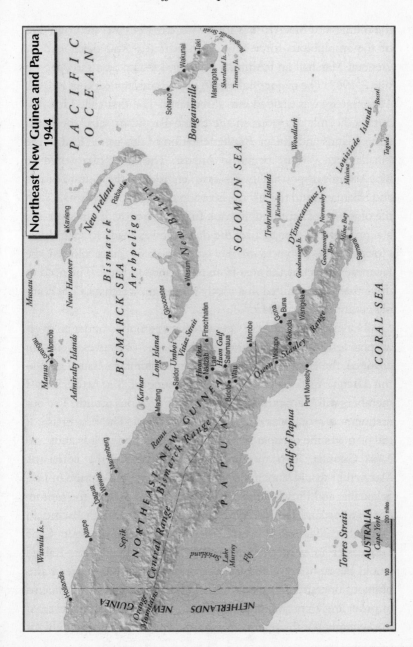

Northeast New Guinea and Papua
1944

the thinness of MacArthur's forces in early 1943 was the condition of the amphibious force. The overall strategy was developed by General Marshall and Admiral King and issued as a directive on July 2, 1942. The major goal was to isolate and later capture Rabaul. The strategy was divided into three tasks. The first called for Admiral Ghormley's troops in the South Pacific to seize the Santa Cruz Islands and Tulagi. Implementation of this would lead to the Guadalcanal venture begun in August. The other two would be MacArthur's responsibility. Task two envisioned the capture of Lae and Salamaua, and the last the invasion of eastern New Britain with the objective of capturing Rabaul. In order to provide air cover and a supply base closer to Lae, the decision was made to take Buna. However, the slowness of the occupation of Buna allowed the Japanese to occupy the area from Sanananda to Buna. The need to drive them out resulted in a costly campaign, which was not completed until January 1943.[13]

The planning for these operations was grouped under an overall plan called Elkton. Although the major objectives were not changed, the Elkton plan was revised and ultimately issued as Elkton III on April 26, 1943, after a meeting of MacArthur's staff members with Nimitz at Pearl Harbor the previous month. The operation as a group was code-named Cartwheel. The first phase of the plan was the occupation of Woodlark and Kiriwina Islands and New Georgia. Two months after the start of the offensive, MacArthur would launch the second phase with the capture of Lae, Salamaua, and Finschhafen. Phase three would involve the capture of the Shortland Islands and Bougainville in the South Pacific. In December MacArthur would then send troops to seize Cape Gloucester in western New Britain. Shortly thereafter, Rabaul would be captured.[14] The Cartwheel plan called for thirteen amphibious operations in six months. There were no serious problems in providing ships and landing craft in Nimitz's area. However, at the beginning of the year MacArthur had practically no amphibious equipment or experts in these kinds of operations. The only units available then were the Army's Engineering Special Boat Brigade, which operated a few small craft.

The man who would be responsible for the amphibious assaults during much of the coming campaigns was Rear Admiral Daniel Barbey. On January 10, 1943, he took command of the forces that would later be designated the 7th Amphibious Force. Barbey immediately established good relations with MacArthur, who eventually came to trust him as much as he did his air force commander, General George Kenney. However, Barbey had little to work with. There were no amphibious training facilities available, and therefore he immediately established bases at Toobul Bay, near the mouth of the Brisbane River, and Point Stephens. It was necessary for his permanent party personnel to build their own facilities at each station.

Equipment that was readily available in other theaters was at a premium. As early as mid-1942, MacArthur had requested more small craft and transports, but because of European and central Pacific priorities, little had been done to build up the amphibious capabilities of his command. Even as U.S. and Australian troops arrived, Barbey's officers had to improvise. MacArthur wanted the troops trained in debarking from larger ships down cargo nets to smaller landing craft. However, Barbey did not have an attack transport (APA), which was a key vessel for this kind of operation. A partial solution was to rig the nets from cliffs. The first LSTs and LCTs did not arrive until mid-January, and it was not until Easter Sunday that thirteen LCIs were delivered; this gave little time before the first operations to train crews how to use them.[15] One should not be surprised that the first operation, mounted in late June against Kiriwina and Woodlark Islands and the Huon Gulf, showed a number of serious deficiencies. By then the 7th Amphibious Force had grown to four old destroyers converted as troop carriers, six LSTs, and thirty assorted landing craft. Barbey had received an APA transferred from the South Pacific, and the Australian government had promised him almost all the small metal boats then under construction.[16] With these additional landing craft and more experienced personnel, many of the problems were solved before the September landing of the Australian 9th Division at Lae.

Soon after his arrival in Australia, MacArthur developed an antipathy to his air force commander, Lieutenant General George Brett. This was partly personal and partly an ignorance of how the desperate situation in Australia limited what the Air Force could do. As soon as he could, he replaced Brett with Major General George Kenney, who reported on July 30, 1942. MacArthur soon altered his attitude toward the Air Force, as Kenney and his air commander in New Guinea, Brigadier General Ennis Whitehead, installed a more positive attitude in the personnel in Australia and New Guinea. New airfields were built, and Kenney was able to convince General Henry "Hap" Arnold, the air force commander in Washington, to send more planes of all types to the southwest Pacific. At first the attacks on Japanese bases, particularly Rabaul, were minimal, partially because of the distances involved. Gradually the newly designated Fifth Air Force received better planes, and as the airfields near Port Moresby were improved, the medium-range bombers became more active in striking at Rabaul and in support of the U.S. and Australian actions in the Buna-Sanananda region. By early 1943, the standard bomber was the versatile North American B-25 and Kenney's fighter squadrons were receiving more Lockheed P-38s to replace the older Curtis P-40s and Bell P-39s. The P-38 could match the vaunted Japanese Zero and Oscar fighters. The Japanese concern over Guadalcanal and the central Solomons drew the bulk of the Japanese air force away from Papua and thus while Kenney was still building his airpower, the Fifth Air Force and the Royal Australian Air Force (RAAF) ruled the skies over Papua during the crucial Buna-Sanananda campaign.[17]

The key factor in the success of that campaign was Kenney's transport aircraft. At first he was almost desperate for these planes and at one time took over aircraft from Australian civilian airlines. However, by the fall of 1942 he had enough Douglas C-47s and a few other transports to promise MacArthur that he could transport most of the U.S. 32nd Division to the Buna area. He not only succeeded in delivering the troops, but even before adequate airfields had been provided, his transports were delivering the bulk of supplies needed by the U.S. and Australian ground troops.[18] The airfields, particularly the seven located near Dobodura on the north coast, allowed Whitehead to advance his bomber line to make it easier to attack Rabaul, Lae, and Salamaua. Modifications to the bombers allowed an increase in their range, enabling them to strike Japanese targets that had earlier been considered out of reach. By spring 1943, the number of aircraft of all types available to Kenney had grown to 1,400. Despite the reinforcements made by the Japanese at Rabaul and Wewak, the Allies continued to control the air. Throughout 1942, the larger numbers of available transport aircraft allowed even quicker movement of troops and supplies than at Buna. In March 1943, these once again became the main factor in the Australians' defense of the key village of Wau in the immediate interior of Salamaua.

An ongoing problem for MacArthur was his staff and field command arrangements. It was not only Leary and Brett who caused him concern after he arrived in Australia, but also the defense structure that he inherited. Throughout the year he was busy transferring those who did not meet his standards or whom he did not like. From his perspective he had the nucleus of senior commanders whom he brought from the Philippines. Members of this "Bataan Gang" filled the most important posts on the Southwest Pacific Command staff. He continued the acerbic Major General Richard Sutherland as his chief of staff, with Brigadier General Richard Marshall as his deputy. As his G-2 he kept his Philippine adviser, Colonel Charles Willoughby. Despite suggestions from Marshall and the president, he had no Australian or Dutch officers on his staff. His excuse was that Australia had first call on the few experienced senior officers for its rapidly expanding army. This was false: there were many Australians available, most with more combat experience than the Americans. He simply wanted to be surrounded by men he knew and trusted. He also realized that after the first defensive phase of the war was over, the war would become primarily the United States' responsibility. He did not want to prejudice future operations by having Australians functioning in an organizational system with which they were not familiar.[19]

As soon as he could without causing too much trouble, MacArthur arranged the removal of those whose abilities he questioned. Brett was replaced by Kenney and Leary by Carpender. In August 1942, Major General Robert Eichelberger arrived as commander of I Corps, which at that time consisted only of the 32nd and 41st Divisions. During the Buna operations MacArthur and his staff were critical of the Australian and U.S. commanders. Without having direct knowledge of the actual situation, they criticized the slowness of the campaign along the Kokoda Trail and ultimately removed Major General Harding from command of the 32d Division. Although he had no direct command of the Australian ground forces, MacArthur used his good relations with Prime Minister Curtin to pressure General Thomas Blamey, commander in chief of the Australian army, to remove ground commanders in New Guinea. However mistaken some of these actions were, by the close of 1942 they served the purpose of gaining subordinate commanders of whom he approved.

In February 1943, MacArthur reorganized the command structure of the U.S. forces in Australia. He established the U.S. Army Forces in the Far East (USAFFE) and the Sixth Army. The former was to act as the administrative headquarters for the Sixth Army, which was to supersede I Corps as the senior U.S. force. To command the Sixth Army, MacArthur requested Lieutenant General Walter Krueger, then commanding the Third Army in San Antonio, Texas. This was a surprise not only to Marshall but also to Krueger. Marshall concurred in the appointment, and Krueger was notified on January 13. Krueger, who had by then served forty-three years in the Army, was one of the Army's senior officers. He had commanded 300,000 men of the Third Army in the great Louisiana maneuvers of 1941 against Lieutenant General Benjamin Lear's Second Army. Among other soon-to-be major role players during the war, Colonel Dwight D. Eisenhower had been one of Krueger's senior staff officers. Krueger had concluded that due to his age, he would not have a combat command, and he did not fully understand why MacArthur had selected him. He requested that he take his full Third Army staff with him. This request was denied, although a significant number were transferred. He officially took command of the Sixth Army on February 15 and established his headquarters ten miles west of Brisbane. At first his command consisted of the 32nd Division in Australia and the 41st Division in New Guinea. The 1st Marine Division, then refitting at Melbourne, was also temporarily under his command. In addition, he had the 503rd Parachute Regiment, the 158th Infantry Regiment, the 98th Field Artillery Regiment, and the 40th and 41st Anti-Aircraft Brigades. Later the Sixth Army would be reinforced by the 1st Cavalry Division and the 24th Infantry Division.[20]

MacArthur also created an independent organization that until July was named the New Britain Force and afterward the Alamo Force. Its staff was almost identical to that of the Sixth Army. Ostensibly the new force was to undertake operations against New Britain and the Trobriand Islands, while Blamey's New Guinea Force would be responsible for continuing the campaign there. The reason for this reorganization later became obvious. Krueger would write his conclusion:

The reasons for creating Alamo Force and having it, rather than Sixth Army, conduct operations were not divulged to me. But it was plain that this arrangement would obviate placing Sixth Army under the operational control of CG Allied Land Forces [Blamey], although that army formed part of those forces. Since CG Allied Land Forces, likewise could not exercise administrative command over Sixth Army, it never came under his command at all.[21]

General Krueger's conclusion was borne out by his deputy chief of staff, Major General George Decker, who commented that the Alamo Force had been created "to keep control of Sixth Army units away from General Blamey."[22]

MacArthur's actions with regard to Alamo Force simply reflected his overall negative attitude toward the Australian armed forces despite his good relations with the prime minister and the defense minister, Frederick Shedden. From the first he was unhappy that he had no choice but to accept that the bulk of the fighting in defense of Australia and New Guinea would be done by Australians. In organizing his staff he purposely excluded Australian senior officers, but he had to accept General Blamey as commander of the Allied land forces. This did not mean that he liked the arrangement, and he made sure that no American served on Blamey's staff, in spite of Blamey's requests. By contrast, the headquarters of the Allied air forces had both American and Australian officers. General Eichelberger confirmed MacArthur's antipathy toward the Australians when he later recalled:

> Shortly after I arrived in Australia, General MacArthur ordered me to pay my respects to the Australians and then have nothing further to do with them. This order I carried out to a very large extent throughout my service in or near Australia. I imagine General Krueger, when he took com-

mand of Sixth Army in May [*sic*] 1943, was given similar orders because he was conspicuous in his avoidance of the Australians, either militarily or socially.[23]

During the defense of Port Moresby and the later offensive along the Kokoda Trail, MacArthur and Sutherland criticized the performance of the Australian troops. Without having adequate knowledge of the problems presented, they believed that the slowness of advance was due to lack of aggressiveness and poor leadership. In a series of discussions with Defense Minister Shedden in early January 1943, MacArthur replied to the question of why the Buna-Sanananda campaign had taken so long, completely ignoring the deficiencies of the U.S. troops and concentrating on those of the Australians: "He regretted to state that his criticism of slowness in exploiting advantages and following up opportunities applied to all Australian commanders including General Blamey." He further observed that he believed that "Blamey had an easy time in New Guinea."[24] The successful defense of Milne Bay by the Australians was marred by MacArthur's continuing criticism of Major General Cyril Clowes's tactics even while the action continued.[25]

MacArthur's staff was not alone in criticizing Blamey. One reason given by Major General Robert Richardson, MacArthur's first choice to command I Corps, in turning down the command was his reluctance to serve under Blamey. Blamey also had his detractors in the Australian government and military. MacArthur in his discussions with Shedden intruded into political affairs when he noted without much evidence that Blamey did not "command the fullest support of all in the Australian army." He suggested that Blamey should be made commander in chief of the Home Defense Forces in Australia. In his place Lieutenant General Sir Leslie Morsehead, then returning from commanding the 9th Division in North Africa, should command the Australian part of the Allied Expeditionary Force.[26] MacArthur's suggestions, although considered, were not acted upon. Blamey remained commander of the Allied land forces, and despite the creation of Alamo Force, most of the fighting during 1943 would be undertaken by Australian troops under Blamey's overall command. The bulk of the Allied force during the year would consist of the three Australian Imperial Force (AIF) divisions that constituted the I Australian Corps under Morsehead. The bulk of the corps was at first located in northern Queensland. Blamey's lieutenant as head of the New Guinea Force was Lieutenant General Sir Edmund Herring, who would be in command throughout most of the year. He would be briefly replaced by Lieutenant General Sir Iven MacKay, who had commanded the 6th Division in the Middle East. Herring returned as commander in time for the assault on Lae and Salamaua in early September. General Eichelberger, who had temporarily been in charge of the New Guinea Force after the capture of Buna, returned to the mainland to oversee the refitting of the battered U.S. divisions. Except for relatively minor actions, U.S. troops would not be used extensively during the year.

Long before MacArthur issued his operational orders for Cartwheel on May 8, laying out the Allied goals for the year in New Guinea, Australian army units were engaged in a desperate fight with inadequate forces to hold the key positions around the village of Wau in the interior from Salamaua. If the goal of capturing Lae and Salamaua were to be achieved, any Japanese offensive there would have to be checked. Following this, the Australians would have to gain the ridgelines between Wau and Salamaua.

Two

THE AUSTRALIANS
DEFEND WAU

The Japanese threat to Port Moresby in mid-1942 was thrust not just over the Kokoda Trail and the landings at Milne Bay, but also from the newly occupied bases at Lae and Salamaua on the north coast. From there the Japanese could conceivably mount an offensive against Port Moresby, 150 miles to the south, by occupying the interior areas of the Bulolo and Markham River valleys. Prior to the war this region had been an important gold mining area, with its center at the village of Wau, at an elevation of 3,700 feet. It was possible to exploit the mineral resources there primarily by using airplanes to supply the miners with the most necessary supplies; the mining companies had constructed a series of small airfields for that purpose. The most important was at Wau, with an airstrip 1,100 feet long. Without an airborne supply system it would have been almost impossible to conduct any profitable operations. The high Kuper mountain range, which rose to almost 10,000 feet in places, cut off the coastal centers from the interior, where, in a deep cleft, the Watut and Bulolo Rivers flowed several thousand feet above sea level. The Bulolo passed through Wau before dividing into a number of streams. In the area between Wau and Salamaua were a number of other rivers. In the interior south of Salamaua were the important, wide Bitoi and Francisco Rivers. Further south was the Buisaval River, which flowed northeast before joining the Bitoi a few miles from the key village of Mubo and thence to the Markham River, which flowed to the sea south of Lae.

Travel between villages was made difficult not only by the altitude but by the terrain features. The streams were fast-flowing, and movement had to be up and down the many rocky ravines. The foothills were generally steep and covered with high kunai grass, above which was thick, almost impenetrable jungle. Vines and undergrowth impeded progress, and at places the sun was blocked out by the tree canopy and vines. Any deviation from the established native trails was nearly impossible. The heat and moisture created a perpetually damp, fetid condition all along the trails.

The miners had constructed a motor road from Wau through the village of Bulolo to a camp called Sunshine, located approximately fifteen miles to the northwest. Even this improved road became almost impassable during the heavy rains. Otherwise there were only narrow native trails connecting the villages and mining locations. The interior line of communication with Port Moresby passed through a location to the southwest named Bulldog and along an undeveloped trail to the Lakekuma River and then to the coast, a hundred miles from the town.[1] The other main trails leading east from Wau were the Black Cat Trail and the Buisaval Trail. The former followed the Bitoi River past the Black Cat Mine to Copper House and then through the village of Waipali to Mubo. The Buisaval began at the village of Kaisanik and then ran along the Buisaval River, where it joined the Black Cat at the village of Guadagasal, five miles south of Mubo. To the northeast of Wau, a trail to Powerhouse ascended to 9,000 feet before descending steeply to Pilimung and Missim villages through a cold, wet forest area. It was almost impossible to evacuate wounded over this trail. The trail from Sunshine to the broad, muddy Markham River was very difficult for even healthy troops and could not be used for moving stretcher patients.[2]

The nature of the terrain dictated in large part both the Australian and the Japanese operations. Flanking movements were, as on the Kokoda Trail, nearly impossible; thus it was necessary for the defenders of Wau to confront the enemy along the trails. The oppressive heat, combined with the high altitude, sapped the strength of the troops, and there was a high rate of illness. One Australian commander estimated that only one third of his men were fit for work at any given time.

Supply and reinforcements for the defenders of the Wau region were nightmares, particularly after large numbers of troops were brought in. Fortunately, the airfield at Wau allowed a reasonable level of supplies for most of the defenders later in 1942. However, during much of 1942 there were few transport aircraft available and supply to the Buna-Sanananda area was considered to be more important. Later the changeable weather prevented a regular air supply system to operate. Throughout the first months of the war, supplies had to be carried around the south coast from Port Moresby to the mouth of the Lakekamu River by steamer. From there they were transshipped to smaller craft and moved up the river to the village of Terapo, where they were transferred to canoes for a two-day journey to Bulldog and then made up into fifty-pound loads to be carried to Wau by native carriers. This last journey, over high mountains, normally took seven days.[3]

The problem of supply at Wau was academic for the troops operating along the trails toward Mubo and further on to the vicinity of Lae. Here the supply system could be maintained only by the troops themselves or by native carriers. During the early stages of the defense of Wau, when the Australians were retreating, it was particularly hard to recruit an adequate number of natives to deliver more than a minimum of the most necessary supplies. Men in the forward areas suffered from a chronic lack of food, although it was possible in places to secure some from the native villages. However, good relations with the natives were often difficult since they were aware of the dominance of the Japanese. The situation in July and August 1942 became critical as the Japanese reacted to the Australians' raids on the Salamaua area. Reserve dumps of food were discovered by the Japanese, and their planes made movement along the trails even more hazardous than usual. Recruitment of native laborers and carriers all but ceased, and forward-area troops simply went hungry.

The medical situation, as elsewhere in New Guinea, was extremely challenging. Malaria was epidemic at the lower elevations. Fortunately, those at Wau were protected by the altitude. The only prophylactic for malaria at first was quinine in tablet form, and many soldiers could not tolerate it. Atabrine was not available. The troops also suffered from a variety of tropical skin infections. Many men developed septic sores due to infection from scratches, and their dirty clothing made them liable to rashes and other infections. Food supplies were constantly low, particularly along the trails, and the diet of the troops consisted mainly of bully beef. There were few vegetables or fruits available. Gastritis and diarrhea were common afflictions. In September 1942, the medical officer of the 2/5th Independent Company reported that, measured by a lax standard, of the 117 men he had examined, 29 were not fit for tropical service, and he recommended that they be evacuated to the mainland.[4] A later medical officer surveying 114 men of the company declared only 8 fully fit and 56 temporarily unfit; 12 were so sick that he recommended immediate evacuation.[5]

Medical facilities at first were primitive. There was an advanced dressing station with thirty-five beds under tenting located 1.5 miles southwest of the Wau airfield. By the time of the Japanese offensive in February 1943, it had been expanded to hold 124 patients. At that time a surgical team was also posted forward to the Black Cat Mine area to provide for the wounded forward on the trail. At the height of the action, because of the danger of being outflanked, this group of sixty medical personnel was moved back closer to Wau. Because of the nature of the terrain along most of the trails, removal of wounded to medical stations was difficult. It was hard for even healthy troops to navigate the trails; in places it would take an hour to move a mile. Once a soldier was wounded, he had to be transported along these same trails. Native bearers, when available, were used to move those too seriously wounded to walk, and near Mubo it could take up to twelve bearers to carry a wounded man on a stretcher. A medical officer, Captain B. H. Peterson, described one such operation:

> I took a squad of stretcher bearers forward and two squads of 2/2nd Field Ambulance bearers formed relay posts along the steep, rough, narrow track at intervals of about 300 yards. (100 yards on this track was like a mile.) Anticipating the steepness and difficulty of the track, we used the boat-shaped wire-netting stretchers used by the miners. We could not have evacuated stretcher cases without them as they had to be half slid, half carried down. They had to be strapped in these stretchers as it was. It was very hard work, but the stretcher bearers did a great job.[6]

The most seriously wounded were treated at forward stations and then carried as quickly as possible to Wau, where they were evacuated by air to the better facilities at Port Moresby.

When the Japanese surprised MacArthur and his staff by landing troops at Lae and Salamaua in March 1942, the only force in that vicinity was two companies of the New Guinea Volunteer Rifles (NGVR). The NGVR was composed of civilian residents of New Guinea: gold miners, planters, and government officials. After blowing up vital stores, they retreated into the hilly country behind Salamaua and began harassing the Japanese whenever possible. Later that month, the Australian High Command decided to strengthen the position at Wau and to make the guerrilla operations near the coast more effective. They created a new command called Kanga Force. The most important addition to the NGVR was a part of the 2/5th Independent Company. However, the larger portion of the 2/5th was held at Port Moresby to counter a possible Japanese landing there. After the Battle of the Coral Sea, it was released, and, along with a platoon of the 2/1st Independent Company and a mortar platoon, it was flown to Wau. Immediately the forward elements at Bulolo and near Mubo were reinforced.[7]

Harassing of the Japanese continued until late August, when a strong Japanese force occupied Mubo. The Australian commander at Wau, Lieutenant Colonel N. L. Fleay, estimated that the Japanese strength moving up the trail was approximately 1,000 men. New Guinea Force Headquarters, faced with the crisis along the Kokoda Trail, informed him that he could expect no further reinforcements. There were only thirty men at Mubo, and thus it would be impossible to hold the village. Fleay concluded that the Japanese had every intention of taking Wau. He estimated that if the enemy wished, its advance elements could be at Kaisenik, a village at the beginning of the Buisaval Trail five miles from Wau, within twenty-four hours. Fleay then gave orders to evacuate the trail and to lay waste to the Bulolo Valley. He moved his headquarters to the village of Kudjeru on the Bulldog Trail fifteen miles south of Wau. On September 1, a small Australian patrol advanced to the outskirts of Mubo and observed the Japanese for three weeks. It became obvious that the Japanese, who numbered far fewer than early estimates, had no intention of immediately moving toward Wau. Fleay's order to destroy anything useful to the enemy, however understandable given the situation at the time, meant that the installations and facilities so quickly destroyed had to be reconstructed. Supply to the forces for the next three weeks became even more critical than normal. Thus it was fortunate that the Japanese, in a decision they later regretted, had no intention at that time of undertaking a further push into the Bulolo Valley. The main reason for the occupation of Mubo was merely to send a message to the Australians at the same time as they were landing in the Buna-Gona area.[8]

When it became apparent that the Japanese had no intention of occupying the Bulolo Valley, the Australians moved back to the positions occupied before the retreat and began trying to reorganize their chaotic supply system. At this juncture Fleay authorized an ill-timed attack on Mubo by sixty riflemen. The Japanese were alerted, and the attackers were forced into a fighting retreat. The attack did not change the situation along the trails appreciably, although the raid was estimated to have caused fifty Japanese casualties. On October 4,290 men from the 2/7th Independent Company were flown in to Wau. Most were sent forward immediately to support those of the force who were holding key positions along the trails. The engineering sections were kept busy restoring the damaged hangars, workshops, and power supply at Wau. They also improved the trails and rebuilt the bridges destroyed by Fleay's actions. Except for aggressive patrolling, the situation in the Bulolo Valley remained quiet through December. Meanwhile, the few troops of the 2/5th located on the south bank of the Markham River settled into a routine of patrolling and gathering information on the Japanese in the vicinity of Lae. The lull in fighting in both valleys was welcomed by General Herring at New Guinea Force Headquarters, whose major concern was to destroy the Japanese force entrenched in the Buna-Gona-Sanananda sector. Any major action against the Japanese in the Mubo area would have to wait until those vital areas were well on the way to being captured.[9]

In early January 1943, the relative quiet was broken by the Australians, who planned to use the newly arrived troops to strike at Mubo. The objective was to cause as much damage to the Japanese there as possible. If all went well, they believed it possible to occupy the town. Fleay planned a three-pronged attack, supported by three hundred native carriers. One force of sixty men, commanded by Major T. F. B. MacAdie, was to seize Vicker's Ridge, which dominated the eastern side of the gorge. Another force of forty men was to take the key bridge across the Bitoi that linked Mubo with Vicker's Ridge. Captain N. L. Winning, with a hundred men, would occupy Mat Mat Hill on the western side of the gorge, and from there another section of fifty men would move forward to another key position on Observation Hill, which overlooked the Mubo airfield. A reserve force was retained 1.5 miles down the trail at a key position named the Saddle.

The attack was scheduled to begin at midmorning of January 11, as soon as Winning's men were in position. They were delayed because they had underestimated the difficulty of the terrain. It took more than ten hours of scrambling up the slopes in a driving rain before they were in position. MacAdie, on Vicker's Ridge, waited until 1320 before receiving a signal that the troops on Mat Mat were in position. The first mortar rounds from the Australians on Mat Mat surprised the Japanese, killing a large number. The Australians continued to sweep the area with machine-gun fire. The troops on Observation Hill charged directly into the Japanese gun positions on Garrison Hill. However, mortar fire from Vicker's began to fall too close, and they retired. These successes were not matched by the troops on Mat Mat, who were defeated by the terrain. They could not advance down the steep slopes and were kept out of the fight. MacAdie built a defensive system on Vicker's despite continuing rain and on the thirteenth surprised Japanese reinforcements approaching Mubo, killing a large number. However, poor communications among the various attacking elements convinced Fleay to order a general retreat. Before this could be accomplished, the Japanese, estimated at 350 men, began a systematic attack on MacAdie's force late on the sixteenth. This was con-

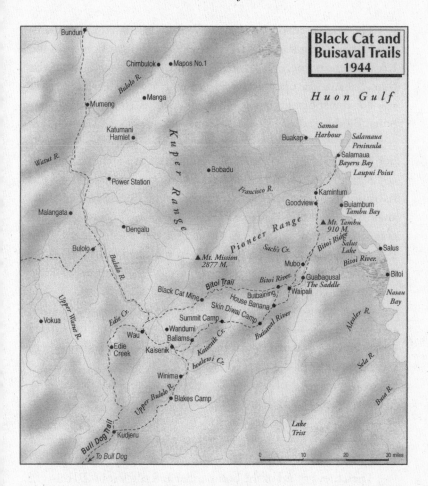

Black Cat and Buisaval Trails 1944

tained, and the Australians began a well-coordinated pullback. By the next day they reached safety, to discover that advance elements of the 17th Brigade had moved into support positions. These troops had been flown in to Wau three days earlier. Fleay's attack on Mubo, although not accomplishing all of its objectives in this operation, showed the Japanese at Lae and Salamaua how much they had erred by not seizing Wau and the other bases in the Bulolo and Markham valleys months before.[10]

The small garrisons of Kanga Force could not have been maintained without air support. Even when the Fifth Air Force and the RAAF were preoccupied with the twin tasks of supporting the Buna-Sanananda operation and striking at Rabaul, there were enough transport aircraft to allow operations from Wau to continue. By the end of the year, Kenney could make a much larger commitment to the Lae-Salamaua sector. The Guadalcanal operation was winding down, and thus bombers from Henderson Field could take over a larger share of attacks on the Solomons and Rabaul. The nearly stalemated situation in the Buna-Sanananda triangle was also almost finished. The Allied air forces could now operate from seven airfields near Port Moresby and three at Milne Bay. The fields at Dobodura had become major forward bases. More supplies and better aircraft had reached the southwest Pacific during the last quarter of the year. Kenney had available six squadrons of medium-range bombers. The older Martin B-26s and Douglas A-20s were being phased out, replaced by the sturdy North American B-25s. Many of these were modified, giving them more firepower.

A former pilot of the 38th Bomb Group recalled the changes made in the B-25 and its use:

> Originally we had a nine-man crew which included a bombardier and we attacked from altitude but with poor results. Then they got rid of the bombardier and stuck four .50 caliber machine guns in the bombardier's compartment and also two in blisters on each side making a total of eight which could spew out a lot of lead very fast. All of the conversions were done in either Australia or in New Guinea.[11]

The bomb racks on these B-25 strafers could carry sixty small fragmentation bombs and six 100-pound demolition bombs. Each plane had tremendous firepower. Pilots were trained in low-level skip bombing at levels of 50 to 75 feet and attacks with delayed-action fuses.[12] The 43rd Bomb Group had fifty-five Boeing B-17s, and in early January the 90th Bomb Group had sixty Consolidated B-24s. The basic fighter plane was the fast, maneuverable Lockheed P-38, which replaced the Bell P-39s and Curtis P-40s, and these could challenge the Japanese Zero fighters. Later models of the P-38, which had auxiliary tanks, could accompany bombers on long-range missions. The attacks on Rabaul forced the Japanese to concentrate their air resources there, leaving the Allies virtual control of the air over Papua. At Rabaul, Lae, and Salamaua, when Japanese planes challenged Allied fighters, they were destroyed at a high rate. Ultimately the Japanese could replace neither the planes nor the pilots.[13]

The Troop Carrier Groups had done yeoman service in shifting thousands of troops to the Buna-Sanananda area and then keeping them supplied during the long, exhausting battle there. The situation had dramatically changed in the months following the Japanese invasion of New Guinea. Then Kenney had had to commandeer Australian civilian aircraft to transport reinforcements to Port Moresby. By early January 1943, the 317th Troop Carrier Group arrived in Australia with fifty-two new C-47s. These were quickly sent forward and shifted to the 374th Group, while the 317th took over the mixed complement of C-47s, C-49s, C-60s, and B-17s.[14]

Faced with mounting losses at Guadalcanal and Buna-Sanananda, General Hitoshi Imamura, commanding the Japanese forces in New Guinea and the Solomons, acting on orders from Imperial Headquarters on January 4, 1943, ordered the evacuation of the remnants of his army from both places. By early February, under the most difficult circumstances, 3,500 troops were evacuated from the Buna-Sanananda area and 13,000 from Guadalcanal. Most of these, however, were sick and exhausted from the fighting, and it would be months before many of the units of the two

Japanese armies could be reconstituted. The Japanese had lost more than 35,000 killed in the futile campaigns.[15] Never again would they enjoy the strategic advantage in the southwest Pacific. However, General Imamura and his deputy, Lieutenant General Hatazo Adachi in New Guinea, had no intention of conceding Papua to the Allies. They decided to reinforce the garrisons at Lae and Salamaua preparatory to an offensive to secure the Bulolo and Markham valleys.

Allied patrol planes noted a heavy concentration of shipping at Rabaul in late December 1942. There were a total of ninety-one ships, including twenty-one warships, there. MacArthur's intelligence group correctly concluded that such a large number of ships indicated that the Japanese were planning to reinforce Lae. This projection proved correct when reconnaissance planes sighted a convoy of two cruisers, four destroyers, and four transports along the south-central coast of New Britain on January 6. These were protected by a Japanese fighter screen. Despite bad weather, Allied bombers attacked the convoy as the fighters challenged the Japanese planes. In the running fight, two transports were sunk and Allied pilots shot down an estimated fifty planes while losing only ten. Despite these heavy attacks, the Japanese were able to reach Lae on the eighth and unloaded an estimated 4,000 troops. The Japanese commander at Lae now had a sufficient number of troops to begin an offensive aimed at Wau and its vital airfield.[16]

The Japanese troops that landed at Lae were from the 51st Division and veterans of the war in China. They were brought from Indochina as a part of General Imamura's strengthening of Japan's remaining bases in New Guinea. The centerpiece of the division was the 102nd Regimental Group, commanded by Major General Teru Okade. There were also transport, medical, and signal units and one battalion of field artillery. Although weakened because of the air attacks, it was a formidable force. After the bulk of the division was ferried to Salamaua, the garrison there amounted to approximately 6,500 men. Okade sent a few hundred men down the coast to help evacuate the survivors of the Buna-Gona battle. The continued aggressive action by the Australians convinced the Japanese High Command to undertake a major offensive against Wau. The commander of this effort undertaken by the 102nd Regiment, with 2,500 men, was Colonel Maruoka. He moved quickly toward Mubo. From there he planned to move toward Wau along a little-used trail between the two main trails. As was the case with the earlier attack toward Port Moresby along the Kokoda Trail, the Japanese knew little of the terrain between Mubo and Wau. They had no maps and did not accurately calculate the time it would take to move troops over the difficult terrain. More important, they did not provide supply dumps. The only supplies the soldiers had were what they could carry.[17]

General Blamey was fully aware of the danger posed by the reinforced garrison at Lae. He wrote to General Herring on the eighth:

> Whether the intention of this force is to push forward from the Lae and Salamaua area towards Wau remains to be seen. This event has always been present in my mind and I have kept the 17th Brigade A.I.F. intact either to meet this threat or as the spearhead of an advance in this area.[18]

In this dispatch he laid out his plans for the disposition of Allied forces in New Guinea. The U.S. 41st Division would be retained in the Buna area, while the battered 32nd was withdrawn to the mainland for refitting and training. It would be replaced by two Australian brigades, one of which would replace the 17th Brigade at Milne Bay. The 17th, under the command of Brigadier Murray J. Moten, would be sent to defend Wau and its approaches. This scheme depended upon the quick delivery of the 2/6th and 2/7th

Battalions. On the thirteenth, leading elements of the 2/6th were landed at Wau, and the following day another ten transports landed. However, bad weather the next few days hampered the buildup. On the fifteenth, six aircraft carrying Moten and the main section of his headquarters were forced back to Port Moresby. Despite the weather and the dangerous landing zone, the bulk of the 2/6th, a total of 28 officers and 535 men, were landed by the nineteenth. Clearing weather enabled the rest of the 2/6th and leading elements of Moten's second battalion, the 2/5th, to arrive. Moten immediately sent Lieutenant Colonel P. D. S. Starr, commanding the 2/5th, with that portion of his battalion down the trail to the Mubo area. The 2/6th was given the task of defending the Bulolo valley.[19]

General Herring promised that he would expedite the movement of the rest of the 2/5th. The main body of that battalion arrived on the twenty-seventh. Moten believed that the recent forward movement of the Japanese in the Guadagasal Gap area was purely defensive and that there was no cause for worry about the security of Wau. He had noted this in a dispatch to Blamey, stating, "The raid on Mubo has undoubtedly disturbed him [the Japanese commander] and I feel he fears that it may be a preliminary to an attack on Salamaua similar in strength to those which have defeated him at Buna and Sanananda."[20]

This sanguine conclusion was immediately proven wrong. On the twenty-fourth, Captain Winning's patrols confirmed that the Japanese were moving toward Wandumi village along a seldom-used trail that was almost totally covered by vegetation that paralleled the Black Cat Trail. Brigadier Moten decided to use the 2/6th in an offensive launched from the Black Cat Mine area with the objective of destroying the advancing Japanese between the Black Cat and House Copper. This was forestalled by the difficult terrain and the Japanese commander, who used the main trails to confuse the Australians. On the twenty-seventh they struck a company of the 2/6th one mile north of Wandumi. The Australians were forced back and established a defensive position in the high grass. They kept the Japanese force at bay for forty-eight hours. This stand gave the Australians time to fly in more troops of the 2/5th and 2/7th, although bad weather prevented the bulk of the 2/7th from leaving Port Moresby. On the twenty-sixth, fifty-seven transport planes landed troops and supplies at Wau, and the next day an additional sixty-five planes braved small-arms fire to bring in troops, artillery pieces, and field ambulance teams.[21] In another of its many errors, the Japanese air force did not attempt to disrupt the air transports until later, after the Japanese were beaten and retreating. Then it lost forty-one planes to Australian and U.S. fighters in a two-hour air battle.[22]

The Japanese plan was to use the 1st and 2nd Battalions and keep the 3rd in reserve. After taking Wandumi, the Japanese force would divide, one part forming the right flank following the Bulolo River to attack Wau from the northeast. The other would advance along the main road. Headquarters was to be established along Crystal Creek. The Japanese plans began to unravel quickly as the Australians attacked the advancing column before Mubo, causing 116 casualties. There was continual heavy fighting along the Bulolo River and on the Crystal Creek road as the Australians retreated to defensive positions around Wau. Lieutenant Colonel Seki's 2nd Battalion, advancing along the main road, was held up by the Australians for forty-eight hours near Wandumi, suffering seventy-five casualties, among whom was the commanding officer. Wings of the Japanese attack were mauled by strafing by Allied planes.[23] On the twenty-eighth, a contingent of approximately sixty Japanese moving along the Crystal Creek road got within four hundred yards of the airfield before being discovered and destroyed. One problem facing Colonel Maruoka was that a key battalion ran into steep ravines and did not reach its battle positions until too late to affect the outcome. Nevertheless, a general attack was planned for the following day. This was thwarted by the arrival of the transport planes bringing in a total of eight hundred more troops of the 2/5th and 2/7th. They were rushed into defensive positions. Two twenty-five-pound artillery pieces were also landed and quickly reassembled, ready to take part in the defense by early afternoon of the thirtieth.

Moten ordered the 2/7th to counterattack toward the Japanese position at Leahy's Farm. One section of the battalion occupied the high ground to the west of the farm, while the larger group advanced toward a key spur under artillery and mortar support. This company, commanded by Major K. R. Walker, was pinned down momentarily by heavy machine-gun fire. At this juncture an estimated four hundred Japanese, seemingly oblivious to the Australians, began to move along the road from Leahy's Farm. When they drew close, Walker's men, augmented by artillery, poured heavy fire into the Japanese column, killing a large number. Within minutes Australian Beaufighters swept in and added to the carnage. Despite these losses, the Japanese held firm and stopped Walker's further advance while the men to the west of the farm were blocked by the terrain and heavy vegetation.[24]

Fighting for the next few days was confused and centered on the defense of Wau against the main Japanese thrusts from the southwest. Reinforcements continued to arrive, so that by February 1 Moten had 201 officers and 2,965 soldiers of other ranks. The Australians actively patrolled the Black Cat and the new lateral trail discovered by the Japanese, which was named the Jap Trail. Although the greatest threat to Wau was in the Crystal Creek area, where the 2/5th Battalion was blocking the Japanese, small units nevertheless attacked the Japanese near Leahy's Farm and the Black Cat Mine. On the third, Moten notified New Guinea Force Headquarters that the crucial period in the defense of Wau had passed and he was releasing a larger portion of his force for offensive operations. A new trail was cut eastward to the Jap Trail above the junction, to be used as an approach to cut off the Japanese retreating down the trail. The small-unit actions were successful, and on the fifth the Australians took Leahy's Farm and burned any buildings that later might prove useful to the enemy.[25] Illustrating the lack of cooperation between the Japanese air force and its ground troops was the belated attack on Wau on the morning of the sixth. Eight P-39s on routine escort duty of a flight of C-47s stumbled into the midst of the Japanese attackers. The Allied pilots claimed to have destroyed eleven planes. Shortly afterward, a flight of eight P-40s swooped down on the planes bombing the airfield and shot down a further seven planes. Later in the day Allied pilots claimed another five planes. Thus, in this day's engagement, the Japanese lost twenty-three aircraft and did only minimal damage to the airfield.[26]

The Australians soon reached the main Japanese headquarters area in the Crystal Creek region near the junction of the Wau road and the trail to Wandumi village. On the morning of the ninth, two companies of the 2/5th began a series of attacks against these defenses. Backed by mortars and machine guns, the Australians systematically reduced the Japanese strongpoints, killing an estimated 250 troops.[27] With the reduction of the Japanese positions in the Crystal Creek area, the destruction of the Japanese in the Wau valley was complete. By then the defense of Wau had cost the Australians 207 casualties. As was true elsewhere in New Guinea, the sick far outnumbered the battle casualties. Medical officers reported a total of 335 sick. The actual number was probably many more.[28]

By the end of February, the Australians controlled the area from Waipali to Buibaining as well as much of the Mubo valley. Vigorous patrolling and setting of ambushes was all the Australian High Command had authorized because they did not have a sufficient force to undertake further major offensive operations. In early March, General MacKay communicated his fears to Blamey that the Japanese would try once more to capture Wau. He believed that even with the projected arrival of the 4th and 15th Brigades he would be outnumbered. MacKay estimated that the Japanese still had 7,500 men in the Lae-Salamaua area and were maintaining strong defenses in the Mubo region and southeast of Missim. He therefore planned to restrict activity to patrolling, to prevent the Japanese from moving back toward Wau, and to building up his defenses, particularly near the airfields. Patrols were also active in the Markham valley regions, and permanent bases had been established on some of the heights near Mubo and the Bitoi River region.[29]

Supply continued to be a major problem, although the increase in the number of aircraft at the Dobodura airfields near Buna made it easier to bring in men and matériel to Wau. In early February, General Whitehead confided to MacKay that his two squadrons of eighteen operating planes were pressed to the utmost and that bad weather was greatly restricting the ability of the Air Force to increase the amounts delivered. He correctly projected that the bad weather would continue for the next six weeks, which would mean that under the best of circumstances, there would be only a two-hour window each day for the delivery of supplies and reinforcements.[30]

Attempting to improve the supply situation, in early January General Blamey had authorized the construction of a Jeep trail from Bulldog to Wau. During the previous fall, surveyors had reported that the best route would be to follow the Elva River as far as Kudjeri. This was altered late in the upper reaches, when it was discovered that the terrain was too formidable. Instead, from Center Camp it diverged to the northwest through Ecclestone Saddle. Work was begun at both ends; that from Bulldog was begun first, with native workers doing most of the work. Retention of the natives proved difficult since the work was hard and the weather miserable. The 9th Field Company, aided by more than 500 natives, was responsible for the work from Wau to the Ecclestone area. It would take four months to complete the sixty-eight-mile trail. The highest elevation of the trail was 9,800 feet. Another Jeep trail to

Summit was begun later. Although these trails were an improvement over previous native trails, they tended to break down during the heaviest rains.[31]

By early April, the Australians increased the tempo of their activities. In the Mubo area, the 2/7th Battalion relieved the 2/5th and the independent company occupying the heights called the Saddle and Vicker's Ridge and artillery was emplaced on the Saddle. Interdiction of the Japanese positions near Mubo was restricted because of the shortage of ammunition. On the twentieth, the Australians attacked a heavily timbered Japanese position on Green Hill. Its possession would later prove valuable for an attack on the fortified positions on Observation Hill. On April 23, Major General Stanley Savige of the 3rd Division opened his headquarters at Bulolo. Kanga Force was dissolved; henceforth the 3rd Division would be responsible for action in the Wau-Lae-Markham area. This showed that with the Buna-Sanananda area pacified, Blamey was prepared, with more troops, to take a more active offensive role against the Japanese.

While the focus during the previous months had been on the defense of Wau, the Australians had also maintained a small force eleven miles from Salamaua to guard the entrance to the Markham valley. There the 2/3rd Independent Company was located in the vicinity of Missim village along the Francisco River on the trail between Powerhouse and Salamaua. In early April, they began a systematic reconnaissance of the area and established staging camps preparatory to a platoon-sized attack on Komiatum village to the southeast. This was made on the fourteenth, and much to their surprise, they found no Japanese there. They later found that this was not Komiatum, which in fact was located a few miles away. Attacks on the second village were halted by the terrain and bush cover. However, on the night of the twenty-first they ambushed a column of Japanese, estimated at sixty soldiers, near the village, killing approximately twenty and wounding fifteen. Soon after, the commander of the 2/3rd was notified by Moten of the impending offensive against Mubo, which was to begin on the twenty-fourth. His unit was to cooperate by harassing the Japanese southwest toward Mubo as the main effort was directed against the enclave and the strong positions on the heights around the town. This action was postponed until more men could be shifted to the area. The 15th Brigade arrived on June 8. It would be used in conjunction with an amphibious landing by U.S. troops to reduce the Japanese presence in the immediate interior from Lae and Salamaua.[32]

This offensive was dictated by the March 28 directive from the Joint Chiefs of Staff and was a part of General MacArthur's Elkton III plan for subsequent operations in New Guinea. By this time, the portents for success in driving the Japanese from the Mubo area were excellent. Allied airpower was dominant, although the Japanese could still stage air attacks on installations at Wau, Milne Bay, Dobodura, and even Port Moresby. However, these raids basically had only a nuisance value. The Japanese garrisons at Mubo and Salamaua were all but isolated. The Battle of the Bismarck Sea in March had convinced the Japanese High Command to stop any major efforts to aid them. The Japanese forces were left to their own devices to confront the ever-increasing Allied power. The capture of Lae and Salamaua would be only a matter of time.

Three

THE BISMARCK SEA BATTLE
AND CARTWHEEL
PRELIMINARIES

Allied success during the campaign for Buna-Gona had depended largely upon control of the air, and this would continue to be a vital factor in all subsequent operations. The Japanese, from their major air and naval base at Rabaul, posed an ongoing threat to that superiority and proved a continual worry for MacArthur. Blanche Bay provided the Japanese one of the best natural harbors in the southern Pacific. Encircled by hills, it was six miles long and two and one-half miles wide. It and three other extensive harbors could provide anchorage for a large number of ships. Seven wharves provided service for many ships. At one time as many as sixty ships had been noted in the harbors. The Japanese had built extensive service facilities, and these and the harbor were heavily defended by more than three hundred antiaircraft guns. By the fall of 1943, the Japanese had 97,870 men stationed at Rabaul, the majority of whom were army troops. Nevertheless, the Southern Fleet Force had more than 21,000 men there under the command of Vice Admiral Jinichi Kusaka. The air strength at Rabaul varied depending on the reinforcements provided by the Combined Fleet, but in early 1943 there were enough to constitute a major threat to Allied operations if utilized properly.[1]

From the beginning MacArthur was deeply concerned about Rabaul. Theoretically he had a number of options on how to negate the Japanese threat. In mid-1942, despite earlier objections to seizing a base in the southern Solomons because of paucity of forces, he proposed a full-scale attack on New Britain to seize Rabaul. In order to accomplish this, he requested a major augmentation to his land force and the buildup of a large naval force. It is difficult to know how serious he was, given the weakness of his amphibious capability and the lack of charts of the coral reefs available at that time. Taken at face value, it would indicate a complete lack of understanding of the military situation in mid-1942. In all probability his proposal was simply a part of his frantic attempts to get more ships and men at a critical time. General Marshall and the Joint Chiefs did not seriously consider MacArthur's proposal and continued to dole out quantities of supplies and men to the southwest Pacific far under MacArthur's requests. However, well into 1943 MacArthur insisted on an invasion of eastern New Britain. He disagreed with the decision to use airpower to negate Rabaul. Despite the long-drawn-out, bloody campaign for Buna, he declared that the decision to bypass Rabaul would "go down in history as one of times' greatest military mistakes."[2] Later he not only agreed to the bypass strategy but claimed it had been a part of his strategic plans.[3]

However questionable MacArthur's early suggestions were, there was no doubt of Rabaul's importance and the need for the Allies to neutralize the Japanese threat there. It was the major Japanese base in the southern Pacific, providing anchorage for main elements of their fleet, and the naval air forces operating from five airfields covered all the major operations in the eastern and central Solomons. Most of the planes stationed there belonged to the Eleventh Air Fleet. Fortunately for MacArthur and his air commanders, there was not a unified command at Rabaul. Although the Army and naval senior commanders cooperated on a friendly basis, their plans and objectives were often counterproductive. The Army had fewer planes regularly based at Rabaul, and it was its responsibility to cover operations in New Guinea. Throughout 1943, the naval air force was primarily concerned with the ongoing Solomons campaigns, in which they would eventually lose 393 planes and irreplaceable pilots. Thus, throughout the first half of 1943, the Fifth Air Force had to contend with only a fraction of Japanese airpower.

During the first year, the attacks directly on Rabaul by Kenney's airmen were minimal mainly because the shortage of aircraft dictated a concentration on support of the ground attacks in the Buna-Sanananda sector. Another factor was that after the conclusion of the Guadalcanal campaign, the Thirteenth Air Force's heavy bombers took over the majority role in neutralizing Rabaul. The continual air strikes by both U.S. air forces forced the Japanese to continue with the tactical plans and defend the port and also support the ground activity in the central Solomons.[4] Only after the loss of Lae and Salamaua would the Japanese rebuild the airfield at Wewak, and between August and October they would send 250 planes of the Fourth Air Army there. The strategy to bring a significant air presence to protect the remaining enclaves in New Guinea, however well thought out, was late and would not prove a major deterrent to Allied control of the air.

The best illustration of the inability of the Japanese to provide air cover for major operations was their disastrous attempt to reinforce their Lae and Salamaua garrisons. The advance of the Australians toward Mubo after the defeat of the Japanese at Wau and the planned-for offensive against Lae was made possible by the devastating losses in early March suffered by the Japanese convoy containing reinforcements during the Battle of the Bismarck Sea. This ensured the isolation of the Japanese garrisons in Papua. By mid-February 1943, the Japanese commanders at Rabaul, Lieutenant General Imamura and Vice Admiral Kusaka, recognized the need to reinforce their units at Lae, Salamaua, and Wewak. On February 19, a three-ship convoy made an unmolested voyage to Wewak. This emboldened the Japanese to brave Allies' aerial superiority and send a major force of combat-experienced troops to the Lae-Salamaua area. The Air Force would give the convoy cover as it reached areas dominated by the Fifth Air Force. Vice Admiral Gunichi Mikawa, advising Kusaka, estimated that in the worst case, half of the reinforcements would get through.[5]

On February 28, a convoy of sixteen ships commanded by Rear Admiral Masatomi Kamura set out from Rabaul. Six of these were transports, one was a tanker, and the other was loaded with much-needed supplies. All were combat loaded so that supplies and men could quickly be off-loaded in order to minimize turnaround time. A total of approximately 7,000 soldiers, mostly from the 115th Regiment of the 51st Division, and a small number of marines were crowded on the transports, which were guarded by eight destroyers. Lieutenant General Hatazo Adachi, commander of the Japanese Eighth Army, and his staff were on board one of the accompanying destroyers while Lieutenant General Hidemitsu Nakano, commander of the 51st Division, and his staff were on another.[6]

The planned route was along the north coast of New Britain to the Bismarck Sea to Cape Gloucester and thence through the Vitiaz Strait to the Huon Gulf. The Japanese believed that their movement would be masked by bad weather. However, in the late afternoon of March 1, the convoy was spotted by a B-24 patrol bomber that gave the alarm. Despite attempts to shadow the convoy, it was lost five hours later. At this time General Kenney had 207 bombers and 119 fighters available in New Guinea. He and his deputy, Major General Whitehead, had already planned for a massive attack. Now he authorized an all-out effort directed against the convoy.

The convoy was not located again until 8:15 A.M., on March 2 as it prepared to enter Dampier Strait. Eight B-17s promptly took off to attack it. Twenty more soon followed, and at approximately 10:15 the first flight dropped its 1,000-pound bombs from an altitude of 6,500 feet. Within the hour the second, larger flight also attacked. Although their claims were exaggerated and conflicting, it was confirmed that the large transport *Kyokusei Maru* had been sunk and two others damaged.

Two destroyers rushed in and rescued the survivors and were then ordered to race ahead to Lae to unload the 850 men who had been saved. The destroyers soon left Lae to rejoin the convoy, which continued on its course eastward as if the earlier attack had not been a portent of future major air attacks. A further strike was made late in the afternoon as the convoy entered the Vitiaz Strait and registered two hits. The convoy of thirteen ships entered the Vitiaz Strait shadowed by an Australian PBY that kept Allied headquarters informed of its position. By dawn of the third, joined by the two destroyers, it was on a direct course toward the Huon Gulf, only ninety miles away.[7]

On the morning of the third, the convoy, now spread out, was within easy range of a variety of Allied aircraft. The first attack that day was made by RAAF Beaufort medium bombers carrying torpedoes. It met with little success. However, by midmorning, thirteen heavily armed Beaufighters arrived and, flying at five hundred feet, raked the convoy with cannon and machine-gun fire. At the same time, thirteen B-17s dropped their bombs on individual targets as conventional B-25s swept in at medium altitude. The Japanese air cover of approximately forty Zeros was too high to provide a good defense against these attacks, and they were quickly engaged by Allied fighters. The final and most damaging attack of the morning came from the modified B-25s with their forward-firing .50-caliber machine guns striking at individual targets. They dropped their 500-pound bombs, whose fuses had been set for a five-second delay. Out of thirty-seven bombs dropped, it was reported that twenty-eight scored. The attacks by B-17s and B-25s continued during the afternoon with claims of many more direct hits.

The morning attacks were almost as destructive as the pilots returning to Port Moresby claimed. The destroyer *Arashio* was hit three times, and, out of control, it struck the service vessel *Nojima*. Both ships would sink. The destroyer *Shirayuki*, the flagship of the convoy, was hit, causing a major explosion, and it was later abandoned. The destroyer *Tokitsukaze* took a number of hits and later sank. During the afternoon the destroyer *Ashoshio*, engaged in attempting to save the soldiers from the crippled and sinking transports, was also sunk. By the end of the day all the transports had either been destroyed or were in sinking condition and their troops were scattered in the water, hoping for rescue by one of the surviving destroyers from the convoy and another sent out from Kavieng. Before dark the four remaining destroyers retreated to Rabaul as quickly as possible. Japanese submarines were also dispatched to try to rescue as many as possible and managed to save 275 men.[8] One survivor wrote in his diary his feelings about the attack: "The Boeing [B-17] is most terrifying. We are repeating the failure of Guadalcanal! Most regrettable!"[9]

The trials for the surviving Japanese were not over. On the fourth, PT boats searched out two damaged ships and sank them. They surprised a submarine that had a large number of men on deck and forced it to dive. They then destroyed the three large landing craft near where the submarine had dived. Fifth Air Force planes joined the PTs, searching for any survivors, and ruthlessly machine-gunned them. One pilot recalled an incident: "As per instructions, we flew around to see if some ships were still afloat. Some were sinking and burning—we saw a lifeboat with about 20 people. I thought these poor guys. But we had a job to do because if they got to shore, they were going to kill our guys. So I came around and strafed them. One of the cruel things of war which had to be done."[10] Whether this was an official policy is difficult to ascertain. However, another pilot remembered, "At the briefing, Australian officers had told us we must not permit a single enemy to reach the shores of New Guinea. They explained the suffering, agony, and loss by our troops in having to hunt down and kill a suicidal Jap."[11] Despite such attempts to prevent any survivors from reaching shore, several hundred managed to do so, and many were later killed by natives and by Australian army patrols. One small group sailed more than seven hundred miles to Guadalcanal, only to be killed by an American patrol.[12]

Officials at the Advanced Air Echelon (ADVON) at Port Moresby, sifting the claims made by the pilots, believed that many more and larger ships had been destroyed. The Allied Air Force Summary of March 6 indicated that additional ships had joined the convoy, and ADVON's official report of April 6 stated more specifically that an additional seven ships had joined the convoy. The conclusion by air force officers—widely believed by General MacArthur's headquarters—was that twelve transports, three cruisers, and seven destroyers had been sunk. An argument would later challenge those figures, and this would refocus attention at higher headquarters away from the reality of the stunning victory. Japan had lost four destroyers, and all eight transports had been sunk. Although accurate figures on the number of troops lost were never ascertained, the Japanese admitted that 3,000 soldiers had been killed during the three-day battle. This did not count the hundreds of sailors lost with the transports and destroyers and the irreplaceable pilots of the many Japanese planes shot down.[13] Thus the Bismarck Sea battle was strategically a defeat for Japan, second only to that of the Coral Sea, confirming their inability to control the air and ensuring the isolation of their forces in New Guinea. The Japanese commanders would never again send transports or capital ships into the waters off Papua. Henceforth their garrisons would receive only meager supplies brought in by submarine or barges. The thousands of troops manning the defenses at Lae and Salamaua would be left on their own to face the growing Allied military superiority. MacArthur was fully aware of the importance of the victory, which he considered to be the "decisive aerial engagement" of the war in his theater, marking the "end of the Japanese offensive in the Southwest Pacific."[14]

Even before the stunning victory of the Bismarck Sea, General Blamey was planning the seizure of Lae and Salamaua. In February, as his troops closed in on Mubo, he suggested that Lae be taken first. He planned to use Salamaua as a decoy, hoping to convince the Japanese commander that it would be the main objective and thus freeze the largest portion of the Japanese there. General Herring disagreed and stated in June that notwithstanding Blamey's suggestions, he planned to take Salamaua as soon as possible. In this he was supported by Kenney and Whitehead, who wanted Salamaua captured immediately. Toward the end of June, Blamey met with Herring and convinced him that Salamaua was of little significance other than to pin down a large number of Japanese who otherwise could be used to check the drive toward the more defensible Lae area. The matter was not finally settled until two conferences with MacArthur in late July, where, on the twenty-eighth, Blamey's plan of operation was approved. General Sir Frank Berryman, Blamey's chief of staff, visited General Savige's headquarters on August 19 to make certain that he was fully informed as to the intentions of higher headquarters.[15] Before the assault on Lae, there were changes in the command structure in New Guinea. Herring was moved to command the Australian I Corps, which comprised the Australian 5th, 7th, 9th, and 11th Divisions and the 4th Brigade, as well as Wampit Force in the Markham Valley. Blamey assumed command of New Guinea Force, and Major General E. J. Milford replaced Savige as commander of the assault on Salamaua.[16]

The reduction of both Lae and Salamaua was a part of the Cartwheel plan for operations in the following six months. As part of this plan, operations were coordinated with the action of army and marine units in the Solomons and Nimitz's operations in the central Pacific. Elements of the Army's 43rd Division landed on New Georgia on June 30 and in a surprisingly drawn out campaign would control the island by early September. Continuing pressure on the Japanese outer defense ring was achieved by the simultaneous assaults on Tarawa and Makin in the Gilbert Islands. The final operation against the Japanese was to be at Bougainville on November 1, to secure air bases close to New Britain that would enable the thirteenth Air Force to assume the larger burden of the air war against Rabaul.

Having reviewed the actions in the Buna-Sanananda operations, MacArthur exclaimed, "No more Bunas!" He had no intention of committing the same types of mistakes that had proved so costly and had stretched out the time necessary to drive the Japanese from their entrenched positions. The Allies' situation had improved so much in the six months following the initial attack at Buna that MacArthur could hope to make good on his promise. Although still complaining about the lack of support from the Joint Chiefs, by the end of February 1943 he had in hand a total of 20,000 men in New Guinea, the bulk of whom belonged to the Australian I Corps. There were 8,396 U.S. troops of the 41st Division located in the Buna area.[17] A short distance from the active front he had available elements of three Australian divisions and one other U.S. division. His ground forces were adequate to finish the Lae-Salamaua action and move quickly to secure strategic enclaves up the coast and in the interior. Those actions would depend in part upon his admittedly inadequate naval force.

As soon as MacArthur had arrived in Australia, he began to be troubled by the lack of naval support. He blamed the highest-ranking officers, particularly the chief of naval operations, for the meager flow of even the smallest naval vessels. Reflecting this attitude, Admiral Nimitz refused to part with a substantial portion of his still outnumbered fleet. Only rarely would he allow major fleet units to operate in the southwest Pacific, and he never relinquished control over them to MacArthur.

MacArthur did not approve of the naval commanders who ostensibly were under his command. First Vice Admiral Leary and later Vice Admiral Carpender seemed to the supreme commander to be working more for the Navy than for him. The refusal of the Navy to commit larger ships to support the Buna campaign prolonged that operation and resulted in many more casualties to the Allied ground forces.[18] It would not be until November 1943 that he would have a compatible naval commander. However, in January 1943 he did receive a first-rate amphibious commander, Rear Admiral Daniel "Uncle Dan" Barbey, whom he came to trust implicitly and who would emerge as the most successful amphibious commander of the war. However, when Barbey arrived in Australia, he found almost no facilities for training and few landing craft of any type. The bulk of the seaborne troop movement had been done by small boats of the Army's Engineering Special Boat Brigade.

During their first meetings, MacArthur made it clear to Barbey that he expected to have his troops trained in amphibious operations. He could not depend upon air transport alone for the coming campaigns. Among the first actions Barbey took was the establishment of two training bases, one at Toobul Bay near the mouth of the Brisbane River, the other at Port Stephens. The permanent party and the first assignees to these bases had to build their own facilities. The chronic lack of ships is best illustrated by the fact that at first he did not have an attack transport (APA) available, even though MacArthur wanted his troops trained in disembarking from APAs. This problem was partially solved by stringing cargo nets down the face of a cliff. LSTs and LCIs were not available until mid-January, when the first of these craft arrived. On Easter Sunday, thirteen LCIs were delivered. Barbey and his staff had a daunting task to prepare the naval and army personnel in a short period because the first amphibious operations were scheduled for late June.[19]

The plan for capturing Lae and Salamaua as eventually approved called for the Australian forces in the interior to continue the assault on the ridges with the objective of taking Mubo and its airfield. In order to facilitate its capture and the troops' later movement toward Salamaua, the 162nd Regiment of the U.S. 41st Division would be carried from Milne Bay by Barbey's ships, covered by planes of the Fifth Air Force, and landed on the coast of Huon Bay. From there they would move into the interior to assist the Australians. The landing was scheduled for the night of June 29–30. At the same time, other units would be transported to seize Kiriwina Island, 125 miles from New Britain, and Woodlark Island, 200 miles from Bougainville. Despite many problems, Barbey's rudimentary amphibious force, strengthened by a loan of ships from Nimitz, successfully carried 16,000 men from Milne Bay to take these undefended islands.

MacArthur's headquarters and the press lauded the first amphibious action undertaken by Alamo Force. Indicative of the tension between Australian and U.S. commanders was General Blamey's attitude, which he confided to his memoirs. He wrote:

> It [the Woodlark operation] was hailed as a fine operation of war by the news hungry. It was, in fact, one of the jokes of the war. There were not one Japanese on the island and had been occupied by a small number of troops for some time. It had the effect, however, of holding up material and vessels urgently required for the following operations against Lae.[20]

Despite criticism, the occupation of the two islands did secure airfields that would be used in continuing air operations against Rabaul.

After arriving at Milne Bay, the 162nd Regiment, commanded by Colonel A. R. MacKechnie, had been posted to defend the beaches in the Sanananda-Killerton area and outposts at the mouth of the Kumasi River. On February 28, elements left by boat and leapfrogged up the coast to Katura, Oki, and Douglas Harbor, reaching the mouth of the Mambare River by March 15. Coming under the command of at first the 3rd and then the 5th Australian Divisions, the unit secured the mouth of the Waria River and Moroke Harbor, searching for Japanese survivors of the Buna-Sanananda fighting. The troops were supplied by air and suffered from the usual problems of operating in the tropical environment. By the end of March, some of the companies had been reduced to only thirty-five men because of hardship and disease. Nevertheless, they had killed 1,272 Japanese while losing 89 men to combat. Having had two months to recover from this, the regiment, now battle-tested, was ready for action against Salamaua.[21]

The plan for the landing of the 1st Battalion, 162nd Regiment, at Nassau Bay, eleven miles south of Salamaua, was for the Australians to support it by attacking toward the coast in two places. The 58/59th Battalion launched a drive on the Japanese high-ground positions at Old Vicker's, Coconuts, and Bobdubi. At the same time one company of the 2/6th was sent east from the Lababia Ridge to attract the attention of the Japanese. On the twenty-ninth, a PIB company captured outposts at Dinga, blocking the best escape route of the Japanese into the interior. Attacks on Japanese positions on Roosevelt Ridge—named for the battalion commander, Colonel Archie Roosevelt, a son of former president Theodore Roosevelt—north of the landing zone and on Bitoi Ridge were made during the afternoon of the twenty-ninth. The landing itself, on the night of June 29, was hardly a model exercise. It was conducted in the dark during a storm that created a ten- to twelve-foot surf. The leading elements were brought in by PT boats, each carrying seventy men. A total of three hundred men was to be landed to secure the beaches. However, those of B Company could not land. When the barges bringing the bulk of the landing force arrived, a PT boat cut across their path, causing more confusion. The barges were rammed into the beaches. Of the eighteen involved, only one could be backed off. This was indicative of the confusion on the beach. The supply situation would not be improved for almost a week as landing parties struggled to sort out those supplies that had been indiscriminately dumped. Despite such problems, men of A and C Companies quickly moved approximately three hundred yards into the interior against increasing Japanese resistance. By midmorning of June 30, the four 75 mm guns of the 218th Field Artillery Battalion had been brought in to support any future infantry advance, and MacKechnie had more than 1,400 men available ready to support the Australian drive on Mubo. The Japanese resistance was minimal. By the time the Japanese withdrew toward Bitoi Ridge on July 1, they had lost an estimated fifty men. The 1st Battalion casualties were eighteen killed and twenty-seven wounded, caused by a fierce firefight between different elements of the 1st Battalion that had erroneously believed they were surrounded by the Japanese.[22]

Roughly following the south arm of the Bitoi River, movement into the interior toward Mubo was complicated by the terrain. There was a series of ridges that could be defended by the Japanese. Flanking the landing area was Roosevelt Ridge, one of the two ridges guarding the hill masses named the Pimple, Green Hill, and Observation Hill. Above Mubo were Lababia Ridge and Bitoi Ridge, which was heavily defended. Although there was some confusion at Japanese headquarters concerning the Allies' objectives, General Nakano was certain that Salamaua was the main target, and on the twenty-ninth he ordered Major General Chuichi Muroya, commander of the 51st Division infantry, to protect and fortify Salamaua. As part of this defense force, he moved approximately 1,000 men to halt the U.S. forces if they moved up the coast toward Lake Salus.[23] Assault on the Japanese positions was delayed until the entire 1st Battalion had been landed on July 6 and MacKechnie, in accordance with orders from Major General Horace Fuller, commanding the 41st Division, had sorted out his problems in the beach areas.

The attack against the Bitoi Ridge line in conjunction with the Australian attack on Observation Hill northwest of Mubo began at 8 A.M. on July 7. This was supported by 159 bombers and fighters dropping 109 tons of bombs on enemy positions. Both attacks were supported by U.S. artillery. The ridges to the west of Bitoi Ridge were taken by July 9. Three days later, against weakening Japanese resistance, the Australian 2/6th captured Green Hill. On the twelfth, a platoon of A Company of the U.S. 1st Battalion made contact with the Australians on Bitoi Ridge. That same day, the Australians took the height called the Pimple and drove on to secure Green Hill to the north; Mubo airfield was also captured. By then the Japanese had been cleared from outposts along the river and the Bitoi Ridge line. Mubo village was captured by a company of the 2/5th Battalion on the fifteenth. The Japanese lost an estimated 973 men in the defense of the village. The last of the defenders, numbering only 46 men, retreated toward Mount Tambu to the southwest.[24]

The Allies' success in the difficult tasks of driving the Japanese from their excellent defensive positions near Mubo was marred by an unseemly squabble between Australian and U.S. commanders. This was caused by unclear lines of command. General Savige assumed, as did Herring, that all U.S. troops of the 162nd had come under Australian control after landing. General Fuller, though in the rear area, obviously did not agree and refused to relinquish control. The problem became serious when Brigadier Moten, commanding the 17th Brigade, ordered MacKechnie to move inland immediately to occupy Bitoi Ridge. The plan was to coordinate the U.S. attack with the major attack on Mubo on the seventh. MacKechnie refused, explaining that his order from Fuller was not to make any serious move until he had adequate supplies, and thus most U.S. troops would remain near the beaches until the supply situation improved. Savige then ordered MacKechnie to obey Moten and coordinate an advance with the Australians. As order was gradually restored to the beachhead, U.S. forces moved to comply and U.S. troops occupied Bitoi Ridge. However, the question of command remained unsolved. Brigadier General Ralph W. Coane, chief of the artillery of the 41st, was designated by Fuller to command the recently landed 3rd Battalion in a drive up the coast. Fuller had told him that his battalion was a separate command from MacKechnie's. On the fourteenth, Colonel Archibald Roosevelt refused to obey an order from MacKechnie stating that he was not under either Australian command and would move only when he received orders from Fuller. The situation was not clarified until the nineteenth, when Herring issued an order stating clearly that the Australian commander of the 3rd Division was in charge of operations in the Nassau Bay region and northward to Salamaua. MacKechnie, who was caught in the center of the controversy, was removed from command by Fuller, who charged him with advancing against Bitoi Ridge before the beachhead had been secured. He was eventually reinstated as executive officer to Coane Force. Under other circumstances, these differences could have proved serious. However, the 162nd's role in the offensive in late July was minimal. The Australians continued to bear the brunt of the fighting.[25]

Moving past Observation Hill, troops of the 17th Brigade made contact near Goodview Junction, southwest of Mount Tambu, with elements of the 15th Brigade, pressing south from the Old Vickers area. Old Vickers itself was captured by a company of the Australian 58/59th Battalion on the twenty-eighth. A company of the 2/7th Battalion moved into that position and stubbornly held off multiple Japanese counterattacks. By this time, with the loss of Mubo and Lababia Ridge, the Japanese held a rough arc of defensive positions in the heavily timbered ground from Bobdubi on the south bank of the Francisco River through Komiatum village to Tambu Peninsula on the coast. The Japanese commander,

Lieutenant General Nakano, rising to the bait as Blamey had hoped he would, poured more men into this area in order to defend Salamaua from what he believed to be the next major Allied goal. The fighting over the razorback ridges and through the gorges from Wau to the Salamaua area was described by General Savige as the roughest country over which the Australians had fought.[26] After having caused the enemy an estimated 6,000 casualties, the stage was now set for the three-pronged attack on Lae, one arm of which would be provided by Barbey's amphibious force landing the Australian 9th Division.

Four

SALAMAUA-LAE OPERATIONS

General Blamey's plan for the capture of Lae, code-named Operation Postern, as approved by MacArthur's headquarters, was complex and reflected the growing power of the Allied forces. Even before the invasion of Woodlark and Kiriwina, MacArthur's operational instructions, followed by amendments, projected the seizure of Lae and the Markham and Ramu valleys. The Markham operations were to be based on Port Moresby while the north coast operations were to be staged from Buna and Milne Bay.[1] For Operation Postern, Blamey moved to New Guinea to take overall charge and Herring reverted to command of I Corps to conduct the actual tactical operations. The key to quick success lay in convincing General Adachi that Salamaua was the primary target for any major action. To accomplish this, it was necessary for the Australian and American forces, located only a few miles from Salamaua in late August, to continue their attacks on the ridgelines to drive the Japanese from the key positions but not to attack Salamaua directly. For these attacks Blamey brought in the 5th Australian Division, commanded by Major General E. J. Milford, to replace the worn 3rd Division.

The main offensive, scheduled for September 4, would be an amphibious assault on beaches adjacent to Lae by Australian Major General George Wootten's 9th Division. This attack would be co-ordinated with troops of General George Vasey's 7th Division, attacking down the Markham Valley to assault Lae from the rear. This latter movement was dependent upon the seizure of airfields in the immediate interior that would enable the 7th Division to be flown in. This task of securing airfields to support amphibious landings would continue to be the hallmark of MacArthur's advance up the coast of New Guinea.

For the planned operation to be successful, the Allied air forces had to continue their dominance of the air. This meant that in conjunction with bombers from the South Pacific Theater and naval planes, Rabaul was subjected to continual attacks. The number of Japanese aircraft at Rabaul varied, but generally at least three hundred planes, mostly fighters, were located at the four airfields. Most of these were from the Combined Fleet, attached to the 11th Air Fleet. The attention of the Japanese commanders there continued to be drawn to the Solomons because of the American landings on New Georgia in July. The bulk of the planes at Rabaul were committed to two tasks: the defense of their bases on New Britain and then the central Solomons. The Japanese army had control of operations in New Guinea with the major airbases within striking distance of Lae at Wewak. Most of the army's planes, along with their crews and supplies, had been shifted from Rabaul to Wewak and further up the coast at Madang.[2]

In order to cover the invasion of Lae adequately, it was imperative to have an air base forward of Wau. MacArthur's headquarters had already determined that the prewar Australian airfield at Nadzab, lightly held by the Japanese, should ultimately be taken. In late 1942, General Whitehead had broached the idea of using the newly arrived 503rd Parachute Infantry Regiment to seize the airfield. Nothing had been done at the time because there had not been enough transport planes available.[3] However, the idea had been kept alive and became the centerpiece of the occupation of the Nadzab area. The initial plan was to have Australian troops move overland from the Lakekamu River to the Bulolo valley and then to the Markham valley. This would depend upon the completion of a road to the Bulolo valley and be coordinated with the parachute attack on the airfield by one of the 503rd's battalions. The road building did not proceed fast enough, so eventually the decision was made to use the entire parachute regiment.[4]

Before launching the Nadzab operation, headquarters decided to construct an intermediate airfield closer to Lae. The task of locating the site for this field was left to an aviation engineer, Lieutenant Everette Frazier, who was flown to the Bulolo valley in late May, accompanied by an Australian officer. He trekked through heavy jungle, avoiding Japanese patrols, and eventually located an old airstrip at Marilinan on the Watut River, fifty miles west of Lae. With native help they began to clear the runway. On June 9, Frazier began another trek to Wau, from which he was flown to Port Moresby. He reported that the field would be usable only until the rains began in September. However, it could be used as a staging field to assist the construction of the Nadzab field. Engineers from the Fifth Air Force surveying the area decided that another old airfield located nearby at Tsili Tsili was better suited for an interim base. Native workers began clearing operations at Tsili Tsili, and by early July, C-47s could land there. These planes brought in engineering troops and construction equipment, and despite bad weather, the 4,200-foot runway was improved and work began on extending it to 7,000 feet.[5]

A young Australian district officer who had spent months in the deep bush recorded his reaction upon seeing the airfield the first time. He wrote:

Where a week ago had been a sleepy native village, a tent
town straggled through the fringes of the jungle, inhabited
by American troops and airmen, both white and negro,
Australian soldiers and airmen, Papuan infantrymen, native policemen, carriers, and labourers. On the rough earth
air-strip, hastily cleared, DC-3 [C-47s] transports roared in
and out, unloading troops, stores, and construction equipment. A major operational base had sprung from the earth
just at the back door of Lae, the enemy's main stronghold.[6]

An Australian battalion was flown in to provide defense, and by
early August the field could handle as many as 150 planes daily.

Surprisingly, the Japanese were at first unaware of the new airfield so close to Lae. However, by August 15 they sent twelve
bombers escorted by fighters to attack the field. One transport
plane on the ground was destroyed, and flights into the field were
briefly interrupted. The bombers were engaged by U.S. P-39 fighters, which shot down most of them. A further strike occurred the
following day, but P-38 and P-47 fighters rose to meet the attackers
and destroyed fifteen fighters. The Fifth Air Force bombing attacks
on the Japanese airfields at Wewak that began on the sixteenth
would remove the major threat to the security of the airfield. Continued air strikes against Japanese positions were aimed at Wewak,
and on September 1 a large-scale raid hit the Madang area further
up the coast. The strikes at Wewak targeted the harbor and sank
two small transports.[7]

Aerial photographs of the various fields at Wewak on July 30
had shown only 30 planes there. Two weeks later, surveillance
showed that there were 176 aircraft, including 107 bombers. It was
obvious that such a concentration would pose a substantial threat
to the proposed attack on Lae. General Whitehead decided to hit
the Japanese installations there in the largest air strike since the Bismarck Sea operation. Indicative of the growth of the Fifth Air
Force, he had available eight squadrons of heavy bombers as well as

the deadly B-25 strafer aircraft. The proposed air strikes would be guarded by newer fighter aircraft, mostly Lockheed P-38s. A total of 127 fighters would be on call during the attacks. On the evening of August 16, forty heavy bombers took off from Port Moresby to begin the assault on the Wewak airfields. There was a series of mishaps that limited the effectiveness of the attack. Reconnaissance showed that only eighteen Japanese aircraft had been destroyed. The next morning two squadrons of B-25s left Port Moresby for the five-hundred-mile flight to Wewak. Three additional squadrons of B-25s left Dobodura for the shorter flight to the target. Only three of twenty-six B-25s from Port Moresby reached the Dura airfield at Wewak. They destroyed a reported seventeen aircraft. The flight from Dobodura was more successful. It struck at Boran and the main Wewak fields and afterward reported destroying an estimated 125 planes with parafrags and strafing. The escorting P-38s also took part in the attacks.[8]

A further attack against the Wewak complex was mounted on the eighteenth with both heavy and medium bombers. The escorting fighter pilots also claimed to have destroyed fifteen enemy fighters. The bombing offensive continued throughout the month, with minimal losses to Allied bombers and fighters. Kenney's headquarters claimed at that time that the bombing offensive had destroyed 200 enemy planes. A later review reduced the enemy losses to 175 planes. The Fifth Air Force continued the air offensive against Madang on September 1 and on Wewak the following day, concentrating on the harbor area and sinking two small transports. On the third the Lae airfield was heavily bombed.[9] These strikes all but destroyed the Japanese air strength at Wewak and its ability to interfere seriously with the ground actions at Nadzab and Lae. General Charles Willoughby, MacArthur's intelligence chief, correctly stated, "The Allied air attack against Wewak this week is unquestionably a milestone in the Pacific war. This is the first major reversal suffered by the Japanese Army Air Service in the Pacific."[10]

A key element in General Blamey's overall plan was the seizure of the small but usable field at the village of Nadzab, which could be rapidly improved. For this operation he would use Colonel Kenneth Kinsler's 503rd Parachute Regiment, which had earlier arrived in Australia from the United States, to augment MacArthur's flexibility. Kenney committed a total of 302 aircraft to the operation. The 1,700 men of the regiment boarded ninety-six C-47s at Port Moresby on the morning of September 5. A detachment of the 2/4th Australian Field Regiment with 25-pound artillery pieces was also to be dropped if the Japanese mounted a major counterattack. After a brief delay due to bad weather over the Owen Stanley Mountains, the transports, arranged in six plane elements, took off from Port Moresby. The transport armada was later joined by bombers and fighters from Tsili Tsili and other airfields in New Guinea. In the lead were six squadrons of B-25 strafers, which hit the small Japanese garrison at Nadzab with machine-gun fire and parafrag bombs.[11]

On schedule, the pilots of the eighty-one C-47s that had made it across the mountains brought the planes down to less than 1,000 feet for the airdrop. There was no ground opposition, and the paratroops seized the airfield and fanned out to their assigned locations. Two battalions took up blocking positions to the north and east while one battalion immediately began to work on the airfield. During the day, B-17s dropped supplies. During the drop, high above, circled three B-17s that Kenney called the "Brass Hat" flight. He observed the operation from one while MacArthur was in another. This was not just an act of bravado but another instance when MacArthur decided to risk his life because he believed that the troops would be inspired by seeing him. He had inspected them at Port Moresby, and as he later wrote, "I decided that it would be advisable for me to fly with them. I did not want them to go through their first baptism of fire without such comfort as my presence might bring to them."[12] As he noted, however, they did not need him. It went like clockwork. The operation cost three dead and thirty-three wounded, all from accidents.

Australian units—the 2/2nd Pioneer Battalion, the 2/6th Field Company, and one company of Papuan Infantry—had already left their base and marched hurriedly down the Watut River valley. They made contact with the 503rd on the afternoon of the fifth. All units worked throughout the night preparing the airfield. The next morning, the first C-47 landed, bringing in elements of the U.S. 87th Airborne Engineer Battalion and some of its equipment. On the sixth, Headquarters of the Australian 7th Division arrived along with troops from the Australian 25th Brigade who had earlier been flown in to Tsili Tsili. By the tenth, there were enough Australian troops on the ground that the 503rd could be relieved. Within two weeks of the landing, the engineers had gouged out two parallel airstrips 6,000 feet long and begun work on six others. The complex would be a vital part of MacArthur's air link in all subsequent operations.[13]

Despite the success of the airborne operation, the main part of the attack on Lae would depend on the Navy. Admiral Carpender had received considerable criticism from both Australian and U.S. Army commanders for the Navy's virtual absence during the Buna campaign. Even after the Solomon Sea routes had been surveyed, there was little activity except by PT boats from Morobe until mid-August. The PTs had sortied from their base, targeting the Japanese barges bringing supplies and reinforcements to Lae and Finsch-hafen. By the end of August, barge traffic had been seriously disrupted. Only a few reinforcements could be brought in, and most of these were landed from submarine transports. However, in a rare occurrence, two Japanese destroyer transports landed 1,560 men and 150 tons of supplies at Cape Gloucester. Reflecting a changing attitude, on August 20 Admiral Carpender ordered Captain Jesse Carter, commanding a destroyer squadron at Milne Bay, to make a sweep of Huon Gulf during the night of the twenty-second. The destroyers *Perkins, Smith, Mahon,* and *Conyngham* made the run to Buna and thence northeast to the Huon Gulf. They bombarded a number of shore targets, including a ten-minute strike at Finsch-hafen. Little damage was done, but this action indicated that the Navy would henceforth be more active off Papua. Carpender's staff looked forward to the upcoming Lae operation to make up for the Navy's former quiescence. One member said, "It will be worth while to prove the Navy is willing to pitch in, even if we get nothing but coconuts."[14]

Barbey called a final conference with the senior officers at Buna on August 31. One problem that had not been addressed was placing buoys and lights in the dangerous waters to ensure safe passage of the invasion flotilla. Responsibility for this was given to Commander G. C. Branson of the Australian navy. With considerable ingenuity, the waters around Cape Nelson were lighted to provide for the proposed night passage of the fleet. The Buna area provided a number of problems that were solved by improvising lights and laying buoys, making Buna a safe twenty-four-hour port. Four U.S. PT boats under Commander Morton Mumma at Morobe had been alerted to sweep Huon Bay just before the landings to check on enemy ships. Nine Australian Fairmile motor launches were to be available to harass any barge traffic along the Huon Peninsula.[15]

The main Lae attack force, the Australian 9th Division, loaded on Barbey's ships at Milne Bay on September 1. In direct contrast to the lack of ships just nine months earlier, the 7th Amphibious Force had available six destroyers in the cover and escort group and the destroyers *Conyngham* and *Flusser* to directly protect the landings. In addition, there were the destroyer transports *Brook, Gilmer, Sonds,* and *Humphreys.* Initially there were twenty-seven LSTs and twenty LCIs. Later more ships and men joined the convoy at Buna and Morobe. On the night of the third, Commander Mumma's PT boats swept Huon Gulf, searching for enemy ships. The main elements of the task force were off the targeted beaches in the early-morning hours of the fourth. Barbey had insisted upon daylight landings because of lack of information about the selected beaches and their approaches. At 4:45 A.M., four destroyers sailing parallel to Beach Red fifteen miles east of Lae and Beach Yellow, a further three miles east, began an intensive bombardment. Following this, planes of the Fifth Air Force made strafing runs on the beach. At approximately 6:30 A.M., the first assault troops, in sixteen rubber boats, began landing on both beaches to establish a perimeter. Fifteen minutes later, advance elements of the 20th Brigade began landing at Beach Red near the Bulu plantation. At the same time troops of the 26th Brigade landed on Beach Yellow east of the Bulu River. No opposition was met at either beach.[16]

Although meeting no Japanese opposition, the Australians, particularly those at Beach Red, were confronted by swampy areas extending almost to the beaches. Despite this, the leading units moved quickly inland and established defensive perimeters in case of Japanese counterattacks. The LCIs were followed in to the beaches by the LCTs and six big LSTs and LCTs carrying guns and supplies. Supplies for the troops had been offloaded by 9:30 A.M. By midmorning, 7,800 troops were landed and advance elements of the 2/24th Battalion had crossed the Busia River. The only casualties suffered during the operation were when six Japanese fighters and three bombers attacked the force with machine guns and bombs. A stick of bombs struck LCI 339, killing seven men and wounding twenty-eight. A much larger attack of eighty planes was mounted from Rabaul in the early afternoon, but the destroyer *Reid*'s radar picked up the incoming flight and vectored in Allied fighters that destroyed twenty-three of the attackers. A few planes slipped through and attacked a small fleet of six LSTs and three small minesweepers off Cape Ward Hunt. Six bombers concentrated on LST 493 and scored two hits, killing six and wounding thirty-one. Another attack, on LST 471, was even more devastating, killing fifty-one crewmen and troops and wounding eighteen. Both ships were saved. The attack was a reminder that although Allied airpower was dominant, the Japanese air forces still retained the capacity to inflict heavy losses.[17]

Three battalions of the 26th Brigade had crossed the Bungu River by nightfall of the fourth, and during the next day the brigade secured a line north from Tali village to the west side of the Singuau plantation. Other units, advancing along muddy trails and along the beach, reached positions just east of the Buiem River, and a patrol reached the mouth of the Busu River. Engineers bulldozed a trail from the Busu River westward that allowed three-ton trucks and Jeeps to bring supplies forward. The advance was sustained mainly by a number of small support vessels—ultimately a total of twenty-one LCMs and twenty-one LCVPs—that brought supplies forward to a series of dumps. The first contact with the Japanese was made on the sixth, when more than a hundred were discovered moving east of the Bungo River. A fierce firefight ensued, and the Japanese were driven back.

On the night of the fifth, the reserve brigade, the 24th, landed and was immediately sent west to support the other units. The weather during most of the advance was terrible. Heavy rains, particularly during the sixth and seventh, filled the weapons pits and forced the troops at night to abandon them and try to find shelter above ground. Although the troops continued to advance toward the Busu River, the major obstacle before Lae, the continued rains flooded all the streams and turned the trails into mud.[18]

By this time the bad weather, harsh terrain, and lack of adequate supplies had taken a toll on the Australian infantry. Under the best of circumstances, the daily ration was monotonous and scanty. The main sources of protein were bully beef, beans, and sausages. Four men were designated to share each tin of beef, six each tin of beans, and ten a tin of sausages. Coffee and tea were rationed to only two pounds each for every hundred men. Such niceties as sugar and margarine were almost nonexistent. This scale of rations had been determined by higher headquarters before the operation despite complaints from the commanders of all the brigades. The ration level was based upon a projected few days of operation but was in fact continued throughout the campaign.[19] On September 11, Captain J. F. Davies, the medical officer of the 2/23rd Battalion, noted that the rations were "quite inadequate considering the strenuous effort involved. Symptoms of malaria and vague dyspepsia are frequent and men are constantly complaining of weakness and inability to stand up to work. Unless the quantity of food is increased the men will not be able to carry on under existing conditions."[20]

Fortunately for the men of the 9th Division, the campaign for Lae was almost finished and the supply of food would be increased in quantity if not quality. The major reason for the Australians' success in moving eastward across the flooded streams was the lack of any substantial Japanese opposition, particularly in defending the major river crossings. On August 24, General Nakano, still believing that Salamaua was the Allies' major objective, had stated his resolve when he assured his troops, "Holding Salamaua is the Division's [51st] responsibility. This position is our last defense line, and we will withdraw no further. If we are unable to hold, we will die fighting. I will burn our Divisional flag and even the patients will rise to fight in close combat. No one will be taken prisoner."[21] This fanatical stance obviously applied to Lae. By Nakano's directive there were few troops at Lae on September 6. There were about 2,000 troops left at Lae, and these were mostly members of base units, such as hospital, artillery, and engineering personnel. Nakano had sent remnants of three regiments of the 51st Division and some naval troops to oppose the Australian 7th Division, advancing down the Markham Valley. He had committed a number of different units, the largest of which was the 238th Regiment less the 2nd Battalion, to counter the Australian 9th Division east of the town. Nakano had fallen into Blamey's trap in the disposition of his forces. Thus he had to withdraw the Salamaua garrison to reinforce the defenses at Lae.[22]

Given the previous suicidal Japanese defenses, such a decision as that made by Nakano on August 24 would have meant a desperate struggle for both Salamaua and Lae. However, Generals Imamura and Adachi had different ideas. They saw that the advance of the Australian 7th Division from Nadzab and the 5th, ringing Salamaua, threatened the destruction of the entire 51st Division. They considered it foolhardy to try to hold if the bulk of the division could be extracted to fight again. They decided to hold the Ramu Valley and Finschhafen with troops that could be extricated along with those of the 20th Division, which had been ordered from Madang to Finschhafen. Nakano and Commander Shoge, in charge at Lae, were ordered to evacuate their positions and move around the advancing Australians to the north coast of the gulf. The first units at Lae began the evacuation by September 12. The Salamaua garrison completed its move to Lae by the fourteenth, and these troops also began the trek north. The last of the main elements of the 51st Division left Lae by the next day. Thus, in the closing days of the campaign, the Australians did not meet the kind of resistance that could have delayed the eventual capture of Lae for weeks. The main Japanese line to defend Lae from the east was along the west bank of the Busu and then 1,000 yards west, near Malahang Anchorage.[23]

General Wootten at first had no intimation that the Japanese might abandon Lae and expected them to bring up considerable force to defend the Busu line. The situation became crucial after the 2/28th Battalion reached the east bank in late afternoon of the eighth. They found the river swollen by heavy rains flowing into a series of channels near the mouth. The main channel was reported to be five feet deep and was flowing at 10 to 20 knots. Patrols reported that there was no good crossing within at least 1,000 yards up from the mouth. Nevertheless, on the morning of the ninth an attempt was made to cross using the sandbar or the mouth. This was halted by Japanese fire from the west bank. Concerned that the Japanese would bring up many more troops, Wootten ordered the 2/28th to establish bridgeheads on the west bank no later than the morning of the tenth. A heavy bombardment by the brigade's artillery of suspected Japanese strong points preceded the preliminary attack at 5:30 P.M. on the ninth. The men were to attempt to wade across the wide eastern channel to Rookes Island, the largest of the islands blocking the mouth of the river. The next problem was to cross the main western branch. The decision was made for the lead troops to walk and swim across the swiftly flowing river. The first of the Australians in line stepped into the water, only to be swept away by the current. Some reached the west bank, but many were swept downstream, either to the sandbar or out to sea. A total of thirteen men were drowned, while thirteen were later rescued from the sandbar. The battalion also lost 25 percent of its automatic weapons and eighty rifles. While this near disaster was occurring, another company 100 yards upstream made a crossing by securing a line to the opposite bank. The Japanese did not contest this crossing, and the Australians clambered up the bank and quickly moved inland, establishing a bridgehead 150 yards deep by 650 yards long. By the morning of the tenth, a secure footing had thus been obtained. However, the continuing rain caused the river to rise more than a foot, making reinforcement difficult.[24]

On the afternoon of the tenth, attacks through the swamp westward were mounted against the Japanese on several small islands. Indicative of the collapsing Japanese resistance was their loss of sixty-three killed as well as a large quantity of equipment. The Australians lost four killed and seventeen wounded. Behind the forward positions engineers were hastily cutting roads to the rivers and laying wire for better communications. A troop of 25-pound artillery was ferried forward to a new beach west of the Burep River, and by the twelfth the artillery commander of the 2/12th Field

Regiment had fourteen 25-pounders available. The next day two 155 mm guns were landed at Beach Red. All were involved in suppression and counter battery fire against the Japanese artillery, which remained active even after the bulk of the infantry had left Lae. For example, on the fourteenth, their 75 mm guns inflicted fifty casualties, mainly among men of the U.S. 532nd Engineering Boat and Shore Regiment, who were busy ferrying men and supplies forward.[25] Log bridges and a girder bridge across the Burep and Busu Rivers enabled a buildup of men prior to the planned attack directly on Lae.

A key part of Blamey's plan of action was the diversion at Salamaua. It was imperative that the Japanese commanders believe that the major goal was not Lae but Salamaua. The Australians of the 3rd Division began the last actions on August 16. At first they did not attack the Japanese entrenchments on Mount Tambu but rather assaulted Komiatum Ridge. Its capture isolated the defenders of Mount Tambu from Salamaua, six miles away. General Nakano threw an estimated 1,000 troops against the Australian lines in a futile three-night attack, trying to dislodge the Australians. The Japanese suffered approximately five hundred men killed, and on the nineteenth they abandoned their Komiatum and Mount Tambu positions. Mount Tambu was occupied by the Australian 2/5th Battalion and elements of the U.S. 162nd Regiment. The way to Salamaua was now open. However, the Allies held up any rapid advance. Major General E. J. Milford, commanding the 5th Division, which took over the sector from the 3rd Division on August 25, kept pressure on the Japanese defenders of the ridge and hill lines surrounding the town. After Kela Ridge, 1,200 feet above the airfield, was outflanked, the Australians limited their activities to patrols, scouring the cliffs and ravines to disrupt Japanese supply lines and to set ambushes for unwary Japanese patrols.[26]

The advance toward Salamaua and the north did not continue until early September, when the action at Lae was well advanced.

On September 9, General Milford outlined his plans. In accordance with these, a company of the 162nd captured Scout Ridge and moved north to Logui No. 1 village just south of the mouth of the Francisco River. Heavy rains lasting thirty-six hours hardly impeded the assaults by the Australians against lessening Japanese rearguard actions. The 42nd Battalion overran the artillery position on Charley Hill, killing 133 defenders, while the 47th Battalion took Kunai Spur, another height above the river, killing 70 more. Japanese resistance south of the river had collapsed by the eleventh, while they were still contesting the high ground north of the river. The first concrete evidence Milford had that Salamaua would not be contested was also on that date, when Herring informed him that intelligence showed the Japanese retiring to Lae.

The decision by Imamura and Adachi, faced with pressure from three directions, effectively canceled any last-ditch defense of the Salamaua sector. In order to save the 51st Division and elements of the 20th and 41st Divisions and the 14th Artillery Regiment, on September 4 they ordered the marine commander in charge of the Salamaua garrison to begin evacuation to Lae by barge. Starting two days later, an estimated 5,000 men were taken to Lae, from which they would move with the Lae garrison at the appropriate time through the Markham and Ramu valleys to Kiari on the north coast. An additional 600 naval troops escaped by submarine to Rabaul. An additional estimated 250 men marched up the coast toward Lae.[27] Milford ordered the U.S. 162nd to move north along the coast to capture the base of the isthmus on which Salamaua was located. He changed his mind because of fears that the Americans would not move quickly and ordered the 15th Brigade, which had earlier crossed the swollen river, to move east and block the area to prevent the escape of any Japanese in the village. Other Australian units had also crossed the river; the 58/59th Battalion captured Arnold's Crest and moved north toward Mission Point to block Japanese attempting to move up the coast toward Lae. The

2/7th also moved north, toward Kela Heights and Chinatown on the coast. U.S. troops finally crossed the river and occupied the area between Lagui No. 1 and the airfield. As the 15th Battalion pursued the retreating Japanese along the coast, the other Australian units could relax and wait for their removal to Milne Bay. The U.S. regiment went into reserve.[28]

The capture of Salamaua ended a seven-month campaign that saw the Japanese blocked in their attempt to capture Wau and subsequently the Australian advance over some of the worst territory in New Guinea. The Japanese losses were estimated at more than 2,850 killed, and they sustained total casualties of more than 8,100. Australian casualties during the period April 23 to September 13 amounted to 470 killed and 1,120 wounded. The U.S. 162nd Battalion, during 76 days of action, lost 81 killed and 396 wounded. Salamaua itself proved to be of questionable value. At one time Allied planners had hoped to make it a major base. However, when Herring arrived to visit the town, he concluded that it was unsuitable. The airfield was too small and its location next to a swamp made it an unlikely choice for anything but a feeder base. The town itself was described by one U.S. soldier as "a filthy rat-ridden, pestilential hole."[29] The great contribution of the later Salamaua campaign, as Blamey had hoped, was to draw off large numbers of Japanese troops from Lae.

Although there were real dangers to the pilots and crews of the aircraft flying over the Owen Stanley Mountains into the fog-shrouded airfields, there had been few crashes. Then, early in the morning of September 7, a major disaster occurred. A B-24 heavy bomber with a full crew and 2,800 gallons of fuel attempted to take off from Jackson for Nadzab. It never reached a safe altitude and crashed into trees beyond the runway. There were three trucks loaded with soldiers of the 2/33rd Battalion nearby. Sprayed with flaming gasoline and debris, all were killed. The total casualties from this accident were more than many units had suffered during the entire campaign. Fifteen men died immediately, 44 died later, and 92 were injured but still survived. Nevertheless, the vital airlift continued, halted only by the bad weather, which persisted until September 11.[30]

The third wing of Blamey's plan, the advance from Nadzab down the Markham Valley Road toward Lae, began on September 9, led by the 2/25th Battalion of the 25th Brigade. Troops were still being flown in to Nadzab airfield as Brigadier Kenneth Eather's men, veterans of the Kokoda and Buna fighting, moved down the road toward the village of Old Munum despite the fact that workers of the last battalion of the 25th would not arrive until after the heavy rains and fog had subsided on the eleventh. Nevertheless, the advance continued almost unopposed by the Japanese. Old Munum, directly east of Nadzab, was reached by afternoon of the ninth, and the 2/25th was soon joined by elements of the 2/23rd, crossing over from Tsili Tsili. By the next day, the Australians had reached a point 200 yards past the junction of the Markham Valley Road and the trail leading to Jensen's plantation. Bad weather postponed a general advance further down the road until September 12. However, patrols moved along the trail to Jensen's plantation, encountering only a few Japanese patrols. Another Australian unit named the Wampit Force had also advanced east from the Wampit River to attack the Japanese defenses at Markham Point. All attempts to take the strongly entrenched Japanese positions there failed. Not until the eighteenth did the Australians discover that the Japanese troops of the 2nd Battalion of the 238th Regiment had abandoned the position.

On September 12, the 2/2nd Pioneer Battalion of the 25th Brigade began the final advance toward Lae, moving along the main road followed by the 2/25th, which by late afternoon reached Jenyns Trail behind the main Japanese defenses. The Japanese, by now weakened by the withdrawal of many troops, nevertheless counterattacked but were beaten back with a loss of thirty men.

The Japanese at Markham Point were more successful in repulsing the Australian attacks. The offensive against the main Japanese entrenched defenses astride the Markham Road resumed on the thirteenth. Eather ordered the 2/25th Battalion to attack directly down the road while the 2/33rd moved around to the left to cut off any retreat. The joint attack was successful, the positions were overrun, and an estimated 100 Japanese were killed. A major Japanese headquarters was captured, and an operations order dated the eighth discovered there was the first proof Eather had that the Japanese had been planning to withdraw.[31]

Meanwhile, units of the 9th Division, who with so much difficulty had crossed the Busu River near its mouth, renewed their attacks on the fourteenth. The 2/43rd Battalion attacked Wagon village, only two miles east of Lae, and after heavy fighting took the village by midafternoon. Further to the south along the coast, the 2/28th Battalion encircled the Japanese defending Malahang Anchorage. The diarist of the 2/32nd Battalion, after the capture of Wagon, noted prophetically that "the rising sun has moved to the western sky insofar as Lae is concerned."[32]

To the northwest, Vasey's 7th Division troops continued their move toward Lae using the Markham Valley Road. One by one the Japanese strong points fell to the 2/25th and 2/33rd Battalions, but only after hard fighting. The Japanese evacuated Markham Point, and it was obvious that Lae would soon be reached. General Vasey was informed that the main Japanese body was probably attempting to escape and was ordered to use a portion of his division, including the newly arrived 21st Brigade, to try to block this. Despite this new worry, Vasey ordered the 25th to continue its drive toward Lae. In a sense it became a race to see which division would enter the town first. After encountering fierce resistance, the 9th Division units penetrated the main defenses west of the Busu by the fifteenth while the 7th was being slowed by near-fanatical resistance by small Japanese units along the Markham Road. By evening of the fifteenth, the 24th Brigade had reached the Bumbu River, the eastern boundary of the town, while the forward troops of the 7th Division were at Cox Road Camp, five miles from Lae.

The first Australian troops to enter the by now nearly deserted town were a patrol of the 2/31st Battalion of the 7th Division, who reached the center of the town at 11 A.M. on the sixteenth. The patrol proceeded as far as Voco Point, only 500 yards from troops of the 2/28th Battalion of the 9th Division who were preparing to cross the Bumbu River. Close behind the lead patrol of the 2/25th was Brigadier Eather, who was anxious that men of his brigade gain the honor of capturing Lae. Without knowing that there were no Japanese in Lae, the artillery of the 9th Division opened up on the town just after noon and forced the Australians in the town to dig in. Earlier, two U.S. aircraft had attacked the area along the road and in Lae with machine guns, and even after the Australians laid out markers, the planes dropped several parafrag bombs, causing two casualties. In retrospect, the lack of serious casualties from friendly fire is amazing since higher headquarters had not designated a dividing line between the two advancing divisions.[33]

The town was devastated by the bombings and artillery fire. As observers had noted at Salamaua and earlier at Buna and Gona, the stench from the Japanese living areas, particularly of the unburied dead, was nauseating. A great quantity of supplies and discarded weapons was captured. Two cargo ships lay offshore, and further down the beach were numerous wrecked landing barges.[34] At the airfield west of the town, the hangars were all wrecked and there were approximately forty damaged aircraft. It was obvious that the field had not been used since the 9th Division had landed.

The numbers of Japanese in the Lae-Salamaua area prior to the invasion had been grossly overestimated by Allied higher headquarters. The intelligence staffs of the two divisions each had estimated differing numbers of Japanese to be present. Wootten's staff estimated that there were 8,240 Japanese at Lae and 6,934 at Salamaua, while Vasey's intelligence service placed the numbers at 6,420 at Lae and 7,041 at Salamaua. General MacArthur, in his triumphant communiqué of September 8, claimed that there had been 20,000 Japanese, who were by then completely enveloped. The truth, as determined later, was that in early September Nakano had approximately 11,000 men, most of whom were members of the 51st Division, though there were also almost 1,500 naval troops there.

MacArthur was wrong. The Japanese had not been enveloped; the majority had escaped by barge or submarine or by taking to the many overland trails in an attempt to move to the safety of the Japanese positions at Finschhafen and on the north coast of Huon Bay. The casualties inflicted by both Australian divisions was estimated at approximately 2,200, which, if correct, meant that Nakano had effected the escape of more than 8,000 men. The cost to the two Australian divisions was minimal, given the nature of the terrain and the tenacity of some of the Japanese defenders. The 7th Division suffered 142 casualties with 38 killed, while the 9th had 547 casualties, including 77 killed.[35]

Lae was scheduled to be the major forward base for further operations, as Buna had been earlier. The plan was to construct what the Australians called Lae Fortress to act as a supply and staging ground. On 22 September, General Milford was placed in command at Lae as well as being in control of the 4th, 15th, and 29th Brigades and the territory as far south as Nassau Bay. Thus the division of authority between Milford's command and Vasey's 7th Division and American forces was clearly demarcated. Milford was specifically forbidden to interfere with the operations of Allied air and naval units or of "striking forces" that might be staging through Lae.[36] The decision had already been made to utilize elements of the 7th Division to pursue the retreating Japanese and secure areas for more airfields in the Ramu and Markham valleys. In addition, the amphibious operation against Finschhafen had been moved up to take advantage of the quicker-than-expected collapse of the Japanese defenses at Lae. Thus it was imperative to quickly improve the facilities at Lae, at the same time planning for a three-pronged offensive against the Japanese in the interior and at Finschhafen.

Five

THE OCCUPATION OF

FINSCHHAFEN

The ease with which Lae was captured caused MacArthur's headquarters to revise the Cartwheel schedule. Originally it had planned to attack Finschhafen, a minor port located on the eastern side of the Huon Peninsula used by the Japanese primarily as a base for barge traffic, six weeks after the conclusion of the Lae operation. The quick capture of Lae, combined with intelligence reports of heavy Japanese reinforcements from Madang headed for Finschhafen and the Ramu Valley, caused MacArthur, on September 15, to order an immediate operation to secure the villages of Kaiaput and Dumpu in the Markham and Ramu valleys and to construct airfields for use by Kenney's planes. The intelligence reports were correct. General Adachi had ordered the bulk of his 20th Division to Finschhafen and one regiment into the Ramu Valley. Lack of air and naval capability meant that the Japanese were forced to march the 200 miles to Finschhafen. This gave MacArthur the chance to assault the port before reinforcements for the garrison could arrive. Another factor was his intelligence chief's assessment of the numbers of Japanese defending the immediate area. How

Willoughby arrived at the figure of only 350 men remains a mystery, but this contributed to MacArthur's and Blamey's optimism about an operation against Finschhafen. Later it was discovered that Adachi had more than 5,000 men available there. Although the low estimate was a factor, it is doubtful whether MacArthur, had he known the actual number, would have altered his plan for an early assault. On September 17, he ordered Admiral Barbey to begin an amphibious attack on Finschhafen as soon as possible.[1]

Before the attack on Finschhafen began, General Milford, at Lae, was involved in clearing the interior approaches to the town against any possible Japanese counterattack and pursuing the retreating Japanese. The successful evacuation by the Japanese of first Salamaua and later Lae had come as a surprise to the Australian commanders despite the fact that they had been informed as early as May of intense Japanese patrol activities along the interior trails. A young Australian political officer had earlier reported his suspicions that the Japanese were surveying these trails for a possible retreat across the mountains.[2] The captured evacuation order of September 8, however, left no doubt that the Japanese had been planning to cross the mountains with the objective of reaching Sio and Kiari on the north coast. Milford's headquarters deduced the line of retreat from the places named in the order; the Melambi River, Boana, Melasapipi, Iloka, and Ulap. This later proved to be deceiving since General Nakano changed the direction of the march to a rough, steep trail along the east side of the Atzera Range and thence to Sio. Most of the Japanese soldiers crossed the Busu River on a rough-hewn bridge by September 22 and thence proceeded to Mount Solawket, and by mid-October they reached the north coast. In late October, a captured Japanese sergeant disclosed that the main body of the Japanese had been organized into four groups, with Nakano in the second. The preparations for the three-week march had hardly been adequate. The troops carried only ten days' rations, and even though conserving, they were on half rations. Thus, although the retreat was a success, the surviving Japanese suffered from hunger in addition to a variety of tropical diseases and dysentery. Nevertheless, approximately 6,400 soldiers reached Kiari. An estimated 1,275 were ill. Approximately 1,500 sailors arrived at Sio. Most were without weapons, having thrown them away on the trek. The Japanese had also abandoned all their heavy weapons after the first few days of the retreat. The defense of Lae and the retreat cost the Japanese an estimated 2,600 lives.[3]

Pursuit by the Australians was late since the main effort had been directed toward Lae. By then the main elements of Nakano's force were beyond the reach of the most forward of the Australian patrols. It was not until September 16 that the 2/4th Independent Company and the 2/24th Battalion were ordered after the retreating Japanese. In a series of small engagements, the patrols killed a number of Japanese who had been left behind. However fierce these local engagements were, the Japanese bands were small and disorganized. Other Australian troops moved north from Nadzab, and one patrol of the 2/14th entered Boana village on the twenty-third. The officer commanding noted how fortunate it was that the Japanese had decided not to defend the village:

> Boana by the way is in a hell of a mess. Nippon pulled out not later than Monday last [September 20]—a hell of a party of him [the Japanese]. It rained here Sunday night and he left after the rain cutting down bridge at Gumbuk on his way. If the battalion had gone to Boana Sunday it would have had a warm welcome. Gun positions of very strong construction commanding road and ambush positions wherever he could put them. At the mission a big gun position was being built—one finished—an excellent job.[4]

By the end of September, the interior approaches to Lae were secure, and elements of the 2/24th and the 24th Battalion were posted in defensive positions. The main area of operations in early October was against the remnants of the Japanese force in the Sonem River valley. As in other sectors, the Australians found that the Japanese had no fight left and were concerned mainly with escaping. Their withdrawal was not well organized. The numbers of each group varied between ten and sixty. They were preoccupied with gathering food and would occupy the native villages until they had eaten all the food available. Normally they paid little attention to flank protection. In such a situation, the Australians found it easy to set ambushes to kill the disorganized enemy. In the ten days after the 2/24th entered the valley, they killed eighty Japanese. Later this number would be increased to more than two hundred. An intelligence survey by the 5th Division at the beginning of November declared that except for a few stragglers, the Sonem valley had been cleared of the Japanese. The last action in pursuit of the Japanese was a patrol along the Sio trail on November 3 that after climbing to more than 6,500 feet abandoned any thought of further pursuit after encountering almost sheer cliffs.[5]

Even before the Finschhafen operations began, the Australian 7th Division was ordered to move into the Markham and Ramu valleys to deny the area to the Japanese and to secure more forward air bases. This had been envisioned by MacArthur in June, when he had advised Herring that this would be a priority operation. On September 16, the day Lae was captured, General Vasey flew to Port Moresby for conferences with senior Allied commanders. Whitehead told him and Herring that he wanted to have fighter planes at Kaiapit by November 1. The major problem was the provision of supplies to Nadzab since the projected road from Lae to Nadzab would take at least two months to build. Whitehead told them that he would not be able to give equal air support to both the Finschhafen and Markham valley operations. After conferring with Blamey, Vasey worked out the plan for operations to seize Kaiapit in the Markham valley, followed by Dumpu, another village where an airfield could be constructed. It was planned for the 2/6th Independent Company and a company of the Papuan Battalion to march overland to seize Kaiapit. The 21st Brigade would follow in a march from Nadzab. Vasey indicated that the 2/27th Battalion could be flown from Port Moresby if necessary. Later the 25th Brigade would be flown from Nadzab and the 18th Brigade from Port Moresby to capture Dumpu after the initial assault by the U.S. parachute regiment. One reason for the planned use of so many troops was the inadequate knowledge of the disposition of Japanese forces, and it was believed that the attempted seizure of the two sites would encounter heavy opposition.[6]

After some delay due to bad weather, the independent company was lifted off the airfield at Port Moresby on September 17 and was landed at a temporary airfield west of the Leron River. Meanwhile, the Papuan Battalion was marching toward Sangat village, near which the 2/6th was temporarily located. The commander, Captain G. G. King, immediately sent out patrols toward the Kaiapit complex of three villages. By the afternoon of the nineteenth, the main body of the Australians had arrived before the Japanese defenses at village No. 1. King ordered a direct attack on the village and defenses. The Australians, in three columns, charged the enemy with bayonets drawn and soon broke through the Japanese defenses. The Japanese, having lost forty-one killed, fled northwest toward the other two Kaiapit villages. Short of ammunition and with its radio not functioning, the 2/6th dug in for the night. King sent a runner back to Sangan with a message for Vasey asking for an immediate supply of ammunition. Early on the morning of the twentieth, the Australians attacked through village No. 2 in the direction of a high area, Mission Hill. By 7:30 A.M., the hill was captured, thus ending all organized Japanese resistance, though sporadic fighting continued against individual Japanese. By noon a relief column of the Papuan Battalion arrived with ammunition and a functioning radio. King could now inform Vasey of what had oc-

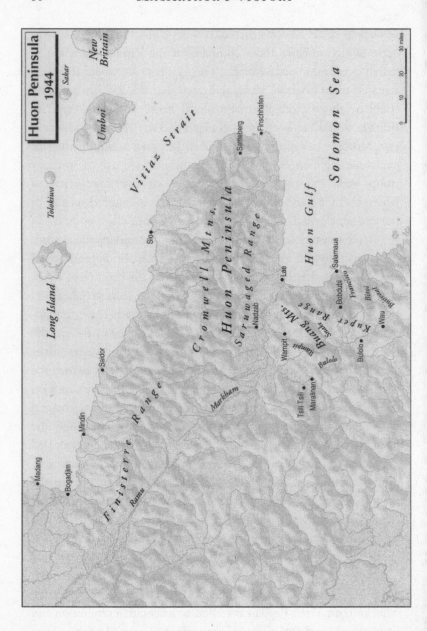

Huon Peninsula
1944

curred and thus assure a concerned MacArthur of the success of the venture. Work began immediately on clearing and improving the airstrip, and the following day the first transport plane landed, bringing in the advance portion of the 21st Brigade. General Vasey, who arrived at Kaiapit that day, learned from captured documents that General Adachi had planned for his 78th Regiment to occupy Kaiapit, but its commander, Colonel Matsujiro Nakai, marching overland, had spent too much time establishing key positions along the route. Only two infantry companies had arrived at Kaiapit to confront the Australians. The quick success of the 2/6th ensured control of the three villages and the airfield. Unfortunately, the field proved too swampy and malarial. However, a new site at the junction of the Gusap and Ramu Rivers provided a good airfield fifty miles in advance of the previous bomber line.[7]

General Vasey was already committed to an advance by the 21st Brigade to Dumpu and beyond to secure the village of Bogadjim. He planned then to build fourteen miles of road to link up with the one the Japanese had constructed. However, he and Herring were concerned with the lack of accurate knowledge of the location and strength of the Japanese. On September 23, he ordered Brigadier Ivan Dougherty, the brigade commander at Kaiapit, to hold up any further forward movement toward Dumpu until he could arrive to directly assess the situation. He ordered the 2/27th Battalion flown in to Kaiapit as reinforcements. After meeting with Dougherty, he decided to bring in the 25th Brigade to reinforce the troops at Kaiapit in case the Japanese attacked the complex. If that happened, he hoped to destroy them completely. By then the patrols of the 2/16th Battalion had moved eastward and crossed the rain-swollen Umi River to occupy the high ground south of the village of Sagerak. This unit encountered a few Japanese, and there was some skirmishing. Vasey's fears of encountering large Japanese forces before his buildup was complete led to his ordering the patrols to abandon their positions in the Markham valley and retreat back across the Umi. Vasey had been informed by Whitehead that the Finschhafen operation had priority for the Air Force for both direct support and supply. There was therefore a delay in moving the 25th Brigade, which was not transported to Kaiapit until the twenty-seventh.[8]

Vasey reversed his position on the twenty-seventh and ordered Dougherty to move elements of the 21st Brigade across the Umi and advance toward Dumpu. Some of his patrols moved toward the village of Kasawi in the Ramu valley. Informed of the advance of a strong Japanese force along one of the trails, the Australians set an ambush. The unsuspecting Japanese were caught in the cross fire. Most of the force of sixty were killed. This small action had major ramifications. General Nakai, already disturbed by the loss of Finschhafen, considered the loss of these few troops a forewarning of a major Australian offensive. His 78th Regiment, in the Dumpu area, was in bad condition. After considering his options, Nakai halted the advance of his 51st Division in the river valleys and instead ordered a concentration at the Kankirijo Saddle in the Finisterre Mountains. General Adachi's main effort would not be in support of Nakai; rather, he would use most of his force in the Huon Peninsula to recapture Finschhafen. This left only remnants of the 78th to contest the Australian advance. This meant that the Australians faced little opposition in their advance. By the twenty-ninth, they had occupied the village of Sagerak, where the small airfield enabled easier supply for the forward-moving troops. The 2/16th Battalion occupied the heights south of Marasawa and, along with the 2/27th, began a steady advance up the valley. Nevertheless, Herring and Vasey were very cautious, even though on October 1 Vasey's headquarters received reports that the Japanese had withdrawn from both the Markham and Ramu valleys. They brought up the 25th Brigade elements, which encountered Japanese stragglers on October 3. In an anticlimax, the 2/16th entered Dumpu by midafternoon of the fourth. Very soon, Vasey moved the headquarters of the 7th Division to Dumpu. Strong patrols branched out in all directions, and soon roads were built leading to the hills to the west and to Kasawi.[9]

While the 7th Division was involved in pursuing the remnants of the Lae garrison and capturing airfields in the Ramu and Markham valleys, the 9th was involved in the major operation against Finschhafen. Admiral Barbey, after being informed by MacArthur of his decision to take Finschhafen, immediately collected eight LSTs, sixteen LCIs, four APDs, and ten destroyers for the amphibious operation. The LSTs were loaded with bulk supplies at Buna, and on September 21, Brigadier Victor Windeyer's 20th Brigade was taken on board. The flotilla was attacked by Japanese planes that evening, but they did no damage. The consensus at higher headquarters was that a brigade would be sufficient since there were few Japanese at Finschhafen. Although the intelligence reports of the numbers of defenders were faulty, there were indeed few Japanese there. Major General Eizo Yamada, commanding at Finschhafen, had correctly judged that the town would be the next target. However, he assumed that the Australians would be advancing overland. He therefore placed the bulk of his 3,000 men south and west of the town, leaving fewer than 1,000 to defend the town and its northern approaches. There were thus only a few troops to defend against the landings at Scarlet Beach, six miles north of the town.

The landing area selected was only 900 yards wide on the narrow coastal strip, which was bounded inland by the steep Kreutberg Mountains. Scarlet Beach had been demarcated by beach groups of the U.S. 532nd Engineering Boat and Shore Regiment prior to landing the Australians. Despite some protests from the Australian commanders, Barbey had insisted that the landings take place in darkness just before dawn on the twenty-second in order for his ships to be under way before the Japanese could launch a major air attack. The destroyers brought the beach area under fire prior to the actual landing, as did some of the assault boats.[10] As was true in many of the early amphibious assaults, there was considerable confusion during the landing. The four assault companies landed on the wrong beaches, missing Scarlet Beach entirely. Not until the third wave did any troops land in the correct place. In addition, the various units of the 2/17th and 2/13th Battalions were mixed together. Some of the LCIs ran into a sandbar, forcing the men to wade or swim through deep water to shore. One soldier recalled:

> We were the second wave this time, and we expected that the first wave of Diggers would have "done over" the Japanese before we hit the sand. But the first wave missed Scarlet Beach entirely in the darkness and ran into Siki Cove and on to coral farther south. Our wave, also of six or eight L.C.I.'s, ran into the cove, but our boat hit coral with a jarring, creaking crash on a small headland between Scarlet Beach and Siki. One gang-plank was immediately out of action, and we began jumping off the other. Odd sniping shots snapped out from the shore. . . . To our left a machine-gun fired a stream of white tracers down on to the beach. . . . Ahead and above us, on top of the headland about 100 feet away, a Japanese machine-gun opened fire with tracers. Its first burst went high into the air, the second into the water beside the boat. The third burst crashed over my head and hit two men behind me; I heard them cry out as I jumped on to the coral and splashed through a pool or two to the beach.[11]

Despite the confusion, the Australians quickly moved off the beaches. They discovered only hastily built beach defenses manned by a small number of troops. These retreated to the interior jungle. The 2/15th Battalion quickly plunged toward Katika village in pursuit of the retreating Japanese. The 2/13th Battalion moved south toward the large Heldsbach plantation and thence down the coast toward Finschhafen. Unloading of men and supplies was soon completed, and by 6 A.M. the APDs and LCIs were on their way to Buna. The retiring flotilla was attacked by forty-one aircraft from Rabaul. Radar from the destroyer *Reid* picked up the incoming flight, and Allied fighters and accurate antiaircraft fire destroyed most of the attackers. Despite wild claims by the Japanese, not a single ship was damaged. Three more heavily loaded LSTs arrived at the beachhead in late afternoon, and once again they were not located by the Japanese air force. The escort destroyer *Flesser* encountered three Japanese barges on the way to Finschhafen and sank them. Movement by Barbey's small naval forces went unimpeded because Admiral Mineichi Koga was afraid of a reiteration of what had occurred during the Bismarck Sea battle.[12]

The Australians moving down the coast encountered a series of bunkers along the Bumi River, and these, defended by a few hundred Japanese, briefly halted their advance. However, on the twenty-fourth, men of the 2/15th Battalion waded across the river and established a firm beachhead on the south bank. The following day, Allied bombers launched heavy attacks on the Salankano plantation area, Kedam Point, and Finschhafen, while Australian artillery pounded Finschhafen. On the twenty-sixth, Yamada launched an attack against Scarlet Beach with his 80th Infantry, but it was beaten off. The Japanese positions on Kakakog Ridge overlooking the Salankano Plantation had to be taken. Men of the 2/15th assaulted this height, crawling up the steep slope through heavy jungle growth. Despite these conditions, they reached the crest and overran the Japanese positions, killing an estimated fifty troops. Meanwhile, the 2/13th flanked the Japanese positions along Ilebbe Creek, moving along the slope of the Kreutberg Mountains.

Windeyer was concerned that the Japanese might launch a major attack against his scattered forces, and he sent a request for the 25th Brigade to New Guinea Force Headquarters. Although General Blamey, now in Brisbane, wanted to reinforce Windeyer immediately, the dispatch of troops to Finschhafen was delayed by a bureaucratic conflict reflecting the dual nature of command similar to what had happened earlier in the Kokoda-Buna operations. On the twenty-second, MacArthur's headquarters had issued orders curtailing amphibious operations beyond those areas already specified. Thus when Herring met Barbey on board the destroyer *Conyngham* and informed him of Blamey's request, the admiral, citing MacArthur's order, refused to transport any more troops. There followed a series of high-level conferences, including Major General Stephen Chamberlin from MacArthur's headquarters and Berryman, Blamey's chief of staff. Windeyer, meanwhile, was repeating his request for more troops and Wootten pressed New Guinea Force Headquarters for reinforcements. Finally, on the twenty-eighth, MacArthur's headquarters approved the movement of one battalion from Lae to Finschhafen. Fortunately, the delay did not cause any setback since the Japanese did not make any serious move toward the beachhead, but it did illustrate the dangers of dual control and micromanagement from a distance.

On the night of the twenty-ninth, Windeyer received his reinforcements: the 2/43rd Battalion of the 25th Brigade, a total of 838 men on three APDs. On retiring, the ships took away 134 walking wounded, many of whom had spent days waiting to be evacuated.[13] These reinforcements gave Windeyer a small reserve to back up his tired troops. Heavy fighting continued until October 1, when the Japanese were forced back with a loss of more than a hundred men. The Japanese withdrew from Kakakog village the next day, and the Australians entered Finschhafen. On October 3, the 2/17th Battalion advanced through Salankua plantation to Langemak Bay. There they linked up with troops of the 4th Brigade who had moved fifty miles up the coast from Hopei. With the capture of Finschhafen, the Allies controlled all the anchorages from Lae to Scarlet Beach.[14]

Even before the capture of Finschhafen, Windeyer had begun tentative movements up the Sattleberg Road toward what was believed to be the main concentration of Japanese troops. At the same time, he positioned a portion of the 2/17th Battalion to protect Scarlet Beach. He also sent a company of the 2/17th by boat north to a trail near the airfield. One aim was ultimately to seize the junction of the Gusika-Wareo Trail, which the Japanese were using to bring up men and matériel to the Sattleberg region. Wareo village, a half dozen miles north of Sattleberg, was on a plateau that dominated the Song River valley and the country inland from Scarlet Beach. Capture of the Wareo-Gusika line would secure Finschhafen and cut off all Japanese south of Wareo.[15] Any serious movement against this Japanese communication line would have to wait until the Sattleberg Mountain area had been cleared. During the first days of October, the Japanese actively attacked the Australian positions in the villages of Kumawa and Jivevaneng, both occupied by companies of the 2/43rd. In all, the company at Jivevaneng withstood five separate strong attacks by units of the Japanese 80th Division. These were contained, but the increased activity convinced Wootten that the Japanese were preparing a major offensive aimed at Finschhafen.[16] He therefore decided to postpone any further serious attempts to capture the Sattleberg or advance to Sio, but to go on the defensive. In stark contrast to the difficulty in having the 2/43rd moved to reinforce Windeyer in late September, the new Australian commander of the New Guinea Force, Lieutenant General Sir Leslie Morsehead, assured Wootten that reinforcements would be swiftly moved from Lae. The difficulties with MacArthur's headquarters and the Navy had been smoothed out; however, some rancor still remained. General MacKay wrote Blamey on October 20:

> Through not being able to reinforce quickly the enemy has been given time to recover and we have not been able to exploit our original success. Through the piecemeal arrival

of reinforcements the momentum of the attack has not been maintained. As was proved in the Lae operations the provision of adequate forces at the right place and time is both the quickest and most economical course.[17]

The landings on Scarlet Beach upset the Japanese plans, which were to reinforce the 5,000 troops in the Finschhafen-Mongi River area. Parts of three Japanese divisions, the 20th, 41st, and 51st, were there. Of these, the most important was General Shigeru Katagiri's 20th Division. Adachi could expect little from the broken 51st, and even the bulk of the 80th Regiment of the 20th, which was in retreat over the Saruwagel Range toward the north coast, was not available. Adachi ordered the main part of the 20th, comprising the 79th and 80th Regiments, to leave by sea on September 15. The plan was to have the 79th lead the way to Sio and then march overland to Finschhafen. When the 80th arrived, Katagiri would have, with the troops already there, the equivalent of a division to defend Finschhafen. These plans were interrupted by the landing of the Australians at Scarlet Beach and their subsequent movement into the interior. Adachi then diverted the troops to the Sattleberg area. The abortive attack by Lieutenant Colonel Takeo Takagi's 3rd Battalion on the twenty-sixth convinced Adachi to suspend active offensive operations until all the available troops of the 80th Regiment had arrived at Sattleberg. It had originally been planned to have them at Finschhafen by October 25, but its loss caused the Japanese to hurry to their concentration points as fast as the terrain permitted. On October 12, Katagiri issued his order for the beginning of the offensive to recapture Finschhafen. He planned a three-pronged attack. The first would be a diversion from the north; then there would be a seaborne attack by a portion of the 79th Regiment to blow up ammunition dumps and artillery positions, and in general cause havoc. The main attack would come from the west by the 80th Regiment along the Sattleberg Road toward Heldsbach village.[18]

General Wootten had received information from higher head-quarters and his advance patrols that the Japanese were planning a major attack. However, until October 15 he had little intimation as to the nature or direction of the attack. Nevertheless, at a meeting with senior commanders, he had warned that the Japanese would probably attack toward the airfield and Langemak Bay. They should be prepared for a land or sea attack or possibly a coordinated attack from both directions. On that day, a copy of General Katagiri's order was captured and soon translated. Wootten's suspicions were confirmed, but he made few changes in the disposition of his defense forces. They were to hold the trail junctions, the high ground two miles west of Scarlet Beach, and the various villages already occupied. Light antiaircraft guns were sited to protect the beach, and two-pound guns were placed along the coast. The 2/32nd Battalion, which had arrived on the fifteenth, and the 2/2nd Machine Gun Battalion formed the reserve.[19]

Wootten's forces did not have long to wait. A bombing raid early on the morning of the seventeenth was the start of a coordinated attack on the beach area from the sea. However sound Katagiri's strategy might have been, he did not provide enough troops. The seaborne invasion was doomed from the beginning. Three barges were detected at dawn on the seventeenth by troops from the U.S. Amphibious Engineer Battalion, manning 37 mm guns. At a range of only twenty-five yards, the guns shredded the barges, sinking two, while the third, riddled with small-arms fire, retired northward. Approximately eighty survivors clambered over a sand spit and made it to land. Approximately half of the Japanese force was killed, and the others were driven across the Song River.[20]

This small-scale attack was but a preliminary. The main attack struck the 2/3rd Pioneer Battalion and penetrated to within 3,000 yards of Scarlet Beach before being halted by the defensive line of the 2/28th Battalion. Troops of the 26th Brigade were sent forward to strengthen the defense of the beach area. On Wootten's request, this brigade had been sent up from Lae in thirteen LCTs and three

LSTs escorted by destroyers, and had made a safe landing despite Japanese air attacks.[21] The 26th would later play a crucial role in the defense of the main Australian front between the Song River and Siki Creek. However, until the twenty-second, the brunt of the fighting was borne by the 20th and 24th Brigades. Much of the fighting was for the village of Katika near the mouth of the Song River, only two miles north of Finschhafen. On the eighteenth, the Japanese attacked in force against the 24th Brigade, defending the village. The fighting continued throughout the day with the attackers launching a series of frontal attacks; in each case they were mowed down by small-arms and machine-gun fire. The only temporary success was when some Japanese managed to establish a wedge between the 20th and 24th Brigades. These reached a point near the mouth of Siki Creek. The Japanese continued their futile frontal attacks on the nineteenth; several of these were senseless bayonet charges. In each case they were repulsed, sometimes by artillery fire.

With his losses mounting, Katagiri pulled his troops back from the Siki Creek and Katika area on the twenty-first. He resumed the attack on the night of the twenty-second. By this time the 26th Brigade had moved forward to aid the defense. The Japanese streamed down the Katika Trail in a massed charge. They were halted, with heavy casualties, by the fire of Australian field guns, mortars, and automatic weapons. This prodigal waste of life was the last major attempt to retake Finschhafen, and three days later a general withdrawal back to the Sattleberg area began, with only blocking forces left around Jivevaneng and astride the main trail. Katagiri had nothing to show for his efforts. There were 1,258 Japanese dead counted by the Australians. In all probability there were many more, and the many wounded and sick meant that the two Japanese regiments were in no position to successfully resist any general Australian offensive against their positions at the Sattleberg and Wareo River line.[22]

Despite their losses, the Japanese had created excellent defensive positions and were aided by the terrain and vegetation. There were great walls of nearly impassable bamboo forests and betel nut palms growing out of steep slopes. The Japanese commander had positioned one regiment in the direct Sattleberg area, a mixed force guarding the western approaches, and a battalion in the Gusika area. He held two battalions in reserve in the center of a triangle formed by Sattleberg, Wareo, and Gusika. The main defenses of Sattleberg were in a circle three miles distant from the mountain.[23]

The task of taking the Sattleberg was given to the 26th Brigade, which would have three infantry battalions and a machine-gun battalion backed by artillery. In addition, there were three troops comprising nine Matilda tanks assigned to the main force, the first time that heavy tanks had been used in New Guinea. The plan of attack was for the 2/48th Battalion to clear the main road and attack Sattleberg frontally. On the left would be the 2/23rd, advancing from the west, while the 2/24th, on the right, would cut the Katiska-Sattleberg Trail and then push on toward the mountain. The attack began on the seventeenth, after a bridgehead had been established across Siki Creek. The immediate objective for the 2/24th was a height called Feature 2200 that dominated the spur line along which the trail ran. Attacking early in the morning, the battalion was held up by the heavy bamboo forest and later by withering fire from the Japanese on the high ground. The next day, it was pulled back in order to allow the artillery and mortars to work over the Japanese defenses. Resuming the attack, the Australians made only short gains and the battalion commander requested tanks. Although it was decided to send them, their movement was held up because a bulldozer had to clear a path for them. For the next few days a series of attempts to flank Feature 2200 was tried, with only minimal success. The artillery and mortar fire in support was almost continuous. Finally, with the arrival of three tanks, a further direct attack was planned for the twenty-fifth. This was not necessary since forward patrols discovered that the Japanese had abandoned their positions and the survivors had retreated toward Wareo.[24]

On and around the height, the Australians counted fifty-nine
dead Japanese. One observer described the situation found after
capturing Feature 2200. He wrote:

> Patrols from our own and "B" Company met on the top of
> the feature in the midst of a scene of desolation. Trees and
> scrub had been torn down and tail fins of both 3-inch
> and 2-inch bombs were found in many of the enemy's
> pits and foxholes. There was evidence that a number of Japs
> had been hastily buried there, and later several damaged
> "woodpeckers" and other material were unearthed. Weak
> from lack of food and the strain of continuous shelling and
> mortaring, the few Japs that evacuated the position were ap-
> parently unable to carry their weapons, other than rifles.[25]

Meanwhile, the 2/48th Battalion had moved up the main Sattleberg Road from the junction of Green Ridge and Sisi. On the
seventeenth, the Japanese positions were subjected to fierce artillery and aerial bombardment before the infantry, supported by
tanks, began to advance. Despite this, progress was slow and the
battalion suffered heavy casualties, particularly from a height
known as Feature 2400. Not until the twenty-fourth were the
Japanese forced from this vantage point by a flanking movement.
By that evening, the Australians were within 150 yards of Sattleberg
summit. Here they were held up by machine gunning from a ridgeline directly in front. At this juncture Sergeant Tom Derrick received permission to lead his section in one further attack. Moving
ahead of the section, he threw grenade after grenade at the enemy
positions, knocking out ten posts, and forced the demoralized defenders to abandon the ridge. For this action he would later be
awarded Britain's highest honor, the Victoria Cross. The Australians dug in on the ridge and then attacked the summit the following day. Much to their surprise, they discovered that the

Japanese had abandoned their positions and pulled back to aid in the defense of Wareo.[26]

After the capture of Sattleberg, two companies of the 2/24th began the next stage, pursuing the retreating Japanese toward Wareo, their objective to link up with the 24th Brigade, advancing on the Wareo-Gusika line. The 2/23rd also moved out on the left flank. The first objective was the village of Palanko, one mile northwest of Sattleberg. The village was abandoned, and the Australians pushed on toward Fior, the next village, more than 1,000 feet below, near the Song River. Only a few wandering Japanese soldiers were encountered before the 2/23rd relieved the 2/24th. At the small village of Kuanko, just south of Wareo, a large contingent of Japanese made a stand on December 2. The Australians were driven back from the high ground. For a time the Australian supply line was threatened before a company of the 2/24th drove through to relieve the endangered battalion. After this the advance was briefly held up by the need to cross a huge ravine and by heavy fire from the Japanese entrenched on a promontory called Peak Hill. A two-day battle ensued for the hill before the Japanese position was flanked. After their withdrawal, Wareo was occupied on December 7.[27]

As the 26th Brigade advanced toward Wareo, a secondary attack by the 24th Brigade was mounted to the east. The objective was to cut the trail from Wareo to the sea. This was a major line of Japanese communications between Wareo and the coast. The high point of this defense line was Pabu Ridge. Two companies of the 2/23rd captured this vital point on November 21. The Australians then dug shallow trenches to counter any Japanese attempts to retake the ridge. These were not long in coming. For the next ten days the Japanese bombarded the ridge with mortar and artillery fire interspersed with infantry attacks. As was usual, these were direct frontal attacks as the Japanese commanders wasted their infantry, which was cut down by the Australians' firepower. For a while the Japanese managed to cut the battalion's supply line, and the situation became critical. The defenders soon ran short of supplies, particularly water. For days it was impossible to move the wounded to aid stations. The situation was saved by airdrops, and on the twenty-sixth another company of the 2/23rd, which had been located as a reserve near the Song River, relieved the defenders, backed by Matilda tanks. A successful attack on Pine Hill, a key terrain feature, reestablished the supply line to Pabu Ridge. Moving west along the trail, a linkup was made on December 12 with units of the 26th Brigade, moving northeast from Wareo. The 4th Brigade, which had been held in reserve at Finschhafen during the same period, began its march up the coast and on November 29 took Gusika, the eastern terminus of the trail. Troops of the 4th then prepared to pursue the retreating Japanese up the coast toward Sio and beyond to Saidor.[28]

Support for the troops during the action after the capture of Nadzab and Lae depended upon the quick conversion of airfields that could handle transport aircraft. This work fell to the airborne engineers. The Kaiapit strip was soon put into condition to handle an ever-increasing number of C-47s bringing in reinforcements, as well as more engineers to improve the facilities there and at Nadzab and the Dumpu area. During October work had begun on a 6,000-foot runway and dispersal areas. After the capture of Dumpu, two U.S. engineering battalions were at work at a site near the junction of the Gusap and Ramu Rivers, and construction soon began on all-weather facilities to handle one fighter group and one medium bomber group there with all the necessary service facilities. As early as September 20, heavy construction crews began repairing the airfield, and soon its 5,000-foot runway was usable; by early December a 5,700-foot runway of steel matting was available at Finschhafen. These new facilities were an important part of higher headquarters' planning for further offensives, since they enabled the Fifth Air Force to cover the Vitiaz Strait more thoroughly.[29]

Brigadier General Carl Connell, at the USASOS Advanced Base office in Lae, was in charge of construction in the region. Both Australian and U.S. engineers, aided by native labor, were involved in improving the harbor facilities. Before the New Britain operation, they had constructed two Liberty ship wharves, one petroleum pier, and one small ship pier at Lae. Work was continuing in harbor dredging at Finschhafen, and by early December there was a floating dock there. Another main construction effort besides airfield work was building an all-weather road linking Lae and Nadzab. The official report on the various construction efforts noted:

> The principal road project was the one connecting Lae and Nadzab where troops were dependent for supplies on air shipments. An engineer aviation battalion began improving the primitive track and jungle trail later in September. The project was completed in record time on 4 October, but unfortunately the same drainage oversights that had earlier plagued the airfield workers now haunted the road crews. Stretches of the road were already impassable on the completion date. Two days later, with the road closed, work was resumed; on 15 December it was opened to all-weather traffic, this time in operational condition. Considerable engineer effort was expended on access roads in the Lae-Nadzab region.[30]

By mid-December, the situation for the Japanese in the Huon Peninsula was desperate. In the interior, the 7th Division was firmly in control of the upper Ramu Valley and was reorganizing in preparation for further advances from Dumpu down the Faria River with the objective of flanking the Japanese retreating along the coast toward Bogadjim. The newly arrived 15th and 18th Brigades would ultimately spearhead this advance and would be forced to fight their way through a series of small-unit actions, the most important of which was at a feature called Shaggy Ridge. From Fortification Point north of Gusika, reached on December 21, the 4th Brigade was preparing its coastal advance toward Saidor, which in the end would last three months.

Six

COMMAND RELATIONS

The success of the Allied forces in New Guinea during 1943 was due in large part to events elsewhere in the Pacific. The amphibious operations against Lae and Finschhafen could not have been undertaken if the Japanese air commanders at Rabaul had been able to devote their entire force to the New Guinea area. However, beginning with Guadalcanal, the Japanese High Command had considered maintaining control of the Solomon Islands to be of more importance, and they spent the lives of their troops in a profligate manner to hold those islands. Even more important, a large portion of the Japanese navy and air force was committed to the various campaigns. As American naval power in the central and South Pacific increased, the Japanese, although successful in a few encounters, gradually lost control of the sea approaches. At the same time, their air superiority was lost to American pilots, who by mid-1943 had more and better planes.

The decision of the Joint Chiefs in March 1943 set forth the tasks to be achieved during the year. For MacArthur, the goals were generally agreed upon. The advance should be continued along the north coast of New Guinea, capturing Wewak and Madang in offensives that ultimately would reach the extreme westward land area of the Vogelkop Peninsula. The situation in the South Pacific area was more complicated. There was general agreement in Washington and at Admiral Halsey's headquarters with regard to objectives. One of the main problems that had to be solved was the command relationships. The drawing of the original line dividing the Southwest Pacific Theater from the central Pacific had left the Solomon Islands as a part of MacArthur's command. The need for the quick invasion of Guadalcanal in August 1942, conducted at first by Marine units backed by the Navy, had dictated the redrawing of their line, giving the Navy control of that offensive. Taking the central and northern Solomons from MacArthur's command could not be repeated. Even the naval leaders in Washington, who still believed that the Pacific war should be directed primarily by Nimitz, did not want to cause an interservice rift at that juncture. Therefore, the original division lines remained. Halsey was given the task of operational command in the Solomons. However, the campaigns were to be under the overall command of MacArthur, who would issue general directives for the planned campaigns. Thus for the coming offensives it was important that MacArthur and Halsey cooperate closely with each other.[1]

Halsey at first shared the Navy's negative opinion that MacArthur was a grandstanding prima donna who rightly should have been placed under Nimitz's command. Further, there had been an incident in February 1943 when Halsey's request for additional planes had been refused by MacArthur. The denial had been couched in such a manner as seemingly to question Halsey's competence. At one juncture Halsey had referred to MacArthur as a "self advertising Son of a Bitch." However, by April 1943 he understood that the proposed offensives dictated that he and MacArthur meet and discuss the various key issues. On the fifteenth he flew to Brisbane, where MacArthur greeted him warmly and exercised his considerable charm in their discussions. By the time Halsey left, he had reversed his opinion of the general. He later wrote, "Five minutes after I reported I felt as if we were life long friends."[2] MacArthur also expressed his admiration for Halsey's fighting qualities.

Nothing in subsequent months would shake the mutual respect of the two commanders, and what could have been an awkward command situation proceeded without friction. In the campaigns against New Georgia and Bougainville, Halsey kept MacArthur informed of all phases of the operations. MacArthur, for his part, did not interfere with the campaigns once the plans had been approved. The one major contribution that MacArthur made that directly influenced the Solomons operations was to disapprove the many tentative plans to invade the southern area of Bougainville, where the Japanese defenses were the strongest. Instead, he suggested that the attack be made far up the coast at Empress Augusta Bay. This was accepted, and the subsequent success of the landings there justified his strategic thinking.[3]

For the Solomons operations, MacArthur and Halsey had overwhelming superiority over the Japanese. Three army divisions and one Marine division, a total of more than 275,000 men, were available. They were backed by AIRSOLS and the thirteenth Air Force, with more than 400 planes, and the Navy had two cruiser-destroyer groups. Halsey could also depend on two carrier Task Groups built around the *Saratoga* and *Enterprise* if needed. The first target in the Central Solomons was the island of New Georgia, on which the important Munda airfield was located. The 172nd Regiment of the Army's 43rd Division landed on the south coast on July 2. At the same time, a Marine regiment landed on the north coast with the objective of cutting off a Japanese retreat. The terrain, combined with a brilliant defense by the Japanese General Noburu Saseki, held up the Americans, and it was necessary to bring in elements of the 37th and 25th Divisions before the island was finally secured on August 25. Possession of Munda airfield gave Allied air a position within 450 miles of Rabaul.[4] The next step was a surprise to the Japanese as 25th Division troops bypassed the strong garrison on Kolambangara to occupy instead the island of Vella Lavella. This forced the evacuation of Kolambangara and added two more functioning airstrips to support the landings on Bougainville, the next step aimed at rendering Rabaul useless for offensive operations.

As the attack on Finschhafen was being mounted, MacArthur's and Halsey's headquarters were planning to further neutralize the Japanese in the Solomons and bring more pressure to bear on Rabaul by occupying the Shortland Islands and then seizing a foothold on the large island of Bougainville. Acting on MacArthur's suggestions, Halsey's planners decided to use the 3rd Marine Division to establish a foothold at Empress Augusta Bay. On November 1, the Marines landed and, meeting only slight resistance from a few hundred Japanese, quickly established a defensible position and soon captured the airfield. Joined by the Army's 37th Division on November 8, they moved into the interior and established a larger perimeter that allowed construction crews to begin work on two airfields capable of handling bombers. By the time the Marines were relieved by the Army's Americal Division in early December, the foothold had been developed into a major base located far from the main Japanese elements on the island. The Japanese would mount a major offensive in March 1944 and, after some initial success, were driven back into the hills with huge losses. This was the last serious threat to the enclave. Australian forces would take over the Bougainville defense beginning in November 1944. Contrary to U.S. tactics, they would undertake the conquest of the entire island. This decision ensured that fighting on the island would continue until the end of the war with thousands more casualties, all to no good purpose as the main objective for the Bougainville landings had been achieved long before. The completion of the airfields brought the key Japanese bastion of Rabaul within two hundred miles of Allied aircraft.[5]

Rabaul was the headquarters and main supply base for both the Southeastern Army and the Southeastern Fleet. There were four natural harbors; the largest, at Blanche Bay, was six miles long and two and a half miles wide. The others were Karavia Bay, Matupi Harbor, and Simpson Harbor. The latter was the best developed, with docking facilities for more than 300,000 tons of shipping. There were adequate loading and repair facilities to service all types of ships. The Eighth Fleet, based there throughout 1942, normally had a complement of five cruisers and eight destroyers. During the Guadalcanal and subsequent Solomons operations, the Third or Combined Fleet assumed the responsibility for most offensive action. However, by the end of 1943, losses in all areas of the Pacific had reduced the capability of the Navy to mount serious major actions in the South Pacific. Air units based at Rabaul were also primarily the responsibility of the Eleventh Air Fleet. The bulk of the Army's planes had been transferred to Wewak in August 1943. The number of planes available at any time varied with the presumed needs but throughout most of 1943 seldom fell below three hundred planes of all types. Despite heavy losses, the Navy continued to reinforce its air units with approximately fifty planes a month flown in from Truk. In all of New Britain, the Japanese army could muster 97,870 men. To defend the region around Rabaul in November 1943, the Army had 76,300 men.[6]

Allied leaders at all levels had been concerned with Rabaul since the early stages of the war. At first this concern was defensive because the early air attacks on Port Moresby and northern Australia were generated from there. The occupation of bases in New Guinea was mounted from Rabaul, and the major but abortive Japanese offensive over the Owen Stanley Mountains toward Port Moresby was sustained from Rabaul. Throughout the first months of 1942, the only offensive action that could be carried out against

Rabaul was by General Kenney's outnumbered air units, which had to fly long distances from bases in Australia and Port Moresby. Surprisingly, it was during this dark period that MacArthur broached his plan to capture Rabaul. In May 1942, he suggested that if he were given three divisions, backed by two aircraft carriers, he could capture Rabaul.[7] It is difficult to know how serious he was since he was trying desperately to gain reinforcements to defend northern Australia. More prudent heads prevailed at that time, but the idea that an invasion of eastern New Britain was necessary continued to be part of the overall general strategy of both MacArthur and the Joint Chiefs, who considered it part of the tasks assigned to MacArthur.

In early June 1943, the Joint Strategic Survey Committee, operating under the Joint Chiefs, took an opposite view and recommended the neutralization of Rabaul rather than a costly invasion. On July 21, Marshall communicated this idea to MacArthur. After the proposed capture of Wewak and Manus in the Admiralties and Halsey's capture of Kavieng on New Ireland, Marshall believed that Rabaul would be encircled and could be effectively neutralized using the two U.S. air forces. MacArthur disagreed, arguing that Rabaul had to be taken in order to provide a forward naval base to guard the right flank of any Wewak invasion force. He argued that the Wewak garrison was too strong and its capture would be doubtful if the Japanese there were supported by air and naval forces from Rabaul. This argument was strange because even with his questionable intelligence service, he had to know that the garrison force and defenses at Rabaul were much more formidable than those at Wewak.

Nevertheless, MacArthur persisted. In early August, he submitted to the Joint Chiefs his Reno II plan, in which he continued to stress that Rabaul should be taken before any major leap forward on the north coast. He proposed the capture of Cape Gloucester in western New Britain in order to secure the Vitiaz Strait and prevent the transfer of forces to Rabaul. Further action would later be taken to secure the New Guinea coast as far as the Vogelkop Peninsula, which MacArthur believed could be reached by the end of 1944. The islands of Halmahera and Morotai would be captured as a preliminary to the invasion of Mindanao in early 1945. Washington disagreed on some key elements of this plan. Chief among these was that Rabaul would be neutralized and not captured. There was also the implication that Nimitz's central Pacific offensives would be given higher priority than those in the Southwest Pacific Theater. This caused genuine concern at MacArthur's headquarters that it would be cut out of later important offensives. The decision to neutralize Rabaul was confirmed by the action of the Combined Chiefs at the Quebec Quadrant Conference, which met from August 14 to 24. One of MacArthur's primary concerns was approval of his long-range plans to return to the Philippines. No decision was made concerning his proposal for an invasion of the southern Philippines. His headquarters feared that even if this were approved, it would be left to Nimitz.[8]

In MacArthur's reminiscences there is no hint of this disagreement with his superiors. The only reference is that he instructed Kenney to assist the Bougainville operation by increasing the air operations directed at Rabaul. The main force available to Kenney for this was the 1st Air Task Force, located at Dobodura. At the beginning of October Colonel Frederick Smith, Jr., commanding the task force, had two bombardment groups of regular B-25s and B-26s, a group of A-20 and B-25 strafers, and two fighter groups, one of which was equipped with P-38s. The RAAF maintained Beaufighter attack squadrons at Dobodura and Kiriwina. In addition, there were B-24 heavy bombers sited at Port Moresby, available for attacks on Rabaul. Afterward, reconnaissance planes indicated a heavy concentration of shipping at Rabaul. On October 12, 349 planes attacked the airfields, shipping, and supply dumps. The preliminary estimate of the damage by the Fifth Air Force was that 100 enemy planes had been destroyed on the ground and another 51 damaged. They reported 3 large merchant ships, 3 destroyers, 43 small merchant vessels, and 70 harbor vessels sunk or destroyed. Heavy damage to the wharf areas and airfields was also claimed. The estimate of aircraft destruction was reasonably accurate, though the damage to shipping and shore facilities was exaggerated.[9] On the thirteenth, MacArthur exulted to Kenney, "George, you broke Rabaul's back yesterday," to which Kenney replied, "The attack marks the turning point in the war in the Southwest Pacific."[10] Neither of the comments proved correct. Nevertheless, this large-scale raid had been a great success.

That MacArthur's optimism was misplaced could be seen in the reprisal air attacks by the Japanese on Oro Bay and Finschhafen on the fifteenth and seventeenth. Although some damage was done, the Japanese lost an estimated 100 planes during the attacks, but the strikes indicated that Rabaul could still be an important offensive air base. Thus Kenney authorized further attacks, the most important being a low-level attack on the twenty-ninth that sank a number of merchant ships and during which the B-25s and P-38s shot down 68 planes and destroyed 26 on the ground. The RAAF followed this with a night attack on November 2 and again on the tenth. Halsey sent planes from the carriers *Essex, Bunker Hill,* and *Independence* against Rabaul on the fifth and again on the eleventh. These were in conjunction with strikes by General Nathan Twining's Thirteenth Air Force. The result of these devastating raids was to prevent the Japanese air force from doing any significant damage to the landings at Empress Augusta Bay. More important, by the time the Thirteenth Air Force assumed the major responsibility for attacking Rabaul, it had ceased to be a major threat. Although the air offensive continued in the early months of 1944, the once threatening base had been neutralized. The planners in Washington had been correct.[11]

While the attacks on Finschhafen and Rabaul were proceeding, fundamental changes were occurring that would alter the details of future operations. The first series of changes concerned the Navy. MacArthur's dissatisfaction with King and Nimitz and more specifically with Carpender masked how much he owed to the Navy. The victories of the Coral Sea and Midway in 1942 had greatly reduced the potential threat of the Japanese navy. The Coral Sea victory undoubtedly saved Port Moresby. Even more significant were the many naval battles in the Solomons in which the Japanese fruitlessly attempted to destroy U.S. naval power but lost control of the sea and the air. In the war of words with the Navy, MacArthur's headquarters overlooked the contributions made by the submarine service. During 1943, those operating from Freemantle had claimed 105 ships, totaling 600,000 tons, those from Brisbane had sunk 61 ships with a total of 350,000 tons, while the main effort from Pearl Harbor had resulted in the sinking of 277 ships. Japan's total shipping tonnage was then reduced by more than 1 million tons in only one year.[12] The Japanese garrisons throughout the southern Pacific would find it difficult to receive supplies and reinforcements in the future and would in many cases be reduced to the starvation level.

On March 15, 1943, Admiral King instituted a new fleet numbering system, giving the three Pacific fleets odd numbers. The main blue-water fleet at first would be the Third, commanded by Halsey; the Fifth was under Vice Admiral Raymond Spruance, and MacArthur's Naval Forces Southwest Pacific was redesignated the Seventh. This had little immediate effect on the situation in New Guinea since no change was made in the command structure. Carpender continued as its commander even though it was obvious that MacArthur was dissatisfied with him. Twice in 1943 MacArthur requested that Carpender be replaced, and finally the Navy decided to acquiesce. King and Nimitz, during their meeting in San Francisco, decided to transfer Carpender to command the 9th Naval District and replace him with Vice Admiral Thomas

Kinkaid, who had garnered an excellent reputation as an aggressive fighter in actions from Midway to the Aleutians. However, while he was on his way to the southwest Pacific, it was discovered that the Navy had been guilty of an embarrassing oversight: They had not consulted MacArthur on Kinkaid's appointment. The error was caught in time, and Marshall smoothed over the difficulty by giving MacArthur a chance to disapprove.[13]

Kinkaid arrived in Brisbane on November 23, accompanied by Halsey, and soon met with MacArthur, who had already approved his appointment. Kinkaid's impression of MacArthur was favorable, and the general appeared happy to replace Carpender with a more aggressive commander. Kinkaid assumed command of the Seventh Fleet on the twenty-sixth and established his headquarters in Brisbane in the same building where General Headquarters was located. This meant that MacArthur could, if he wished, have immediate access to his naval commander, a situation that did not apply to his ground force commander, General Blamey, whose headquarters was located elsewhere. Barbey continued to command the amphibious forces. Thus, ostensibly, the Navy had given MacArthur two leaders whom he trusted. However, the problem of command was not totally solved. Kinkaid still had to serve two masters since he depended entirely upon the Navy for ships, men, and supplies, and King retained control of the Seventh Fleet. MacArthur's navy was that in name only, and the future success of joint army and navy ventures depended upon good personal relations between commanders rather than a unified bureaucracy. During all the months he was in command of the Seventh Fleet, Kinkaid was able to deal diplomatically with the difficult situation and MacArthur as the war situation improved. Although never convinced that he was not being slighted by higher naval command, MacArthur made the best of the situation. The success of Barbey's 7th Amphibious Force was a major factor in reducing MacArthur's ire. The forced relations between the Navy and Army necessitated a series of compromises that ultimately proved successful.[14]

A parallel series of developments while the offensive against Finschhafen was progressing had serious ramifications for Australia's premier role in the New Guinea operations. It had been obvious even before the Buna campaign that MacArthur was unhappy about having to depend primarily on Australian troops. Although on the surface harmonious relations prevailed between him and Blamey, MacArthur had been critical of Blamey and the Australian combat record. He had created Alamo Force in preparation for Krueger to assume the chief role in planning and conducting the later stages of the war, thus bypassing Blamey as Allied ground force commander. Already in the spring of 1943, he had planned a shift away from his dependence upon the Australians. This he had done by creating Alamo Force and dividing spheres of activity between the Australian and U.S. forces. New Guinea Force was to continue its operations in the Huon Peninsula and beyond, while Alamo Force commander General Krueger was given the task of occupying Kiriwina and Woodlark and later western New Britain.

One of the first developments leaning in this direction was the political debates in Australia prior to and immediately after the general election in August, which the government won handily. It was obvious that Australia had borne a large burden in the war, providing a significant part of its army to support Britain in the European Theater during 1940–41. Doing so in Malaya, Singapore, and later the defense of Australia had cost much in men and matériel. Now thoughtful Australians believed that Australia's contributions should be scaled back. Blamey opposed the most radical suggestions and warned that a reduction in the size of Australia's strike force below three divisions would be against the national interest. He wanted an army that would not be below 375,000 men in order to maintain that interest both during and after the war. He suggested to Prime Minister Curtin—who passed it on to

MacArthur—that the Americans take over some of the administrative tasks then being done for U.S. forces. On August 24, MacArthur replied that however much he might like to do this, it would be at a considerable cost to the war effort and would not be done. The Australian Defense Committee proposed that the effective strength of the Army by July 1944 should be 371,000 men, as compared to the current 492,000 men. The civilian workforce was targeted for considerable cuts, as was the RAAF. At a meeting of the War Cabinet, Blamey argued against many of these cuts, particularly in view of the need to continue to supply logistical support for the Americans. Nevertheless, the War Cabinet agreed to the cutbacks. These debates and later Curtin's overseas visits in early 1944, on which Blamey accompanied the prime minister, took up much of Blamey's time. This also aided MacArthur in shifting much of the planning and execution of the war away from Blamey. For the record, MacArthur appeared unhappy with the Australian government's decision, although it is difficult to believe that he did not see that the Australians' role would have to be diminished during the coming year.[15]

General Krueger, in contrast to the situation a year previously, had significant troop strength in northern Australia and New Guinea. The bulk of the army units were located in the area from Rockhampton to Townsville in Australia and at Port Moresby, Milne Bay, and Buna in New Guinea. Much of the 41st Division was in the environs of Buna, and the 32nd was refitting and retraining in Australia after the arduous Buna campaign. On July 11, the first elements of the 1st Cavalry Division arrived, and the 24th Division landed the following month. They were joined in January 1944 by the 6th Division. The last arrived too late for the Cape Gloucester and Arawe landings but would be useful in later operations. The most important part of Alamo Force (Sixth Army) in the immediate campaign was the 1st Marine Division which had been recuperating from the Guadalcanal operation in southern Australia and was thus under MacArthur's command. He coveted the Marine unit and tried hard to have it assigned to him permanently. This was ultimately denied since the Navy believed that its amphibious expertise was more needed in the planned central Pacific campaigns. Nevertheless, MacArthur had the Marine unit on a temporary basis, and he planned to use it to secure western New Britain.

Seven

ARAWE AND
CAPE GLOUCESTER

MacArthur's concern about Rabaul dictated in part the decision to secure airfields in western New Britain. A further reason was the belief that they would be necessary to secure control of the Vitiaz Strait between New Britain and New Guinea. General Headquarters planned to use the airfields at Cape Gloucester and on the south coast at Gasmata to help neutralize Rabaul and protect future landings at Wewak and Madang. On May 6, 1943, Alamo Force received the warning order from General Headquarters for future airborne and amphibious operations in western New Britain. The major goal, as stated, was to seize Cape Gloucester and its airfield. For this the 1st Marine Division, which had been refitting and retraining near Melbourne, was designated. Beginning in June, representatives of that division traveled to Brisbane to work on advanced planning for the operation, which was named Backhander as part of the overall operation code named Dexterity. At the same time, General Krueger's staff worked out a plan of their own. One major difference between the two was that the Alamo plan called for more forward staging areas for the invasions. By September 28, a plan had been accepted by Krueger. This was approved by General Headquarters on October 14 with the minor change of moving the 1st Marines, the reserve for the Cape Gloucester venture, forward to Oro Bay. The date for the landing was scheduled for November 14. Lack of shipping—given the operations ongoing on the Huon Peninsula—postponed D-day for Cape Gloucester to December 26. The secondary landing at Gasmata, code-named Lazaretto, was to be undertaken on December 15.[1]

Major changes were made to the original composite plan to conform to the objections of Major General William Rupertus, the Marine Corps commander. The plan, as previously approved, called for landings on two beaches by only one marine regimental combat team, while another would be held in reserve to land as quickly as possible and then to pass through the first. There was to be an airdrop by the Army's 503rd Parachute Regiment south of the airfield. The marines were expected to drive through the jungle to link up with the paratroops. The air commanders did not like this plan because it would create a considerable drain on the available planes, and thus they joined the Marines in objecting to it. Differences between the marine planners and the Army continued until the visit of MacArthur and Krueger to Goodenough Island, where at a conference they heard the Marines' exposition of their objections. The plan for Cape Gloucester was altered on December 15. Instead of a single regiment, the changed plan called for the initial landing to be made by two regimental combat teams. The proposed airdrop of the 503rd, never popular with the Marines, was canceled.[2]

It is difficult to know why an invasion of the southern area was believed to be necessary. One answer at that time was that the Navy wanted a PT boat base at Gasmata in order to operate better against the Japanese barge traffic. However, when the decision was made to substitute Arawe for Gasmata, Captain Morton Mumma, commanding the PT boats, declared that he did not need a base there as long as the Cape Gloucester area was secure.[3] Arawe was substituted for Gasmata because Kenney learned that the Lindenhafen plantation at Gasmata was not suitable for an airfield. At a conference on November 19 with MacArthur, Krueger, and Carpender, he argued further that any airfield there would be closer to Rabaul than to Dobodura. General Headquarters eventually agreed with Kenney despite the statement of his deputy, Ennis Whitehead, that an airfield there was not necessary. Thus Arawe, fifty miles to the west of Gasmata and ninety miles closer to the cape, was declared the next target for Alamo Force and given the code name Director.[4] MacArthur was informed by his intelligence chief that there were only five hundred members of the 115th Infantry of the Japanese 51st Division located at Arawe. MacArthur's major worry about the entire Backhander operation was fear of air attacks from Rabaul and Wewak.

Arawe, the new target authorized on November 22, was the name of an island, harbor, and plantation. The site chosen for the landing was the narrow peninsula that was bounded on the northwest by a large swampy region. There were two good beaches that could be used. One, named House Fireman, was on the west coast of the peninsula, the other at the village of Umingalu on the mainland, a mile from the tip of the peninsula. Elsewhere there were stone cliffs a few hundred feet high covered by mangrove. In order to provide information for the landing, Krueger attached one company of the 1st Marine Amphibian Tractor Battalion to the Task Force to cooperate with the Army's 532nd Engineer and Boat Regiment.

The revised plan substituted the 112th Cavalry Regiment, commanded by Brigadier General Julian Cunningham, for the landing in place of the original regiment of the 32nd Division. True to his word, Kenney kept attacking the Gasmata area until just before Z-day. He then shifted the Air Force's attention to Arawe, dropping more than 400 tons of bombs on the startled Japanese. Meanwhile, during the afternoon of December 13, the troops were taken aboard the LSD *Carter Hall,* HMAS *Westphalia,* and the APDs *Humphreys* and *Sands.* Amphtraks were loaded onto the *Carter Hall.* The convoy was joined by ten bombardment and escort destroyers at Buna. The departure of the cavalry men from Goodenough during a heavy rain was viewed by MacArthur and Krueger along with a number of senior officers, among whom was General Marshall, who was paying one of his infrequent visits to the southwest Pacific.

The plan of operation was for two small assault groups to land ahead of the main effort and secure footholds. Troop A was supposed to land an hour before the main landing and cut the coast road near Umtingalu village, while Troop B landed at Pilelo Island, whose defenders could possibly cover the main passage to the harbor. Troop A was not successful, being surprised by Japanese defenders, whose machine guns and a 25 mm dual-purpose gun sank twelve of the fifteen rubber boats and killed twelve troopers, wounding seventeen. The destroyer *Shaw* quickly opened fire and silenced the Japanese guns. Small boats picked up the survivors and landed them half-naked and without arms at House Fireman Beach.

Troop B was more successful. Its mission was to land at H-hour minus 1 hour on the small island of Pilelo and capture a radio station reported to be operating at the village of Paligmeta. Surprise was lost when the Japanese began firing at Troop B, so the fifteen rubber boats were directed to the side of the island opposite the village. The lead platoon reached the village of Winguru, where it was fired upon by Japanese in two caves. One squad took the caves under fire while the rest moved on to Paligmeta, where they found neither a radio station nor Japanese. Returning to Winguru, they attacked the caves with a bazooka and a flamethrower, killing seven Japanese.[5]

The main landing at House Fireman Beach was preceded by heavy bombardment by the destroyer's five-inch guns, which fired 1,800 rounds in fifteen minutes. Shortly after 6:25 A.M., one of the assigned air squadrons of B-25s bombed and strafed the beach area. The 2nd Squadron of the 112th Cavalry, which was designated to lead the assault, proceeded toward the beach in five landing waves. The first wave, carrying two troops, was in LVT(A) Buffaloes. The next three waves were in the older, slower Alligators. There was initially some confusion as the first wave, without waiting, headed directly for the beach. It was fortunately halted to wait for the subsequent waves. This caused some problems and delayed the landing until after 7 A.M. Even then the second wave landed twenty-five minutes after troops of the first had reached shore. The Japanese, however, were not present in force. There was only sporadic machine-gun fire from the beach, and this was quickly silenced by rocket fire. Once landed, the 2nd Squadron divided, some troops occupying the peninsula while others moved northwest toward its base and established the main line of resistance there. The Japanese had only two companies in the area, and these were quickly silenced. The 1st Squadron, which had been held in reserve landed without incident beginning at 8 A.M. Because of the nature of the beach, there was room for only two LCTs at a time. Thus unloading continued throughout the day. This left Barbey's force vulnerable to air attack. The first of these materialized at 9 A.M., when an estimated thirty planes eluded the U.S. fighter cover to attack the ships remaining on the beach or offshore. The Japanese planes strafed and bombed the beach, the LCTs, and Barbey's command ship, *Conyngham,* without causing serious damage. By midafternoon there were more than 1,600 men onshore, and the two cavalry squadrons controlled the entire peninsula.[6]

The cavalry's hold on the Arawe area was consolidated in the following week as more troops and heavy weapons were brought in. No serious contact was made with the few Japanese left. However, both the Japanese 11th Air Fleet at Rabaul and the 6th Air Division at Wewak sent aircraft to strike at Arawe and later the Marines at Cape Gloucester. In the two weeks following the landing, the naval planes attacked the beachheads seven times while army planes struck Arawe four times. The results for the Japanese were meager: one coastal transport was sunk and another damaged; a minesweeper and six LSTs were also damaged. Despite the lack of antiaircraft guns on shore to defend the lodgment, damage was slight. The Japanese aircraft losses were so heavy over the cape area and at Rabaul that by the end of the month, the Japanese were forced to call off all daylight bombing to concentrate their air defenses at Rabaul and Wewak.[7]

The next phase of the ground action at Arawe was begun on December 18, when two armed Japanese barges attacked a patrol in two of the LCVPs under Cunningham's command. The patrol had been sent westward to discover if there were any Japanese who could threaten the perimeter. The Japanese forced the abandonment of the LCVPs, and the patrol had to march overland to reach Arawe. This was a harbinger of the coming Japanese attempts to retake Arawe. The Japanese in the barges were a part of the 1st Battalion of the 141st Infantry, which had been ordered to move to Arawe by boat and by overland march to come under the command of Major Masamitsu Komori, who had been moving to Arawe from Rabaul before the U.S. landings. Once the two forces joined, Komori was ordered to destroy the Americans.

On December 20, Komori's force arrived at the Pulie River, east of Arawe, and on Christmas Day he attacked and drove back advanced elements of the 112th. General Cunningham believed that Komori was in charge of the lead element of a larger force moving from Gasmata. He therefore requested reinforcements. General Krueger responded immediately, sending a company of the 158th Infantry by PT boats. Reinforced with the troops from the 81st Infantry, Komari, by the twenty-sixth, moved close to the

Americans' main line of defense, where Cunningham had constructed an excellent defensive position only seven hundred yards wide. The cavalry was well dug in, and the mortars and artillery support had time to register in against any possible attack.[8]

On December 25, Komori's 1st Battalion of the 81st Infantry forced the withdrawal of the 112th's outposts, leading to the seizure of Lupin airfield. Komori afterward believed quite wrongly that the Americans' main objective had been the airfield, and his task therefore became to deny it to his enemy. However, during the last week of December, he tried a number of times to dislodge the 112th from its main defense lines. Artillery and mortar fire took a heavy toll in each of the attacks. Bombardment of the Japanese continued even after they had retreated back to their defense line, approximately five hundred yards forward of the U.S. position. On the twenty-ninth, after a week spent wandering about, the 1st Battalion of the 141st Infantry joined Komori's by-now-depleted forces and was given the primary task of defending their airfield. The Japanese proceeded to build a defense in depth with foxholes and trenches from which they could cover all routes of approach. The Japanese, aided by the dense undergrowth, beat off a series of attacks by the cavalrymen. General Cunningham reported to Krueger that it was nearly impossible to see the enemy and he was convinced that continued attacks would simply result in more casualties. He requested tanks to help root out the Japanese.[9]

Krueger agreed and sent a platoon of Company B of the Marine Corps's 1st Tank Battalion from Finschhafen on January 9 along with the 2nd Battalion of the Army's 158th Regiment. Eventually Rupertus released the rest of the tank company then in reserve at Cape Gloucester to participate in the operation. The Marine tankers and Army infantry quickly worked out details of combined operations for the coming attack. On January 16, in preparation for the attack, a squadron of B-24s followed by B-25s struck the Japanese positions. This was followed by an intense artillery and mortar barrage. Then two five-tank platoons, each closely supported by a company of infantry, advanced on a five-hundred-yard front. Despite the swampy terrain and thick vegetation, the tank-infantry teams shattered the Japanese defenses and by midafternoon had achieved their objectives. General Cunningham then ordered a pullback to the main line of resistance. Komori, still obsessed with defending Lupin airfield to the last man, also ordered a pullback. In three weeks of fighting he had lost 116 killed and had 117 wounded. Fourteen had died of other causes, and 80 were so sick as to be unfit for duty.[10] General Cunningham had achieved his goal and was satisfied to allow the shattered Japanese force to slowly starve at an airfield he had no intention of capturing. Komori had drawn that same conclusion and, in his communications with his superiors, began to hint that he should be allowed to withdraw. Finally, 17th Division headquarters agreed that his force was serving no purpose, and on February 24, 1944, he was allowed to begin a retreat to a mid-island position to join other Japanese units covering the withdrawal of Major General Iwao Matsuda's main force from Cape Gloucester.

The Arawe campaign had cost the United States a total of 118 killed and 352 wounded, and almost immediately questions were raised as to the necessity of the operation.[11] Possession of Arawe did little to advance the offensive, as possession of the Huon Peninsula had already assured Allied control of the Vitiaz and Dampier Straits. Once captured, the airfield proved useless for offensive operations, and, true to Commander Mumma's earlier objections, the Navy did not use the harbor for the planned PT boat base. The only positive result appears to have been tying down nearly 1,000 Japanese troops who possibly could have been used against the Marines who were then involved in the main Backhander operation at Cape Gloucester.

The Cape Gloucester operation was much larger and would be much more difficult than that at Arawe. The Japanese forces there had been heavily reinforced as General Imamura, commander of the Eighth Area Army at Rabaul, had earlier anticipated a possible invasion of western New Britain. In May he sent the understrength 65th Brigade to the cape area by barge and small boats. Although it had only a two-battalion regiment, Imamura had attached to it an antitank company with 37 mm guns and an artillery unit with 75 mm mountain guns. In September, partly as a result of the Salamaua operations, Major General Iwao Matsuda was sent to take command of the 65th along with the various shipping companies and a number of troops from rear-echelon units of the 51st Division. On October 5, Imamura appointed Lieutenant General Yashushi Sakai to take over the defense of western New Britain. He was the commander of the 17th Division, which had only just arrived from China. This force was also greatly depleted due to the sinking of two of the transports, one by submarine and another by air attack. The remaining troops were transported by destroyer to Karai-al on the coast and from there were taken by barge or forced to march to their destinations. The main strength of the 17th Division and a further field artillery battalion was assigned to Matsuda to bolster his defense of Cape Gloucester. He deployed his best units along with the regiment's 37 mm and 75 mm guns to defend the vital airfield sector. The Japanese built bunkers and rifle pits along the coastline and in areas they considered most likely for a hostile landing near the cape. Matsuda had to divide his force of 10,500 men to defend Arawe and the region north of Cape Bushing across the island. Nevertheless, he still had a significant force of approximately 4,000 men in the Cape Gloucester area with which to implement General Sakai's order to his troops to carry out "certain death warfare to the utmost, in such a way that not even the slightest disgrace will adhere to your name."[12]

Krueger had formed the Alamo Scouts, a special group operating directly under his command, made up of Australians and U.S. intelligence personnel and natives who knew the region. These scouts would be taken to their objective by PT boats and would be off-loaded on rubber boats. The first party of nine scouts went ashore on September 24 and operated south of Mount Tangi for two weeks, searching for usable trails and the locations of the Japanese. They discovered that the Japanese had earlier evacuated the natives from coastal villages and near the airfields, actions that had alienated most of the population. In mid-October another group of scouts operated for two weeks on Rooke Island, and in early December they landed near Arawe. Admiral Carpender refused to risk the PT boats north of the cape; thus the main beaches near Silimati Point were not investigated. However, another party scouted the region near Tauali and confirmed that the beach was suitable for landings and that they had met no Japanese there. Coast watchers also provided information that was particularly useful to Kenney's planes. In late September, Allied General Headquarters authorized sixteen coast watchers and twenty-seven natives to be landed; they divided into five parties, which scattered to various parts of the interior. Despite all these sources of information, Krueger's intelligence service still knew little of the interior. They depended upon maps based on a pre–World War I German survey augmented by aerial photographs. The latter, though of some use, had very real limitations due to the heavy jungle covering much of western New Britain.[13]

All intelligence sources showed that there was a fringing reef along most of New Britain's thousand-mile coastline with only occasional breaks. The coastline of the western region was generally regular, with a series of small bays. Cape Gloucester, at the northern tip, was free of a reef for one and a half miles on either side. Throughout this area were firm beaches composed of black volcanic sand. There was another break in the reef line near the village of Tauali on the extreme west, bordering Dampier Strait. The narrow beach there was backed by a three-foot bank. From there the ground rose to a series of bluffs. Alamo Force had decided to use this as a

Lieutenant General Hatazo Adachi,
commander, Japanese Eighteenth Army

General Korechika Anami,
commander in chief,
Japanese Second Area Army

Field Marshal Count
Hisaichi Terauchi, commander in
chief, Japanese Southern Army

General Hideki Tojo,
prime minister of Japan, 1941–1944

Major General George A. Vasey,
commander, Australian 7th Division
and, later, 6th Division, just before his
death in March 1945.

Lieutenant General
Sir Edmund Herring, commander,
New Guinea Force, 1943

Lieutenant General
Sir Sydney F. Rowell, commander,
New Guinea Force, 1942

Field Marshal Sir Thomas Blamey,
commander in chief, Allied ground
forces in Southwest Pacific Theater

Major General Richard K. Sutherland, chief of staff,
Southwest Pacific Theater

Lieutenant General George C. Kenney,
Fifth Air Force commander

Major General Robert L. Eichelberger,
commander, U.S. I Corps,
later Eighth Army

Rear Admiral Daniel E. Barbey,
commander, 7th Amphibious Force

Lieutenant General Walter Krueger (left), commander,
Alamo Force and Sixth U.S. Army, and
Vice Admiral Thomas Kinkaid, commander, Seventh Fleet

Lieutenant General Walter Krueger,
commander, Alamo Force and
U.S. Sixth Army

Admiral William Halsey,
commander, South Pacific Area
and Third Fleet

Admiral Chester Nimitz, commander in chief, Pacific Ocean Areas

Admiral Ernest J. King, U.S. chief of naval operations

General George C. Marshall,
chief of staff, U.S. Army

General Douglas MacArthur
and Australian prime minister
John Curtin

General of the Army Douglas MacArthur,
commander in chief, Southwest Pacific Area

backup landing area, code-named Green Beach. The main landings were to be made near Silimati Point on the north coast. The reef surrounding the point had an opening of approximately 1,000 yards; then there was a continuation before another break a few hundred yards away. There was approximately one-half mile of good, although narrow, beach. This was selected to be Yellow Beach 1. The beach closer to Silimati Point was designated Yellow Beach 2.

Behind the Yellow Beaches was an area of mud and standing water. One observer stated succinctly the terrain features in the area of the landings when he wrote:

> Cover and concealment are complete in swamp forest. Ground observation usually is restricted to a few yards. Movement of troops or vehicles is very difficult. Flooded areas virtually preclude movement during the wet season. Large areas of swamp forest occur in the Cape Gloucester–Borgen Bay area: the vegetation behind the landing beaches is a strip of swamp forest which extends nearly to the airdrome area on the west, as well as eastward around Borgen Bay.[14]

The heavy jungle prevented the intelligence operations from ascertaining the real nature of the forest and the swampy conditions before the invasion. Two large hills in the immediate interior rose out of the swamp forest. Target Hill, a 450-foot hill, was close to Yellow Beach 1, while one and a half miles south was Hill 660. West of the beachheads toward the cape was a rolling plain covered by kunai grass. The plain narrowed down near the cape, and it was here that before the war an emergency airfield had been built. Beginning in December 1942, the Japanese started another airstrip there and even began another in April 1943. Air attacks and the need for planes elsewhere had halted construction. By December, one of the runways had already been taken over by kunai grass.[15]

In preparation for the landings, the Marines practiced at Cape Sudest; the last exercise was conducted on December 21. The 7th Marines, reinforced, chosen for the initial landings, loaded on board APDs at Oro Bay on the twenty-fourth, and Barbey's Task Force 76 left on Christmas Day. Later the 1st Marines, from Cape Cretin, joined the convoy. An indication of the growing power of MacArthur's forces in the Southwest Pacific can be seen in the support supplied by the Navy for the landings. Only one year before, the troops of the 32nd Division had been forced to fight for Buna without as much as one destroyer to assist in neutralizing the Japanese defenses. For Cape Gloucester, the transports were escorted by the destroyers *Shaw, Conyngham, Flusser, Reid,* and *Smith.* Task Force 74, the bombardment unit commanded by Australian Rear Admiral V. A. C. Crutchley, comprised the cruisers *Australia, Shropshire, Nashville,* and *Phoenix.*[16]

The convoy proceeded through the Vitiaz Strait without incident, arriving off the Yellow Beaches early in the morning of the twenty-sixth. At 6 A.M. the naval bombardment began. Fire from the cruisers were joined by two LCIs on the flanks firing four-and-a-half-inch rockets. This lasted for ninety minutes before the APDs in the lead lowered the landing craft. At this juncture the bombers, including B-24s, bombed and strafed the beaches and Target Hill. Whitehead had also provided five fighter squadrons for high-level cover. The bombardment was halted as the landing craft neared the shore. In all, the planners had designed the landings in seven echelons, six of which aimed at the Yellow Beaches. The fourth echelon, with 1,500 troops, landed at Green Beach in what was code-named Operation Stoneface. The task given to Lieutenant Colonel James Masters, commanding the 2nd Battalion of the 1st Marines, was to land, then move inland to establish a roadblock and prevent Japanese reinforcements from moving north to join Matsuda's main force. According to schedule, destroyers and aircraft gave support to the leading elements of the 1,500-man force. The

Marines landed at 7:45 A.M., encountering no opposition. They discovered good defensive positions that had been abandoned. Moving inland, they established a 1,200-yard perimeter approximately 500 yards from shore and sent out patrols. These encountered a few Japanese but no large units. The main action did not come until the early morning of the thirtieth, when approximately 100 Japanese attacked the lines during a driving rainstorm. In all, the Japanese commander launched four attacks, each of which was contained. At the conclusion of the action, the Marines counted eighty-nine Japanese dead. The few survivors melted into the jungle. This was the only threat to the beachhead. When it became obvious that no large Japanese force was in the south, Rupertus ordered the battalion to abandon the position. Beginning on January 5, the battalion and its stores were taken northward by sea to rejoin the rest of the 1st Marines.[17]

At Yellow 1, the first echelon consisted of five APDs, which offloaded the 3rd Battalion Landing Team of 720 men. At the same time at Yellow 2, an equal number of men of the 1st Battalion were landed. Soon after, the second echelon landed the 2nd Battalion at Yellow 1 and the 3rd Battalion at Yellow 2. There was no opposition on the main beaches, but as the marines began to deploy to the west they ran into a few Japanese and a brief firefight took place. The beaches were good for the landings, but they were narrow and immediately behind them was a swamp that made maneuvering difficult. There the marines had to wade through waist-deep water. Despite these difficulties, on the first day Barbey landed a total of 12,500 troops and 7,600 tons of equipment.[18]

General Matsuda was surprised by the marines' landing on the Yellow Beaches. He had believed the swampy conditions would obviate any such landing, and therefore he had deployed his troops to the right and left of the swamp. Only thirty minutes after landing, Colonel William Whiting's 1st Marines swung to the right and began an advance toward the airfield, roughly following the coast road. They soon encountered a roadblock consisting of four machine guns in a bunker supported by infantry in trenches. Bazooka rounds striking the earthwork did not detonate, and the Marines' flamethrowers did not work. During this attack, the commander of K Company, the attacking company, and his executive officer were both killed. The position was finally reduced when an Amphtrack rammed the bunker and the marines clambered over it to destroy the supporting infantry. On the left, Colonel Julian Frisbie's 7th Marines had occupied Target Hill by noon of D-day, but further progress was blocked by the swamp and jungle to the east. However, by the afternoon, bulldozers had been landed to begin clearing the jungle. Artillery and Sherman tanks were also landed. By the end of the day, the marines held a perimeter a thousand yards inland and had not encountered any significant resistance except in the instance of the roadblock.

At 2:30 P.M., the Japanese struck at the beachhead with approximately twenty-five VAL dive-bombers and sixty fighters. Little damage was inflicted on the perimeter, but during the attack, the Marine gunners confused a squadron of B-25s then attacking Matsuda's headquarters with the enemy and shot down two B-25s. Further confusion led the B-25s to bomb a Marine artillery position on Silimati Point. The Japanese attackers were finally intercepted by P-38s, P-47s, and P-40s, which destroyed twenty-two of the bombers and an estimated twenty-four fighters, but not before the bombers inflicted serious damage on the Navy's support vessels. They attacked the destroyers *Hitchins, Shaw,* and *Brownson,* which were taking evasive action eight miles north of the cape. Two of the VALs attacked the new destroyer *Brownson* from the stern. Their bombs sheared off everything on the main deck from the forward gun mount back to the stack. This attack cost 107 lives, and by 3 P.M. the *Brownson* sank. The *Shaw* and another destroyer, the *Mugford,* were also hit. The *Shaw* was saved only by the most heroic efforts. This air attack was the most serious that day. A second attack was made at 5:15 P.M., when torpedo bombers attacked the LSTs. These were intercepted by P-47s, which destroyed sixteen of them. The last serious air attack occurred on December 31, when U.S. fighters shot down twelve planes. Little damage was done in this raid. The onset of bad weather and the need for the Japanese to defend Rabaul from the constant attacks in January spared the Marine and naval forces from further attacks. Between December 15 and 31, the Japanese lost 163 planes at Arawe and Gloucester.[19]

The 1st and 3rd Battalions of the 1st Marines, advancing toward the airfield on the twenty-eighth, encountered a strongly defended position that the Marines dubbed Hell's Point. This consisted of twelve large bunkers with approximately twenty men in each. Sherman tanks were brought up and fired their 75 mm guns directly at the bunkers. The commander of K Company, 3rd Battalion, recalled, "If the Japs stayed inside, they were annihilated; if they escaped out the back entrance, the infantry would swarm over the bunkers and kill them with rifle fire and hand grenades."[20] Despite the onset of the northwest monsoon, the airfield was surrounded on the twenty-ninth and occupied the following day.

Rupertus radioed Krueger, "First Marine Division presents to you an early New Year's gift of the complete airdrome of Cape Gloucester. Situation well in hand due to the fighting spirit of Marines, the usual Marine luck and the help of God. Both strips occupied at noon. Consolidating around drome."[21] Krueger replied that he was delighted. Soon MacArthur also added a glowing, if somewhat overblown, message of congratulations. The capture of the airfield ended the first part of the campaign, which had cost the Marines 250 casualties. Matsuda had lost an estimated 1,000 killed.[22] Despite all the congratulations, the hardest part of the campaign was still ahead.

The torrential rains, with as much as sixteen inches falling in one day, continued unabated for the next nineteen days. Combined with the high winds, they made any but localized gains impossible.

All the streams flooded, and the trails became seas of mud. One marine recalled:

> We had no idea of the severity of the rains. We were able to move off the beach in the same direction of the airstrip and followed a creek up toward the volcano and found a spot about 1,000 yards and north and a little west of the airstrip to establish our headquarters. We had two rivers that converged right at the site of our headquarters. We had no more than set up when one of the creeks flooded and washed away our mess kits and half the guys clothes. It rained then constantly for at least 15 to 20 days. We just never saw anything but rain. . . . Anyone who was there didn't think of the rain first. The electrical storms started and were horrendous. Having been in naval shelling and every type of bombing, nothing was as terrifying as the electrical storms at the Cape. I have seen lightning strike and balls of fire like sparks roll out across the ground, the only thing is they would be ten feet in diameter setting the kunai grass on fire. We had five men killed in one tent when lightning struck the tent pole and arced to the nails in their shoes and killed them all in place. When it started we all had foxholes to climb into, but they were just holes with water in them and no help in an electrical storm.[23]

The general conclusion concerning the weather was later echoed by Major General Harold Deakin, then on Rupertus's staff, who stated unequivocally that Cape Gloucester had been worse than Guadalcanal.[24]

Despite the weather conditions, Rupertus wanted to press the attack on the left flank. He ordered his assistant division commander, Lemuel Shepherd, to extend the beachhead and clear the Japanese from the Borgen Bay area. For this he had a task force comprising the 7th Marines and the 3rd Battalion of the 5th, newly arrived from the Green Beach area. On January 2, 1944, Shepherd anchored his left flank on Target Hill and moved his right flank units eastward. Blocking the advance was a small stream, now much deeper because of the rains. Behind this a battalion of the Japanese 53rd Infantry Division had constructed a long line of interlocking defenses in the deep undergrowth. As the leading elements of the Marine companies clambered up the eastern bank, the Japanese opened up a devastating fire. The marines could not see their enemy and were forced to fall back across the stream, dragging their wounded with them. Other units continued to probe for weak spots but could not find any, taking casualties in the attempts. Finally, by late afternoon, the marines dug in along the west bank of the stream, now dubbed Suicide Creek.

Soon after Shepherd began his offensive, Matsuda ordered Colonel Kenshiro Katayama, commander of the Japanese 141st Infantry, to attack the marines' positions around Target Hill. The Japanese grossly underestimated the numbers of marines and the strength of the defenses, and thus, on January 3, Katayama launched his attack with only a single company in the lead. He was ready to commit a thousand men if there were a breakthrough. Preliminary artillery and mortar fire did little damage to the Marine defenses. The frontal attack was broken up by a combination of machine-gun and rifle fire, and the Japanese retired after sustaining heavy losses. Despite the defeat, Katayama, in a face-saving report, informed his superior that his troops had taken Target Hill only to be driven back by superior forces.[25]

The stalemate at Suicide Creek was eventually broken. Tanks were ordered to support the stalled offensive, and Lieutenant Colonel Lewis "Chesty" Puller, the executive officer of the 7th Marines, was ordered by Rupertus to take command. The movement of the tanks and half-tracks was excruciatingly slow as engineers had to build a cordwood road over the swampy terrain. Late on the afternoon of the fourth, the tanks arrived, accompanied by a bulldozer that was immediately put to work knocking down the stream banks to fashion entry points for the tanks. Two of the drivers were shot by snipers before a third managed to complete the job. Puller had told his officers that they were to ignore regimental orders in the attack to guide both right and left, which he castigated as ridiculous. He planned to attack frontally and said, "We have enough power to drive and we are going to drive." The following morning, after a brief artillery preparation, the tanks and half-tracks moved across the stream. Their big guns soon destroyed the enemy bunkers, and the survivors fled eastward into the jungle. The Marines pursued, driving forward several thousand yards by day's end. However, the Japanese defense slowed the advance and caused 240 casualties.[26]

The marines' next major objective was Hill 660 near the coast, overlooking Borgen Bay south of the marine lines. However, on January 11, before attacking the hill, Shepherd sent a portion of the 7th Marines Weapons Company with tanks and half-tracks down the coast road to establish a roadblock between the bay and the hill. By the afternoon of the thirteenth, it had destroyed pockets of Japanese in the lowlands. Despite the rain, the armor was in position, having been pulled out of the mud by a bulldozer. The Marines also captured a dump, denying the Japanese defenders' much-needed supplies. That same day, the 3rd Battalion of the 7th, commanded by Lieutenant Colonel Henry Buse and supported by a special weapons force of tanks, 37 mm guns, an army DUKW capable of firing rockets, and half-tracks began the attack on Hill 660.[27]

There was a heavy preparatory bombardment by planes and artillery before the 3rd Battalion moved out at 8 A.M. The Japanese defenses were obscured by the heavy foliage, and the tanks that were to move with the infantry became mired in the mud. The slopes were very steep, and in places the marines were forced to crawl. The lead company was halted by heavy fire, and Buse's attempt to flank the defenses with another company failed; the marines were forced back into more defensible positions. The attack was resumed the following day with artillery and tank support. Mortar fire silenced most of the Japanese machine guns and artillery and the marines reached the crest, driving many of the surviving Japanese directly toward the roadblock, where, during the night, the marines picked off stragglers. Heavy rain day and night halted Japanese counterattacks on the Hill. However, early on the morning of the sixteenth, remnants of two companies charged screaming up the hill, attempting to close with the marines. They were driven back, and heavy mortar fire killed most of the attackers. Later patrols discovered 110 bodies. At the same time, the Japanese attacking the roadblock lost forty-eight men. The repulse of the Japanese on the sixteenth was the end of Matsuda's defense of the Cape Gloucester area. In the following weeks, the Japanese would attempt to escape from western New Britain in the face of continuing Marine pressure.[28]

By now Matsuda had lost approximately half of his troops, and he began withdrawing them along the coastal trail toward Iboki. His action was approved on January 21, when Imamura ordered the retreat of all Japanese troops to the Talasea area. Colonel Jiro Sato, who had been on Robben Island, had crossed to the mainland and, with approximately three hundred men arrived at Nakarop village, a few thousand yards from the north coast. Since his men were relatively fresh, Matsuda gave Sato the task of acting as rear guard for the majority of the retreating troops. On January 24, Major Komori also received an order to withdraw from the Arawe area. His force moved north on a trail through Didmop village and made a junction with Sato's troops at a midisland trail junction, where they became a part of the rear guard action.

After the capture of Hill 660, Marine patrols in both platoon and company strength began their long pursuit of the retreating

Japanese. At first it was believed that the bulk of the Japanese were retreating south because most of the trails seemed to be in that direction. However, the main trails soon turned eastward. Nevertheless, on January 30, one of the earliest major patrols of 1,400 men, comprising elements of the 1st and 5th Marines led by Puller, began a search-and-destroy mission from the village of Nakarop. The patrol was distinguished mainly by the extreme hardship on the troops caused by the terrain, the continuing rain, and the lack of supplies. At first supplies were carried by native bearers, but later the marines had to be supplied by light aircraft dropping C rations. By the time that they reached the village of Agulupella, having met no Japanese, it was obvious that the main Japanese force was not in the south. Because a large force was not needed, Puller's command was reduced to fewer than four hundred men and the native carriers. A bridge had to be built over a branch of the Itni River before the reduced command moved out on February 6. They reached the river opposite Gilnit three days later. Puller was ordered to remain there until army patrols moving north from Arawe reached them on the sixteenth. Puller's patrol then moved back along the trail, having assured higher headquarters that no Japanese units were in the south. The only Japanese encountered during the two-week excursion were sickly scavengers, some of whom were bayoneted, causing Puller to refer to the "pig sticking" being fine.[29]

The main effort against the Japanese was along the coastal trail adjacent to Borgen Bay and in the immediate interior. Colonel John Selden's 5th Marines were given the primary task of dealing with the Japanese rear guard. Colonel Sato's weary and hungry troops were nevertheless tenacious in holding certain key points to allow Matsuda's main force the time to escape. On January 20, a company of the 1st Battalion, 5th Marines, ran into a strong set of defenses. Later investigation showed that the Japanese had at least a hundred men manning fifteen machine guns at the base of Borgen Bay. In addition, a 75 mm cannon was emplaced to the rear of their line.

The marines brought up tanks, called down air strikes, had DUKWs firing rockets from offshore and even involved heavy 155 mm guns before the Japanese position was broken on the twenty-second. The remnants of the holding force fled up the trail toward Agulupella village.

The next major block was at the Natano River, where the Japanese held up the marines' advance for five days. When the marines finally crossed the river on the twenty-ninth, they found that the Japanese had abandoned their defenses and pulled back along the road past Natomo village, which units of the 1st and 5th Marines reached on February 2. The next day, MacArthur's headquarters issued a halt order so that the marines could establish the defenses necessary to defend the airfield from a Japanese counterattack. Krueger and Rupertus, then at Finschhafen, concluded that this was another example of the rear echelon not knowing the situation, and they chose to ignore the order. The 5th Marines were ordered to continue to mop up the faltering Japanese. In their advance, they used LCMs to leapfrog ahead by as many as ten miles per operation. On February 24, the Marines reached the large village of Iboki at the head of a major north–south trail near the Aria River, fifty miles west of the Willaumez Peninsula.

As the 1st Marines were pursuing Matsuda along the coast, General Rupertus planned an amphibious operation that would deny sanctuary for the Japanese in the Willaumez Peninsula. Codenamed Appease, the operation, commanded by Colonel Oliver P. Smith, would utilize two battalions of the 5th Marines that would land on the western side of the peninsula near its base. The landing site, named Red Beach, was located at Volupai, across from the main village of Talasea and Garua Harbor. It was approximately 350 yards wide, bordered by a swamp, and close to two large hills. The major problem was a reef line 300 yards from shore. This meant that the main landings had to be from LVTs, which could cross the reef and deliver the troops directly onto the beach.

For the operation Smith had approximately 5,000 men concentrated at Iboki. By contrast, Captain Kiyomatsu Terunuma had fewer than 600 concentrated in the Talasea area. The movement of the 5th Marines to the landing area on March 6 was uneventful, and the landing of the 1st Battalion was uncontested. The marines quickly established a defensive perimeter, and the 2nd Battalion, commanded by Major Gordon Gayle, passed through, moved quickly to secure the hills, then moved toward Bitokoa village. Backed by Sherman tanks, the marines brushed aside token resistance in the Volapoi plantation area. On March 7, Teranuma counterattacked near Mount Schleuten, but a combination of Marine firepower drove the Japanese back. The next day, Major William Barba's 1st Battalion took Liapo village while the Japanese in front of Gayle pulled back after enduring heavy artillery and mortar bombardment. When the marines attacked the following day, they found Talasea abandoned. The redoubtable Japanese commander, understanding that his main role was the protection of Matauda's retiring force, established a series of roadblocks that were only briefly defended. Nevertheless, the marines' advance was slowed. The final block was overrun on the seventeenth, and what was left of Terunuma's force melted away to join the overall retreat.[30]

By then most of Matsuda's main force had successfully reached safety on the eastern side of the peninsula. With some of the sick and wounded, Matsuda had left by boat earlier and reached safety at Cape Hoskins. However, Sato's and Komori's men were struggling along the trails, hotly pursued by the marines. Komori's small force reached Kandoka, a village near the base of the Willaumez Peninsula, on March 24, but found no food or other supplies there and moved on. Komori kept a meticulous diary in which he recorded in detail the trials of his command, and he noted how his troops were starving, in some cases eating bark from the trees. Sato's group reached Kandoka two days later and quickly left, leaving some of the sick and wounded behind. On March 30, a small patrol of the 2nd Battalion of the 1st Marines encountered Sato's rear guard of approximately seventy men, including the colonel, who was being carried on a litter. Reinforced from Kandoka, the patrol brought the Japanese to battle on the twenty-sixth, and in the ensuing fight the Japanese were wiped out. Colonel Sato was cut down, sword in hand. Major Komori met the same fate on April 9 as he, wracked with malaria and with only three soldiers, stumbled into an outpost of the 2nd Battalion of the 5th Marines. The last entry in his diary, which was recovered, was on March 31, when he noted, "We are very tired and without food."[31]

The suffering of the Japanese in the long retreat was also recorded by a member of a Marine patrol in the Aria River region:

Leaving a native village, we pushed down a broad trail and soon came upon a camp that held a scattering of bare skeletons. It was the beginning of an eerie patrol. A little farther on we came to a camp with two or three hundred skeletons, all bare. There was nothing of value present except the gold teeth in some of the skulls, and we began collecting these. Every half-mile or so along the trail we came to another camp with more such skeletons, sometimes many. During that entire patrol we didn't see a living thing in that damned jungle except the trees, vines, and brush. I don't remember hearing the call of a single bird. There wasn't even a whisper of wind. It was as if the jungle was in mourning.[32]

The Marines' last major action was near San Remo village. Even before this, the decision had been made to replace the 1st Division. MacArthur, pleased with the way the Marines had performed, wanted to retain the division, and he made his argument for this in correspondence and also through his representatives in Washington, including his chief of staff, Major General Richard

Sutherland, who attended a series of high-level conferences in March in which they tried to counter the Navy's position. King and Nimitz wanted to have the division in the central Pacific in order to use it in the invasion of the Palau group in September. MacArthur wanted to retain it at least until operations against Kavieng had been completed and Rabaul was isolated. On March 12, the Joint Chiefs made the decision to bypass Kavieng and ordered MacArthur to return the Marines to Nimitz as soon as possible. The actual negotiation for this was left to the area commander. Even then MacArthur delayed, stating that because of a lack of amphibious vehicles, he could not relieve the marines until late June. He was informed that the transfer had to be done by June 1. This he grudgingly conceded, and by April 8 arrangements had been completed to replace the Marines with the Army's 40th Division, then on Guadalcanal. The 185th Regiment, the first army troops, arrived at Cape Gloucester on April 23. The rest of the division arrived by the twenty-eighth, and Rupertus turned over command to Major General Rapp Brush.[33] Elements of the 40th continued to put pressure on the Japanese stragglers and occupied Cape Naskins airdrome in early May. In June, units of the 40th relieved the 1st Cavalry troops at Arawe. For all practical purposes, the American campaign in western New Britain was completed.[34] The war in New Britain would continue on until the war's end because the Australian 5th Division, which replaced the 40th in November, would unnecessarily continue active operations. Rabaul was never assaulted and its 70,000-man garrison sat out the rest of the war, but after February 1944 the once powerful Japanese bastion was never a factor in the continuing operations in the Pacific.

The conquest of western New Britain had cost the Marines 310 killed and 1,083 wounded. The Japanese suffered at least 4,300 dead. The campaign is remembered by those who fought there for the appalling conditions in the aptly named Green Hell. In all probability, the Cape Gloucester campaign, like those at Tarawa and later Peleliu, was unnecessary. The fears that the Japanese could dominate the Vitiaz Strait from Cape Gloucester were not realistic. By that time, MacArthur's naval forces, and particularly the Fifth Air Force, controlled all the vital areas of operations. The bases later built at the cape and at Arawe were never important and remained forward staging stations at best. Even while the fighting for control of Cape Gloucester was ongoing, the main focus of MacArthur's campaign was New Guinea and the need to negate the Japanese at Saidor, Wewak, and Madang.

Eight

SAIDOR AND SHAGGY RIDGE

Sensing the Japanese weakness in New Guinea and reveling in the Allied air and naval dominance, MacArthur decided to conduct three separate operations in early January 1944 even while the Cape Gloucester operation was under way. The first of these was a continuation of the Australian advance up the coast toward Sio and Madang. The second was the attack in the interior from Wareo toward the ridgelines adjacent to Bogadjim on the coast. The third was an amphibious operation to capture Saidor village up the coast in front of the advancing Australians. If these were successful, they would threaten thousands of General Adachi's troops and force the Japanese High Command to decide whether to confront the pincers movement, with the full expectation of being destroyed, or to retreat by interior trails to move the bulk of their forces to Madang. Each of the Allied offensives was connected with the others since they placed considerable strain on the resources available, particularly the air forces. Nevertheless, the conduct of each would be separate until they merged when the Australian 11th Division reached the coast at Bogadjim.

The coastal action after Finschhafen began on December 5 and was conducted at first by the 4th Australian Brigade of the 9th Division commanded by Brigadier C. R. V. Edgar. The historian of the 2/24th gave a good account of the condition of the 4th Division troops:

> The nine infantry battalions of our division were now extremely weary and depleted, and on the average were not more than half strength. Atebrin supplies had been kept up, but malarial discipline had been difficult to maintain in the conditions in which we had fought. A large number had contracted malaria and the rest had one or more bouts of dengue fever at one time or another, even if they had taken their atebrin religiously each day. Five months of the New Guinea climate, on not too plentiful a ration scale, mainly packaged in tins, combined with the hard slogging labour of movement on jungle trails and the constant carrying of supplies, had worn down the troops to a shadow of the superbly fit young men they had been when they left Australia.[1]

Despite their physical problems, they pressed on against an enemy who was in far worse condition. The Japanese, mostly from the 20th Division, could do nothing more than briefly halt the Australian advance as they retreated from position to position. They were forced from some strong bunker positions by heavy concentration of artillery fire supported by tanks of the 22nd Battalion. At a coconut grove at Cape Sibidia, a combination of tanks and infantry destroyed nearly all of the estimated 200 defenders, some of the Japanese committing suicide by jumping over the cliffs. On December 20, the Australian 2/24, transported by LCVs from Gusika, forced the Japanese from the Masaweng River, and on January 15, 1944, it captured the major base at Sio, which the Japanese had evacuated. The landing of the U.S. 32nd Division troops at Saidor on January 2 blocked the trail from Sio to Bogadjim, forcing the Japanese High Command to make a fateful decision for its shattered forces. Of the nearly 13,000 men present in the Finschhafen area prior to the Allied landings, the action along the coast and in the interior had left General Adachi with only an estimated 4,200 men for the retreat from Sio. The pursuit after Sio was taken up by the 8th Brigade of the 5th Division in the appalling conditions of the monsoon rains. The bodies of many Japanese were found along the trail; they had simply collapsed of fatigue and starvation. During the sixteen days before the linkup with U.S. forces, the Australians discovered more than 1,000 such casualties while accounting for only 267 Japanese killed in action. On February 8, as the Australians neared Saidor, an advance party was sent ahead and contact was made with the Americans at Yagami, fourteen miles east of the town.[2]

In December, MacArthur finally decided to act upon a suggestion earlier made by Chamberlain that Saidor on the south side of the Huon Peninsula be occupied in order to construct an advanced air and naval base. He waited until two days before the Arawe expedition before ordering Krueger to prepare plans for the action. This was a departure from the previous understanding that New Guinea Force would command all operations in New Guinea. One reason given for this was that Australian units were already committed. The limitation on the date for the action was the lack of available landing craft, but General Headquarters suggested January 2 as the date for the operation, code-named Michelmas. One early idea was to have the 503rd Parachute Infantry assault Saidor in an airdrop. The limited number of aircraft available to do this and continue the assault on New Britain ruled this out. Instead, it was decided to use a regiment of the 32nd Division that had earlier been scheduled to land at Gasmata. When that operation was canceled, it became available. The general outline of the operation was discussed at a conference on Goodenough Island on December 20 attended by Barbey; Major General William Gill, commanding the 32nd;

Whitehead; Colonel Clarence Martin, commanding the 126th Regiment; and its staff officers. Other meetings over the next week fleshed out the plans for the operation.[3]

Intelligence reported few Japanese in the Saidor region. Nevertheless, the plans called for landings in force on three beaches codenamed Red, White, and Blue on the west shore of Dekay's Bay. D-day, as MacArthur suggested, was set for January 2. Admiral Barbey had provided nine APDs and sixteen LCIs for the operation. The task force also included fifteen destroyers for escort and bombardment duties; Admiral Crutchly's cruisers would stand by in case the Japanese navy made an appearance.

The landings went off smoothly as planned. The beaches were pounded by more than two thousand shells in the twenty minutes before the first troops in LCVs landed shortly after 7 A.M. Two battalions of the 126th landed abreast without opposition and quickly established a defensive perimeter. Soon a third battalion passed through and moved to the left to extend the perimeter to the high ground southwest of the unserviceable airfield. Captain Meredith Huggins, who played a prominent role in the capture of Sanananda, recalled his impressions of this seemingly uneventful landing:

> When we landed at Saidor it was an amazing sight. There were dozens of warships bombarding the coast. The sound was like a rolling thunder and the smoke hung along the ground. As we approached the beach, air attacks began. Heavy bombers dropped their load of high explosive from a few thousand feet. Then came in the B-25 strafers shooting everything in sight, clobbering positions. Behind them came fighters to give the Japs a final working over. There was very little opposition when we landed. We found a few Japs wandering around in shell shock. What a contrast from the days at Buna and Sanananda, only a year before, when we were fighting with rifles, grenades, and rocks![4]

Within a few hours, 7,500 men landed with the supplies necessary to maintain them. There was no immediate attack by the
Japanese air force. The number of planes available to it at Wewak
had been reduced to only thirty-nine fighters and twenty-four
bombers, and many of these were on patrol duty over Madang.
When the Japanese finally mounted an abortive attack, Barbey's
ships were safely away from the landing area.[5]

Despite the ease of the landings, Colonel Martin was concerned that the Japanese retreating from the Huon Peninsula would
attack from the east while the considerable force in the Madang
area would attack from the west. He ordered only patrol activity
while he strengthened his defenses. The monsoon rains, which at
the same time were pounding the marines at Cape Gloucester, also
prevented any major forward movement. Martin requested reinforcements, and Krueger responded immediately, sending the bulk
of the 128th Regiment, which arrived at Saidor with the 32nd Division commander on the nineteenth. Army and air force engineers
went to work immediately and by January 9, despite the foul
weather, had constructed a 2,500-foot-long, 250-foot-wide airstrip
for transport aircraft. By early March, a more permanent 6,000-
foot airstrip was completed. Continuous supply for the 15,000-man
garrison was ensured by the construction of dock facilities and an
aviation gas farm.[6]

The Saidor operation was one example of MacArthur's strategic thinking, which paid great dividends over and above the establishment of a forward military base. It interposed a large Allied
force between the significant residue of Japanese from Finschhafen
then retreating from the Australian 4th Division and the much
larger force at Madang. General Adachi, commanding the Eighteenth Area Army, with great difficulty, just before the American
landings, had visited the 51st Division headquarters at Kiari and
then traveled overland to the 20th Division at Sio. Therefore he was
fully aware of the difficult situation facing both divisions. At

Rabaul, the Saidor landings also stimulated a heated high-level debate. Some senior officers wanted to bring all available troops together to attack and retake the town, a course of action that Colonel Martin feared. Others wanted to save as many troops as possible for the defense of Wewak, considered the next major Allied target. General Imamura decided in favor of bypassing Saidor and withdrawing over the inland trails.[7]

After being informed of this decision, Adachi appointed General Nakano, commander of the 51st Division, to take charge of the withdrawal. Convinced that Madang was the next goal of the Allied drive, Adachi ordered eight companies from the Ramu valley to Bogadjim prior to them advancing down the coast to harass the Americans at Saidor. He also had the 41st Division move from Wewak to reinforce the troops at Madang. These were purely defensive moves. The major problem for the Japanese was how to extricate the large numbers of men of the 20th and 51st Divisions from the impending trap if the U.S. and Australian units then moving toward Bogadjim should join. Nakano at first ordered the 20th to retreat up the coast while the 51st would use inland trails. He soon abandoned this scheme and ordered both into the interior to retire as rapidly as possible toward Madang, two hundred miles away. This meant that the exhausted, hungry, and sick Japanese had to deal with jungle growth, rivers, and the mountains of the Finisterre Range. General Gill was informed of this mass movement by a new observation post that had been established in the interior. The report showed that the Japanese were not interested in trying to retake Saidor.[8]

In contrast to the ease with which the 32nd Division had occupied Saidor, the Australian 7th Division, operating from the Ramu Valley in the interior, met stubborn resistance as the Japanese utilized the natural defenses of the Adelbert and Finisterre Ranges. There were few trails that could be used, and many of them were made even more difficult by the onset of the monsoon. One of the worst areas that Vasey's men encountered was the stretch from Dumpu and Kumbarum villages to the Faria River, where there was only one trail. It climbed toward the ridgelines, which ran generally parallel to the coast. The most obvious of these ridges—and the one that protected Bogadjim—was Shaggy Ridge, located six miles north of Dumpu. This razorback ridge, at one elevation of more than 5,000 feet, ran roughly southeast to northwest. The highest point on the ridge was the Kankirjo Saddle. There were also three high elevations along the ridge that the Australians named the Pimple, the Intermediate Snipers' Pimple, and the Green Sniper's Pimple. The Japanese had constructed four miles of defenses along the northern part of the ridge. These positions dominated the trail along which the Australians had to advance. The trail was narrow, only two to three feet wide, and there were drops on either side of 300 to 500 feet. The Japanese had also constructed a rough road on the coast side to a point between the Mindjim and Faria Rivers, making supply to the defenders much easier. The Pimples were the strong points, and the Japanese had built fortified posts with machine guns and deep trenches on each.[9]

Attack on the Intermediate Snipers' Pimple began with heavy bombing by the Allied air forces. The bombing was planned in detail and called for a series of attacks by P-40s, each carrying a 500-pound bomb. They were led to the targets by RAAF Boomerangs, slow Australian aircraft. The Boomerang pilots were able to survey the battle areas and decide where the P-40s should strike. The dive-bombing was conducted from approximately 1,000 feet and was accurate.[10] After the bombing runs, coupled with heavy artillery bombardment, the 2/16th Battalion of the 21st Brigade began a direct frontal assault on the Pimple in a heavy rain. Advancing in single file, the Australians gained and secured the top in hand-to-hand fighting and destroyed the bunkers by using "blockbusters," canisters of high explosives triggered by grenades. By the next day they had control of the Pimple, where they established a firm defensive perimeter.[11]

The main Japanese defenses, headquarters, and supply dumps, as well as their hospital, were located in three villages: Prothero I, Prothero II, and Kankinyo. During the first weeks of January, the Australians made little headway against the honeycombed Japanese defenses. The air force was once again called upon and plastered the ridgeline in a three-day attack called Operation Cutthroat. Beginning on the eighteenth, B-25s from Nadzab and Port Moresby dropped 500-pound bombs on the defenses. Then, on the twenty-first, P-40s strafed and bombed the area. By this time there had been a change in the Australian units on the front line: the 15th and 18th Brigades had relieved the tired 21st and 25th. On the twentieth, after heavy artillery and air preparation, the 18th, led by Brigadier F. O. Chilton, began an attack on Prothero I. Some idea of the difficulties faced by the Australians can be gathered from a report by Captain T. L. James. He described the action of the 2/2nd Pioneer Battalion, which would participate in the attack:

> At 1000 hours we met 2/12 Infantry Battalion at the appointed rendezvous, where I met their C.O., Lt.-Col. C. F. Bourne. We did not stay long at the rendezvous but formed up and commenced the long approach march. It was a gruelling day. The long single file moved silently up the deep ravines, scaling cliff-faces with the aid of ropes and lawyer vines. It took us the entire day to cover the four mile approach.

The following day, he noted, "In one spot that was almost impossible to traverse—a steep-sided cliff—they rigged lawyer vines between trees to act as a handrail and allow us to pull ourselves up."[12] Despite such conditions, the Australians attacked during heavy rain and reached Canning Saddle, then forded the flooded Mene River and moved up a steep slope before the village. A 75 mm gun used by the Japanese caused a number of casualties before it was finally captured.

Further north the 2/10th Battalion dislodged the Japanese from a feature called Cam's Saddle and the 2/9th, in a duel with grenades, seized Green Snipers' Pimple. By this time the Japanese defenses had been reduced to only a one-mile length. Two days later, the 2/12th, supported by heavy shelling from 25-pounders, took Prothero II behind the Japanese forward positions. Fighting then continued through the night as the Australians systematically destroyed the Japanese bunkers. On the twenty-fifth, the 2/9th moved up toward Kankiryo Saddle, where the Japanese were firmly established, as well as on some of its spurs. It was vital that the saddle be captured since it looked over the Mindjim watershed and observers there had a good view of the coastline and any Allied shipping there. The Australians had to attack up another narrow, slippery slope toward two spurs, where the Japanese strongly resisted and even mounted counterattacks. Finally, on the thirty-first, the Japanese resistance was broken. Many Japanese attempted to break through without success. Others jumped to their deaths from the cliffs into the valleys. The saddle was finally occupied, bringing to an end the coordinated Japanese resistance on Shaggy Ridge. The Australian command then consolidated its position and replaced the 18th Brigade in the forward positions by the 15th. Long-range patrols were begun, and on February 18 one of these made contact with the U.S. forces at Saidor. The occupation of Shaggy Ridge had cost the Australians 46 killed and 147 wounded. Of the approximately 800 Japanese defenders, an estimated 500 had been killed. With the linkup of the Australian and U.S. units at Saidor, the Huon Peninsula campaign was finally over. On February 11, MacArthur's headquarters announced that the Japanese 79th, 80th, and 238th Infantry Regiments, the 26th Field Artillery Regiment, and two engineering regiments, a total of approximately 14,000 men, had been trapped and mostly destroyed.[13]

The cost to the Australian forces during the long campaign from Kokoda to Shaggy Ridge had been high. Their success had been obtained under perhaps the worst conditions encountered by Allied troops during the entire war. A closer analysis of the difficulties faced by the Australian troops during these campaigns shows clearly how remarkable their achievements were. For two years they had operated in the interior, where dense jungle gave way to kunai grass in some areas. They had pursued the Japanese over the high Owen Stanley Mountains and later in the Finisterre Range. There were seldom any roads, and during the rainy periods even these were almost impassable. Confined to trails, they were forced over and over to confront the Japanese in frontal attacks since the terrain prevented any flanking maneuvers. If they were seriously wounded, despite the best efforts of native carriers and medical personnel, the odds were that they would die before reaching a facility that could adequately treat them. The supply system, particularly to the forward troops, varied from chaotic to nonexistent. Even the packaging of food supplies seemed designed to plague the infantrymen who had to carry these forward over the muddy trails. U.S. soldiers who were forced to partake of Australian rations found them almost inedible. The basic food was bully beef in cans that in many cases when fires could not be lit had to be eaten cold. In the extreme heat the contents could often be poured as liquid from the tins. The other available foods, such as canned herring and salmon, were roundly disliked. Canned ham and bacon were luxuries not often available. Fresh vegetables were almost impossible to obtain. Substitutes, such as boiler peas, often arrived moldy. Marmite spread, tea, and sugar were normally available even to frontline troops, and chocolate was a welcome treat. Studies by nutritionists had indicated that soldiers needed 3,750 calories per day in order to maintain their weight, and many did not even approach this figure. Patrols normally carried only enough rations for one or two days. Thus, on longer patrols the men went hungry. Doctors surveying a large number of troops found that most suffered from a chronic shortage of vitamins B and C. Most of the men in the forward areas had lost weight and were weak. Many had lesions in the mouth and on the lips and tongue. Thus even those considered fit for duty were far from healthy.[14]

The worst enemy of the Allied forces operating in the tropical areas of New Guinea were the mosquitoes, both *Anophiles* and *Aedes*. They bred even at Dumpu, more than 1,000 feet above sea level. The *Anophiles* types carried the malaria virus. The rate of infection for all of New Guinea in January 1944 was 11.5 per thousand per week. However, at the same time the rate at Finschhafen was 31.1 and in the Ramu Valley 29.1. Some idea of what this meant for the efficiency of the Australian units can be gained from other medical statistics. In the 7th Division, those with malaria made up 83 percent of all casualties, while in the 9th Division, the rate was 60 percent. In the period September 22 to December 10 in the Finschhafen campaign, there were 3,400 malaria casualties, while those killed or wounded in action numbered only 1,328. In the period December 3 to March 1, 1944, in the Gusika-Saidor sector, there were 4,300 malaria casualties, while the number of battle casualties was only 229. In all, in the period September 1943 to March 1944, 9,942 men out of a total of 28,059 troops then engaged in New Guinea, were evacuated to medical units because of malaria.[15] This despite heroic work by mosquito abatement teams and the distribution of the malaria suppressant Atabrine. In permanent locations, where Atabrine could be delivered on a regular basis, the number of malaria cases was drastically reduced. However, distribution to forward troops was a hit-and-miss proposition, and without supervision, many soldiers did not take the medicine.

Although malaria was the greatest scourge, the infantrymen had to contend with a host of other diseases. By the end of 1943, dengue fever, caused by the bite of *Aedes* mosquitoes, had become epidemic, and, although not as dangerous as malaria, it could render a man unfit for duty for days. Scrub typhus was also an ever-present threat. A major outbreak of this occurred later, during the operation at Hansa Bay. These many diseases, while causing the most serious casualties, were generally accompanied by one of several ailments that reduced the Australian units' effectiveness. Various kinds of skin rashes, known collectively as "jungle rot," were almost impossible to cure, given the locale of the action. Then, too, there was dysentery, which afflicted almost every soldier at one time or another. The more serious and minor illnesses would have presented major problems to the Australian military even had they not been involved in a war.

The Australian medical services did yeoman work throughout the various campaigns under the most difficult conditions. The services were logically designed to give maximum care to both the wounded and sick. Advanced Dressing Stations (ADSs) were established as close to the fighting as possible. Wounded would be brought to these as quickly as possible, and for this, native carriers were depended upon to relieve the infantrymen, who otherwise would have had to carry the wounded. The terrain was generally difficult to traverse even without trying to carry a wounded man. The historian of the Australian medical services described one such rescue situation in the fighting for Shaggy Ridge. He wrote:

Native carriers did very good work during these actions, and members of fighting units too had to help with transport. In places the ground was steep and slippery, to such an extent that members of the 2/5th Ambulance detachments sometimes had to pull themselves up with ropes tied to trees. These ropes were also found useful in carrying loaded stretchers over this type of country. During the struggle for the Kankiryo Saddle a few casualties had to be taken from the bottom of a steep declivity at the base of the ridge. This was too precipitous even for a native carrier team, and was sometimes under fire. Some seventy men of a company of the 2/12th Battalion under directions of their R.M.O., Captain J. M. McDonald, took the stretchers up the hill by passing them up a chain of two rows of men to Shaggy Ridge, where ambulance bearers and finally native carriers took over at the aid post. Many of the stretchers were improvised, and to make them and to keep patients warm, half blankets and ground-sheets were fastened together with twine and Japanese signal cable. In spite of fatigue, members of the ambulance detachments were often too cold and wet to sleep.[16]

Once the wounded had been cleared from an ADS, they were transported to a more permanent Medical Dressing Station (MDS), located in a quiet zone such as Dumpu or Finschhafen. At first there was a shortage of tents and the wounded were placed in grass huts. The continuing rains made adequate care difficult, as many of the wards in either tents or huts would be flooded. During military action, these MDSs were overcrowded with wounded as well as sick. By October 1943, the MDS at Dumpu became a major center and at its high point had more than eight hundred patients. Further back, the MDS at Finschhafen had four hundred beds, but there most of the patients had malaria. Operating at these sites were Casualty Clearing Stations, which arranged for the transfer of patients to hospital facilities in Dobodura, Buna, Port Moresby, or Australia. The most serious cases could be flown to larger facilities for better care. Others not so seriously ill or wounded could be transported by sea. This was a long, arduous process as the wounded were transferred from barge to sea ambulance transport, to a DUKW, to an ambulance, to a plane, and finally to another ambulance to transport them to a hospital. For those scheduled for transport from Finschhafen to the hospital at Dobodura, it was a grueling twenty-two-hour trip.[17]

As MacArthur's campaign moved onward, there was less and less actual combat for Australian units to do. Troops of the 15th Brigade pursued stragglers along the trails to Bogadjim, and this key coastal village was occupied on April 13. From there they took up the chase along the coast toward Madang. Halted by the deep, rushing Gogal River, men of the 57/60th Battalion were taken on board boats and landed on the north side of the river. They then occupied Madang, once one of the major Japanese coastal bases, on the twenty-third. The Australian 8th Brigade moved into Saidor, relieving the U.S. troops for later amphibious operations against Aitape and Hollandia. For the rest of the New Guinea campaign, the Australian army would continue to be utilized by MacArthur, but generally in a backup role. The use at Saidor of the Alamo Force under Krueger's command had breached the tactic agreement that operations in New Guinea would be under Australian command.

Although Australian forces would be involved, particularly at Hansa Bay, the advance up the coast would be primarily the responsibility of Krueger's Alamo Force, now generally recognized as being the Sixth Army. Australian troops would henceforth be used in patrolling the interior, as garrison forces, and, by the decision of Blamey and his subordinates, in costly operations at Wewak, Bougainville, and New Britain much later. This shift of responsibility was perhaps inevitable as the Australian army was to be reduced in size and the active divisions that had borne the brunt of MacArthur's offensives had been reduced by casualties and disease. Despite some unwarranted criticism by U.S. commanders, the Australian forces, operating in some of the most difficult terrain encountered by any Allied units, had given MacArthur most of the victories of which he was so proud.

Nine

THE ADMIRALTY
ISLANDS GAMBIT

The Quadrant meeting of the Combined Chiefs of Staff at Quebec in August 1943 laid out in general terms the goals for the coming year in all theaters. For the southwest Pacific, it specified the continuing operations in New Guinea, the occupation of Kavieng on New Ireland, and the seizure of the Admiralty Islands. One of the reasons for these latter actions was the continuing concern with Rabaul. However, there was a further reason for MacArthur to occupy the Admiralty group. His ultimate goal was a return to liberate the Philippines, and although he had not received permission for such a large-scale campaign, he was certain that ultimately, despite opposition from the Navy, this would be approved. He had already received assurances from Marshall that Mindanao would be a future target. The Admiralty Islands, particularly Los Negros, with its fine Seeadler Harbor, would provide a first-rate staging base. An air base on adjacent Manus would give the Allied air forces control of more than 1,000 square miles, reaching out to Biak, Palau, Truk, and Bougainville. For the continued operations on New Guinea, MacArthur recalled that he wanted this base because the harbor could contain a large amphibious force for a full-scale attack not only to the north but also to the west, thus securing his right flank to prevent reinforcements from reaching the beleaguered Japanese garrison on New Guinea.[1]

The Japanese situation in the central Pacific during the first months of 1944 had grown desperate. On January 31, marine and army forces had invaded the Marshall Islands, thus breaching further the Japanese outer defense ring. On February 16, the Fifth Fleet began a devastating two-day air attack on Truk that made this onetime bastion of Japanese naval and air power untenable. In this context MacArthur directed Halsey's forces to seize the Green Islands, north of Bougainville. On February 15, the New Zealand 3rd Division occupied the islands against minimal opposition, cutting off more than 25,000 Japanese still in the central and southern Solomon Islands. By early March, a fighter strip had been constructed there, only 117 miles from Rabaul. Japanese barge traffic there was paralyzed, and the Japanese on the islands, particularly Bougainville, ultimately became more concerned with planting gardens for food rather than participating actively in the war. As MacArthur noted, "For all strategic military purposes, this completed the campaign for the Solomon Islands."[2] This important maneuver, if followed quickly by the occupation of Los Negros and Manus, would complete the encirclement of Rabaul and isolate the large Japanese garrison there.

The major objective in the Admiralties was Manus, the largest volcanic island, forty-nine miles long and sixteen miles wide, which formed the western side of the excellent Seeadler Harbor. The harbor itself was fifteen miles long and four miles wide and could provide anchorage for all of MacArthur's available capital ships. Immediately adjacent to Manus was Los Negros, which had a potentially excellent airfield at Momote, close to the eastern entrance to Hayne Harbor on the eastern side of the island. Although General Imamura at Rabaul considered these islands important, he was not able to spare many troops to garrison them and had difficulty convincing higher authorities to reinforce the small force there. By late 1943, headquarters was finally willing to concede that MacArthur might be planning an invasion and ordered the 66th Regiment, then in the western Caroline Islands, to proceed to the Admiralties. However, on January 16, the transport *Denmarck Maru,* carrying approximately 3,000 troops, was sunk by the U.S. submarine *Whale.* The loss of more than 1,300 men ended this attempt. Imamura then decided to send at least a battalion to Los Negros, and 750 men of the 1st Independent Mixed Regiment of the 38th Infantry Division was landed despite the near-continuous bombing by the Fifth Air Force. He wanted to send more, but the U.S. raids postponed this. On January 30, he dispatched a transport with 850 men, only to have this sunk by a submarine with the loss of 350 men. Finally, on February 2, the last reinforcements, 530 men of the 1st Battalion, 229th Infantry Regiment, landed at Los Negros.[3]

The early plans for the Admiralties operation worked out between MacArthur and Halsey's representatives called for Los Negros to be assaulted on April 1. This plan was issued on February 22. Within three days, MacArthur decided on an immediate strike instead—or, as he called it, a *coup de main.* The reasons for this were twofold. One was the ease with which Saidor had been taken. The other was General Kenney's recommendations. The Fifth Air Force had been active, striking the islands repeatedly in January. Major attacks had been made on February 6 and 13, and the pilots had reported that there were few, if any, Japanese on either island. This was attributable to Colonel Ezakai Yoshio, commander of the Japanese forces on both islands. He had issued strict orders for maximum concealment since he was convinced that an invasion would soon occur.[4]

Kenney's prestige as an adviser to MacArthur can be seen clearly in the debates prior to the invasion over the numbers of

Japanese on the islands. The secret Ultra code-breaking machines had provided MacArthur's headquarters with what later proved to be accurate reports of the numbers of men and their units at Los Negros. This was confirmed by his own intelligence chief, General Willoughby, who had tended to ignore Ultra in the past. This time, by using his own cryptanalysts, who were reading Imamura's communiqués, he came to roughly the same conclusion as Ultra had. His estimate in late January was that there were 3,250 Japanese present on the islands. Later information obtained after the invasion placed the exact number at 3,646 men.[5] However, Kenney argued that there were at most a few hundred men there and suggested that a reconnaissance team be sent to Los Negros to confirm his conclusions. This was agreed to, and Lieutenant J. R. McGowon and five men of the 158th Infantry were inserted by a Catalina flying boat. However, despite Krueger's objections, MacArthur did not wait for McGowon's report and demanded that all concerned, particularly the Navy, put together a feasible plan within days. On the twenty-fifth, he ordered Barbey and Krueger to prepare plans for landing a part of the 5th Cavalry Regiment at Hayne Harbor on the twenty-ninth. On the afternoon of the twenty-seventh, McGowon reported to Brisbane that the place was "lousy with Japs." However, by this time MacArthur considered it to be too late to cancel the invasion. Although fewer than 1,100 men were to make the initial landing, MacArthur believed that the 1,500 cavalrymen and 400 Seabees in reserve at Finschhafen could be sent in quickly if the situation demanded it.[6]

MacArthur's orders came as a complete surprise. Rear Admiral Russell Berkey, who was to command the covering force for the operation, code-named Brewer, was in Brisbane and had to make a full-speed run with the cruiser *Phoenix* to Milne Bay to join his other ships. This force consisted of the cruisers *Phoenix* and *Nashville* and the destroyers *Daly, Hutchins, Beale,* and *Bache.* Admiral Barbey, who disagreed with the speedup, designated his deputy,

Rear Admiral William M. Fechtler, to command the landing. The landing force, consisting of eight destroyers and three APDs, were concentrated at Cape Sudest, where they embarked 1,026 troops of the 5th Cavalry Regiment, commanded by Brigadier General William Chase.[7] These members of the last square division of the Army were untested troops who caused considerable worry at General Headquarters, but MacArthur was convinced that they would perform well. As he explained to an aide:

> I have known this 5th Cavalry for almost 60 years. When I was a little boy of four my father was a captain in the 13th Infantry at Fort Selden, in the Indian frontier country of New Mexico. Geronimo, the Apache scourge, was loose, and our small infantry garrison was to guard the middle fords of the Rio Grande. A troop of this same 5th Cavalry . . . rode through to help us. I can still remember how I felt when I watched them clatter into the little post, their tired horses gray with desert dust. . . . They'd fight then— and they'll fight now. Don't worry about them.[8]

Since this operation was totally MacArthur and Kenney's idea, MacArthur convinced himself that he had to accompany the convoy, explaining to Krueger, who protested that he himself had to go. MacArthur and Admiral Kinkaid flew to Milne Bay on the twenty-seventh to board the cruiser *Phoenix*.

The plan as developed for Operation Brewer was to land the cavalrymen on the eastern side of Los Negros at Hyane Harbor. This presented certain problems. The entrance to the harbor was flanked by two points of land 750 yards apart, from which the Japanese could maintain a cross fire by their artillery against the landing force. The actual entrance to the harbor through the reef was only seventy-five yards wide. Much of the shoreline was covered with a mangrove swamp, but to the south there was a wide sandy beach just 150 yards south of Momote airfield. Had the Japanese posted a larger force near the harbor, they would have had a good chance of throwing back the leading waves since the lack of landing craft meant that only a minimal number of troops could be brought in on the first waves. The first three waves would land at five-minute intervals; then the LCP(R)s would return to either the APDs or destroyers for more. Support from the Air Force would prove to be minimal as the APDs and destroyers moved into position, since a heavy overcast prevented all but three B-24s making their scheduled drops. However, the Navy provided heavy support both before the landings and later in suppressive fire.

Just before the scheduled landing at 8:15 A.M., the Japanese opened fire on the ships with 20 mm guns, later to be joined by heavier-caliber weapons located farther back. These were quickly silenced by the big guns of the destroyers, and support fire continued until only five minutes before the first wave of Lieutenant Colonel William Lobit's G Troop of the 2nd Squadron landed. They encountered only a few Japanese, who retreated back toward the airfield. The Japanese guns opened up, targeting the landing craft, and this fire disrupted the second wave. Thus, after ten minutes, there were only 150 cavalrymen on shore. The destroyer *Mahon* moved to within a mile of the beach and silenced the guns on the south shore while other destroyers continued to pound the north shore. After the fourth wave landed, there was a defensive perimeter 300 yards inland, and within two hours, the airfield was secured. By 1 P.M., the entire force had landed, along with two 75 mm pack howitzers. The casualties were low: only two men were killed and three wounded.[9] Patrols probed northwest a half mile beyond the airfield without encountering any Japanese. Other patrols advanced almost to the skidway, the isthmus connecting the northern and southern halves of the island, before being halted by Japanese fire. Although they encountered few Japanese, they reported back on large installations that indicated the probability of a

much larger force present than headquarters had led Chase to be-lieve.

About 4 P.M., MacArthur and Kinkaid came ashore in the rain and tramped through the mud to inspect the troops and confer with Chase. Kinkaid was uneasy about this venture since the island was far from pacified and he worried that an artillery round would land near the party or a sniper's bullet would find the supreme commander. However, MacArthur, with his usual disdain for personal safety, enjoyed his brief stay, once commenting on the dead Japanese he passed by saying that that was how he liked to see them. He decorated Lieutenant Marvin Henshaw, the first man ashore, with the Distinguished Service Cross. At that time he must also have been aware of the possibility that his intelligence estimates were wrong and that the few troops of the 5th Cavalry were vulnerable. He told Chase, "You have all performed marvellously. Hold on to what you have no matter whatever the odds. You have your teeth in him now. Don't let go."[10]

Muddy and wet, Kinkaid and MacArthur returned to the *Phoenix,* where MacArthur immediately sent a message to Krueger ordering more men and equipment to be sent to Los Negros. Krueger at once ordered the rest of the 5th Cavalry, approximately 1,500 men, along with 400 Seabees, to proceed immediately from Finschhafen to the relief of Chase's by-now-beleaguered force. They arrived on March 2, but by then the Japanese had expended themselves in a series of ultimately futile attacks. Even before MacArthur's visit, Chase had concluded that his small force could not hold the extended perimeter if the Japanese counterattacked in force. He pulled back the troops to the east of the airfield, established a perimeter only 1,500 yards long, and set the cavalrymen to digging foxholes in the hard coral. His supporting arms were only .50-caliber machine guns, mortars, and the two 75 mm guns. However, Berkey, before moving out with the majority of the support ships, left behind two destroyers. Their firepower would prove crucial in the coming days. Chase asked Krueger's headquarters for an airdrop of small arms and mortar ammunition, but especially barbed wire. The air force responded the next day with much-needed supplies but no barbed wire.[11]

General Imamura ordered Ezaki to attack the perimeter at once and drive the Americans into the sea. The main Japanese concentration near Hyane Harbor was the 1st Battalion of the 229th Infantry, commanded by a Captain Baba. Like so many Japanese commanders, Baba did not build up his force for a concentrated attack on one part of the defenders. Rather, beginning at dusk, he sent his troops against the perimeter in a series of uncoordinated attacks. Some of the Japanese managed to infiltrate the lines. A few donned life preservers and swam around to get behind the line. A number of infiltrators even got close to Chase's command post before being discovered and killed. The cavalrymen stayed in their foxholes and shot at anything that moved beyond them. The attacks were a complete failure, and the Japanese withdrew by early morning of the first, leaving sixty-six dead behind. The cavalry losses were seven dead and fifteen wounded.

The weather had cleared, allowing the air force to attack suspected Japanese positions. In a number of runs, they hit the dispersal areas of the airfield and flushed out an estimated one hundred Japanese, who tried to escape westward. Most were killed. During the day, the destroyers and the 5th's howitzers brought Japanese fixed positions in the south and in the Palaka area under fire. A seventeen-man patrol led by Captain Baba, which had infiltrated the perimeter the night before, was discovered. The cavalrymen killed many, while others, including Baba, committed suicide. In the late afternoon, the Japanese launched a series of weak attacks, all of which failed. During the night there were more uncoordinated attacks, one by fifty swimmers. The artillery and the destroyers' bigger guns played an important role in disrupting all these attacks. The two night actions had cost the Japanese an estimated 147 killed.[12]

On March 2, in anticipation of the arrival of reinforcements, Chase decided to expand the perimeter and moved his troops forward to take control of the entire airfield again. Later that day the rest of his command arrived. The Seabees brought with them bulldozers, which were immediately used to clear fields of fire. The cavalrymen dug in as deep as possible in their new positions, strung trip wires with coral-filled tin cans, and set out land mines. Chase positioned his 60 mm mortars to give direct support and massed his 81 mm mortars, along with machine guns, in front of his artillery in the center of his line. Colonel Ezaki wanted to begin an all-out attack that night, but he had problems positioning his men, so that the major attack was postponed until the following evening. Part of the reason for the disruption was the air attacks mounted by the 13th Squadron of A-20s and B-25s of the 499th Group, which strafed and bombed in the north. Later they returned to strike gun positions near the harbor.[13] At dusk on the third, the Japanese 2nd Battalion of the 1st Independent Mixed Regiment delivered the main attack from the skidway toward the east from Polaka against G and F Troops. The Japanese did not attempt stealth but moved openly, talking and shouting. Some advanced boldly through the minefield, taking heavy casualties but continuing to advance despite the heavy small-arms fire. Chase asked for support fire from the Navy. Four destroyers responded and, guided by cavalrymen on land, brought the area of attack under fire with everything from 40 mm to five-inch guns. The destroyers stood by and continued to fire on command during Ezaki's major effort.[14] The 75 mm guns and the larger 105 mm of the 82nd Field Artillery Battalion fired more than 8,500 rounds before the action ended on the fifth.

One fierce combat arena was the attack on a revetment area in front of the main line held by only eight men from G Troop, led by Sergeant Troy McGill. Outnumbered by an estimated ten to one, they held off the Japanese. All of the men except McGill and one other were killed or wounded. McGill ordered the other man back to safety while he stayed behind, mowing down the enemy until his weapon jammed. He then attacked the Japanese, using his rifle as a club, until he was killed. After daylight, a total of 105 Japanese dead were counted in front of the area occupied by the 1st Platoon. For his action McGill was awarded the Medal of Honor, the first for the 1st Cavalry in the war.[15]

Ezaki's big attack was a resounding failure. By the morning of the fourth, he had pulled back what was left of his command. Little skill had been shown by the Japanese in their fanatical attempt to breach the American perimeter. Ezaki had expended his men lavishly as they charged ahead without fear, only to be destroyed. The losses to the cavalrymen had been heavy—61 killed and 244 wounded. However, a total of 700 Japanese dead were counted on the fourth.[16] As MacArthur had foreseen, holding the perimeter was the key to victory. The severe Japanese losses meant that the U.S. offensive to control Seeadler Harbor, however time-consuming, would be that much easier.

Chase had requested on March 2 that the reserve force be brought to Los Negros immediately. There was some difficulty with the Navy in arranging their transport, and Krueger flew to Cape Sudest to confer with Barbey. The admiral agreed to provide three APDs and eight destroyers to move the 1,250 men of the 2nd Squadron of the 7th along with the 82nd Field Artillery Battalion. He also convinced Barbey to land the 2nd Brigade at Salami on the ninth, rather than at congested Hyane Harbor.[17] On the morning of the fourth, the 2nd Squadron landed and was immediately put into line to give the weary men of the 5th some rest. Chase had decided to wait for further reinforcements before beginning any offensive. This waiting was canceled by Major General Innis Swift, the division commander, who arrived on the morning of the fifth. He ordered an immediate advance across the skidway to secure the northern part of the island and another landing area at Salami plantation. The 2nd Squadron of the 7th was to begin its attack northward at noon of the fifth while the 2nd Squadron of the 5th moved back into position on the perimeter. The Japanese attacked from the skidway and Porlaka area during this changeover, but they were repulsed by small-arms and mortar fire. The air force delivered a combined attack by medium and heavy bombers. The Japanese attack postponed the planned offensive for hours. When it was finally under way, the cavalrymen found their advance further slowed by mines. The forward movement was resumed the next day, with the skidway being secured, but it was again slowed by the muddy roads and trails and by the men having to move trees felled by the Japanese along the way. Men of the 12th who had recently arrived bypassed the 7th and, despite the difficult terrain, took Salami after an hourlong firefight against the Japanese entrenchments. Fortunately for the cavalrymen, all the Japanese fortifications had been constructed with the guns facing the harbor in anticipation of an amphibious landing. The defenders were seemingly unaware of the direction of the cavalrymen's attack until it was too late. Captured diaries showed that the Japanese Iwakomri Battalion had lost six hundred men defending the skidway and many of the remainder had tried to cross a five-hundred-yard stretch of water to Papitala Mission in canoes or by swimming. Only a few survived the rifle fire from the cavalrymen, and many drowned.[18]

The capture of Salami and the air strikes against Japanese positions, while important, did not open Seeadler Harbor. The Navy had tried to force an entry into the harbor on the second. The captain of the destroyer *Mullany,* by chance also named Mullaney, had led two minesweepers through the narrow 1,500-foot entrance between Hauwei and Ndrilo Islands. The Japanese responded with heavy, accurate fire from the shore defense guns on the islands. The *Mullany* escaped damage by quick maneuvering, and the captain decided to retire. The group commander quickly brought up three other destroyers to support the *Mullany* in counter battery fire but with little apparent result. The *Mullany* made one further attempt to enter the harbor with the same results as before. The decision was then made to wait for the big guns of Admiral Crutchley's cruisers of Task Force 74. On the fifth, these fired more than four hundred rounds of eight-inch and six-inch shells into the islands, effectively silencing the shore guns. The destroyers and mine sweepers then entered the harbor without drawing fire.[19]

The southern part of Seeadler Harbor was secured by a series of amphibious actions in coordination with the 5th Cavalry attack westward to Porlaka. The village was captured on the seventh. The cavalrymen then crossed Lemondrol Creek to seize Papitalai village. At the same time, men of the 2nd Squadron of the 12th Cavalry at Salami boarded five LVTs with the goal of taking Papitalai Mission at the west end of Papitalai Harbor. Three of the LVTs got stuck in the mud, and therefore only twenty men could be put ashore in the initial landing. They dug in and waited for support. It eventually arrived and the Japanese were driven out, but only after the cavalrymen had sustained thirty-two casualties. The 2nd Squadron of the 7th Cavalry left Salami by boat on March 8 and took Lombrum village without opposition. Seeadler Harbor was now open. The bulk of the 5th and 12th Cavalry spent the rest of the month clearing the Japanese from the most southerly areas of Los Negros. The heaviest opposition came from the Japanese entrenched on Hill 260. These few Japanese repulsed the first attacks, but with heavy artillery and air support, the hill was taken on March 14.[20] Meanwhile, the Seabees and engineers had repaired the airfield. This allowed spotter planes to begin to use it on the sixth, and the following day a B-25 made an emergency landing there. On the ninth, twelve P-40s of the RAAF's 77th Squadron landed, followed by twelve more planes on the tenth. From this time on, most direct air support came from the RAAF planes stationed on Momote.[21]

The next objective after the seizure of Salami was Lorengau village and airfield on the adjacent island of Manus. General Swift assigned the task to Brigadier General Verne Mudge's 2nd Brigade, which had landed at Salami on March 9. Plans for the amphibious attack were completed the following day, though little was known as to the number and disposition of Japanese defenders. It was known that the village and airfield would be heavily defended, with

permanent bunkers and trench networks guarding the most obvious routes of approach. The plan called for simultaneous landings
on two beaches, code-named Yellow 1 and 2, 3,000 yards west of
the main objective near Lugos village. Leading the assault would be
the 8th Cavalry, commanded by Colonel William Bradley. The 7th,
less one squadron, would follow the initial landing. The 81st Engineering Squadron would be landed quickly to bridge the Liei River,
which separated the two landing beaches. After landing, the 1st
Squadron would move east along the coast road toward Lugos Mission and the airfield while the 2nd would take a well-defined trail
into the interior to prevent the Japanese from retreating into the
hills.

Before the main invasion, it was decided to seize Butjo and
Hauwei Islands in order to emplace artillery to support the Yellow
Beach landings. Butjo was occupied without incident on the afternoon of the eleventh, and soon twelve 75 mm and six 37 mm guns
of the 99th Field Artillery Battalion were landed. The Hauwei experience was different. An advance patrol landed from a PT boat
and an LVT on the western part of the island, only to be met with
withering fire from all sides. The small unit retreated back to the
beach, only to find that the PT boat had left after its captain had
been wounded. Some of the men clambered aboard the LVT,
which promptly ran aground on a submerged reef. The cavalrymen,
including the wounded, jumped into the water, where they were
soon joined by the group on the beach. Ultimately another PT boat
picked up eighteen men from the water. The patrol had suffered
eight killed and three missing. Every survivor was wounded.[22]

The following day the 2nd Squadron, less F Troop, returned to
the island on LCMs. There was heavy supporting fire from offshore destroyers and artillery at Salami. In addition, RAAF P-40s
from the 77th Squadron flew a number of suppressive strikes. One
troop landed in the west and another in the south. Considerable
Japanese small-arms fire caused the cavalrymen to dig in for the

night. On the thirteenth, the reserve troop landed and brought with them a Sherman tank. The 61st Artillery Battalion, from positions on Los Negros, fired more than 1,000 rounds, and the destroyers brought their five-inch guns into play. This awesome firepower, directed at a small area, destroyed most of the Japanese trenches and bunkers, so that by noon of the thirteenth, the three troops had secured the island, killing the forty-three defenders. By late afternoon, the 61st Artillery had some of its 105 howitzers in place on the southwestern part of the island, while the 271st's guns were offloaded in the west.[23]

The artillery placed on the islands and in the Salami area, combined with the fire of four destroyers, began to soften the Japanese defenses, first at Lorengau, and then, just before the landings, shifted to Lugos Mission. The air force also assisted by sending over twenty-five B-25s from Nadzab. Troops of the 8th Cavalry were loaded onto twelve LCMs, seven LCVs, and one LCT. The landings began when the LSTs let out seven LVTs carrying A Troop to Beach Yellow 2 and C Troop to Yellow 1. There were no casualties as A Troop drove eastward through the mission on to the coast road, encountering only a few Japanese. Soon the bulk of the 8th were onshore and advancing toward the airfield and village. Meanwhile, men of the 2nd Squadron moved southwest along the trail and over a series or ridges. They were harassed by small Japanese units. The opposition grew heavier as they neared the junction of the trail and the interior road, which they had named Road No. 1. They dug in for the night and waited for reinforcements. These arrived early on the sixteenth, accompanied by one light and two medium tanks led by a bulldozer, which had gouged out sufficient width on the trail. With these, the Japanese position was quickly overrun, allowing the troops to move east. By the evening they had reached a point only eight hundred yards south of the airfield.

In the meantime, the men of the 1st Squadron had advanced along the coast through heavy rain forest and swampy areas. Arriv-

ing at a point one mile east of Lugos Mission, they were halted by
Japanese fire from three pillboxes. A frontal assault failed, and artillery fire from Hauwei was called in, but a second attack also
failed. Tanks were brought up, and RAAF planes attacked the
Japanese. This enabled B Troop to overrun the position and, by late
afternoon of the fifteenth, advance to a ridge near the edge of the
airfield. The following day, the troopers were halted by sustained
Japanese fire from ridges parallel to the line of attack despite heavy
artillery fire on those positions. The troops were pulled back, and
General Mudge replaced the troops of the 8th with those of the
7th. During the night of March 16–17, destroyers and artillery
pounded the Japanese defenses, and this, combined with heavy
mortar concentrations, all but obliterated the Japanese positions.
Thus, when the 1st Squadron of the 7th moved ahead at midmorning of the seventeenth, it found little opposition. The advance to
the Lorengau River was blocked by only a few Japanese survivors.
The river was approximately sixty feet wide and in places twenty
feet deep. However, there was a sandbar near the mouth that could
be used. Later it was discovered that it had been mined; the mines
were connected to a master switch controlled by a soldier in a
dugout. Fortunately for the advancing troopers, he had been killed
earlier, and thus the crossing was made with no casualties.[24]

Lorengau village lay in a cup-shaped valley surrounded by low-
lying hills. Despite this natural defense, on the eighteenth the
troops of the 8th Cavalry met little opposition because of the heavy
concentration of naval and artillery gunfire. Eighty-seven Japanese
bodies were found in the environs of the village. The surviving defenders moved southward along Road No. 2 to the interior village
of Rossum. The Japanese had constructed elaborate defense positions along this road and from these slowed the pursuit of the 7th
Cavalry. Nevertheless, the village of Old Rossum, one third of the
way to Rossum, was captured on the twenty-second. Reinforced by
troopers of the 8th and support from RAAF planes, they systematically cleared the bunkers and captured Rossum on the twenty-fifth.

The cost of this advance was high: 36 killed and 128 wounded. With the capture of the airfield and then Rossum, the campaign for Manus, for all practical purposes, was ended.[25] However, there were still many Japanese in the jungle areas of the interior who had to be tracked down. Thus Manus became a kind of training ground for U.S. units. Most of the patrolling was done by the 2nd Brigade and the 302nd Reconnaissance Troop. Throughout April, acting on information from Australian civil authorities and their own patrols, the individual units would move quickly against these stragglers. Hundreds of Japanese were killed by these patrols in the weeks before General Krueger finally declared the operation on Manus terminated on May 18.

The future operational control of the Admiralty Islands was tied directly to the high-level arguments concerned with future operations in the Pacific. MacArthur had proposed in a radiogram to Marshall on February 2 that after the Marshalls operation, almost all the Pacific forces be concentrated along the New Guinea–Philippines axis. This would include almost all the Pacific Fleet and the bulk of the B-29s. He wanted Halsey to command the greatly augmented fleet. He sent Sutherland to Washington to explain further his proposals to the Joint Chiefs. Nimitz then sent his chief of staff, Forrest P. Sherman, to present his arguments for continuing the central Pacific actions. As MacArthur had suspected, at this juncture the Washington planners were more sympathetic to Nimitz's ideas than his. In late February, Nimitz proposed bringing the Admiralties under his command by placing Halsey in charge of Manus. The argument was that the Navy had more use for the base and that most of the construction was being done by naval personnel. All that was needed was to shift the western boundary of the South Pacific Theater to encompass the Admiralties. MacArthur bristled at this, seeing the suggestion as the latest attempt by the Navy to close out the Southwest Pacific Command in the final phase of Pacific operations. He protested against Nimitz's suggestions to Marshall and volunteered to come to Washington to present his arguments. He even hinted that, at age sixty-four, he might retire if the Admiralties were removed from his command. Marshall reassured him that he would retain control over base operations unless he chose to turn over control of them. However, there had to be a clear understanding that the Pacific Fleet would have unrestricted use of Seeadler Harbor.[26]

MacArthur, still not reassured, contacted Halsey to come to Brisbane for a major conference. Accompanied by his staff, Halsey met with MacArthur on March 3. He was met at first with perfect courtesy and then with a fifteen-minute tirade against any change in the status of command on Manus. MacArthur indicated that he intended to restrict the use of Manus–Los Negros to the Seventh Fleet until the question of jurisdiction had been settled. Halsey replied that if that were done, MacArthur would be hampering the war effort and indicated that he did not care who was in charge of construction as long as the harbor was open to the Fifth Fleet as well as the Seventh. After an hour, MacArthur said that Halsey could have his way. However, the next morning MacArthur stated that he had changed his mind, and in another meeting, the question was argued over again. Again MacArthur backed down. This did not end the controversy; as Halsey remembered, "I'll be damned if we didn't run the course a third time." At the third meeting, MacArthur protested that Nimitz and the Navy had insulted his honor. Halsey, who had held his temper, finally replied, "General, you are putting your personal honor before the welfare of the United States." This shocked MacArthur and his staff. He finally said, "We can't have anything like that," and told Sutherland, "Dick, there will be nothing like that."[27]

That agreement was echoed in Washington when the Joint Chiefs rejected Nimitz's proposal to take over Manus. MacArthur retained control with the provision that Seeadler be open for use by all units of the U.S. Navy.

Construction to improve the air and naval facilities on both Los Negros and Manus began immediately even while the fighting continued. The 40th Seabee Battalion, the 8th Engineering Squadron, and members of the 532nd Engineering Boat and Shore Regiment started working soon after the initial landing on Los Negros. One week later, the Momote airstrip had been lengthened to a usable 3,000 feet. By the time Krueger declared the operation at an end in May, the Momote airstrip was 7,000 feet long by 100 feet wide, complete with taxiways, hard stands, and storage facilities. The airfield at Lorengau on Manus was determined not to be suitable for further expansion, and thus the area of the Makerang Plantation was selected for a new airfield. By May, an 8,000-foot-long by 100-foot-wide strip had been constructed with service facilities, and another, parallel strip was under construction. A petroleum farm was finished near Momote, capable of storing 7,000 barrels of fuel, while another, much larger one was being completed at Makerang. In addition, the engineers constructed camps for RAAF and U.S. units and built roads and bridges, including a 125-foot-long bridge over the Lorengau River. They also completed a floating Liberty Ship dock, and an LST pile dock was under construction.[28] By late spring, the Admiralties had become what MacArthur had envisioned, a major base for further offensive action in New Guinea and ultimately the Philippines. The relatively quick success in capturing them with low casualties removed any immediate direct criticism that could have been leveled at MacArthur for gambling on Operation Brewer with inadequate ground forces.

Ten

HOLLANDIA:

THE GREAT LEAP FORWARD

The pace of the offensive against the Japanese positions in New Guinea accelerated in the first half of 1944. This was partially because MacArthur feared that unless he could move quickly to secure the necessary bases for his hoped-for Philippines campaign, the Joint Chiefs would limit any such action and allow the Navy's central Pacific plans to take precedence. Despite his continuing complaints about the southwest Pacific being shortchanged in supplies and men, he had been provided with the means to carry out the numerous amphibious assaults necessary to gain his eventual goal. The operations in New Britain, Saidor, and Los Negros showed clearly the Allied superiority over the Japanese in numbers of ships and men, and particularly the ability to dominate the air. By early April, MacArthur had almost 750,000 men under his command. The major ground components were six U.S. infantry divisions and one cavalry division, three separate regimental combat teams, and three special brigades. The Australians, though now relegated to a secondary role, could provide five divisions and enough separate brigades to form two additional divisions. Kenney's air force had grown to such an extent that he could mount two-hundred-plane raids on a variety of targets with little fear that the Japanese could seriously interfere with any planned operation. His major limitation was distance. He needed airfields from which his bombers and fighters could reach their most important targets. The Navy, although still operating under a type of dual command and without the capital ships MacArthur wanted, was unchallenged by the Japanese and adequate to carry out MacArthur's strategic objectives.[1]

In retrospect, the Japanese position in New Guinea was hopeless. Although there were more than 350,000 Japanese troops in the southwest Pacific region, many of them were already isolated with little chance of receiving reinforcements or requisite supplies. There was also confusion in the command of the Japanese ground forces, made even more difficult by the distances involved and the relative lack of Japanese naval power. Ostensibly, the overall command of Japanese forces as far as Wewak was exercised by Lieutenant General Fusataro Tshima, whose headquarters was far away at Manokwari on the Vogelkop Peninsula. Reflecting Imperial Headquarters' concern as to MacArthur's next move, on March 25 Tshima ordered General Adachi to withdraw the residue of his 18th Army, consisting mainly of three battered infantry divisions, overland to concentrate in the Hollandia area. Fortunately for later U.S. operations, Adachi procrastinated, believing that the next landing would be at Hansa Bay. Heavy bombing by the Fifth Air Force and systematic shelling of the coast near Wewak seemed to confirm this. However, General Korechika Anami, commanding the Second Area Army at Davao, became concerned about Adachi's reluctance and on April 12 sent his chief of staff to Wewak to convince Adachi to pull out. He finally began the withdrawal and had two regiments on the trail when the U.S. landings at Aitape and Hollandia began. Further command problems were apparent at Hollandia, where Major General Toyozo Kitazono arrived only ten days before the invasion and, for some unexplained reason, never took over command. Thus Tshima appointed an air officer, Major General Masazumi Inada of the 6th Air Division, to assume command.[2]

The Japanese High Command was well aware of the deficiencies in numbers and quality of troops. In December 1943, it managed to bring a division to reinforce Tshima's forces in the Vogelkop area. Attempts to reinforce Wewak during February and early March proved disastrous. The code-breaking Ultra decoded messages from the Eighteenth Army that indicated details for a series of convoys that would bring reinforcements to Adachi. The first of these four ships managed to get through to Wewak. The second, despite air cover, was intercepted by the U.S. submarine *Gato,* which sank the *Diagen Maru.* Approximately four hundred troops drowned. Another submarine, the *Peto,* torpedoed the *Kayo Maru,* a smaller vessel, on February 29. There were forty-five casualties, but the rest of the survivors were taken to Hollandia, not to Wewak. On March 15, Fifth Air Force night patrols sank two small ships and drove another aground. Two days later, sixty miles off Hollandia, B-24s sank the *Yakumo Maru.* The three other ships in the convoy stopped to rescue survivors and were attacked by U.S. heavy bombers and fighter-bombers, which sank all three. Presumably most of the troops and crews were lost. This last attack convinced Imperial Headquarters to order all large ship convoys to Wewak stopped.[3]

General Adachi was not totally incorrect in believing that the Hansa Bay area would be the next target. MacArthur's and Krueger's staffs had been developing plans for occupation of that key area since December. Although they were aware of the proximity of Adachi's main force, they recognized that the potential area for the operation was held by only five hundred troops. Not all the planners at General Headquarters were enamored of this proposed action. Brigadier General Bonner Fellers, the planning chief, was concerned with time factors. Hansa Bay was located only 120 miles up the coast from Saidor, and he concluded that even with moderate opposition there, it would postpone the ultimate conquest of New Guinea and thus allow Nimitz's central Pacific operations to frustrate MacArthur's goal for a return to the Philippines. He therefore recommended that the Hansa Bay operation be canceled and instead a huge leap forward be taken by occupying Hollandia in Dutch New Guinea, five hundred miles from Saidor. His immediate superior, General Stephen Chamberlin, who was committed to the Hansa Bay plan, vetoed any such ambitious undertaking. Fellers then breached protocol, bypassing Chamberlin to suggest the Hollandia proposal directly to MacArthur. Although Fellers was fired by Chamberlin for this breach, he had made a deep impression on MacArthur, who seized upon the idea and rescued Fellers by making him his military secretary.[4] Without crediting Fellers for the original idea, MacArthur, in his autobiography, much later gave the cogent reasons for the change in plans. He wrote:

> The capture of Hansa Bay would mean an advance of only 120 miles, but I now planned a maneuver which at one stroke would move us almost 500 miles forward and at the same time render some 40,000 Japanese troops ineffective. I would by-pass Hansa Bay, by-pass the enemy stronghold at Wewak, and strike well to the rear at Aitape and Hollandia. Once this area was securely ours, we would have airstrips from which our ground-based aircraft could dominate the Vogelkop, and our advance westward would be hastened by several months.[5]

Preliminary planning for the Hollandia operation had been completed by late February. The problem of air cover for the invasion troubled MacArthur. He wanted the Navy to provide it from the many fast carriers of the Fifth Fleet. At a conference in Brisbane with Nimitz's representatives, he reached a tentative agreement with the Navy on temporary support, although the exact use of Nimitz's precious carriers was postponed until later. When the Admiralties campaign was assured of success, MacArthur alerted Krueger on March 5 of the possibility of abandoning the Hansa Bay project and instead attacking Hollandia, with a secondary assault on a closer target that would provide Kenney's planes good air cover for the invasion. The planners had looked at first to Wuvuli Island, 125 miles northeast of Hollandia, and then to Tanamerah Island, but potential terrain and transportation problems had caused them to give up any action there. Instead, they suggested Aitape, where there was already an airfield located 150 miles from Hollandia. MacArthur had alerted the Joint Chiefs that he was preparing this bold move and asked for their approval. This was granted almost immediately, and on March 12 they instructed Nimitz to provide the necessary air cover for the operation.

While Kinkaid and Barbey, in conjunction with Alamo Force headquarters, planned the complex amphibious landings for Operation Reckless, a final conference between Nimitz and MacArthur was scheduled for the twenty-fifth in Brisbane. During this meeting, Nimitz still showed his concern for his big carriers coming close to the considerable Japanese air groups at Hollandia and Wewak. He indicated that the Fifth Fleet was planning a large-scale attack with eleven carriers on the western Carolines between April 1 and 3. They would be in position for direct support of the Hollandia operation by April 20. However, he stated that they would remain in position for only two days. Kenney was concerned that if he could not have an airfield at Tadje near Aitape by then, he would not be able to give the supply ships adequate cover. Nimitz then promised Kinkaid the loan of seven smaller carriers, primarily to support the Aitape landings. Kinkaid could have them for eight days. As the discussion progressed, Nimitz was still fretful about the Japanese land-based air capability. Kenney then surprised everyone but MacArthur by promising to wipe out the entire Japanese air force if elements of the Thirteenth Air Force, operating from Los Negros, would take up the support role for any possible action in the Carolines or Marianas.[6]

Nimitz was not being timid. He and MacArthur knew that the Japanese had been building up their air strength at Hollandia. In mid-February, the 8th Air Brigade there had had only fifty-six airplanes. Ultra evidence on the twenty-third indicated that there were at least 175, and later aerial photos showed more than three hundred lined up along the airstrips.[7] The Japanese commanders took little care to disperse their planes. They believed that Hansa Bay would be the next target and that they would be able to challenge the Allied air cover there. They thought that Hollandia, located more than five hundred miles from the nearest Allied air base at Dobodura, was relatively safe, since they knew Kenney and Whitehead would not commit to large-scale bombing efforts without adequate fighter protection. They were convinced that no Allied fighter had the range to protect the bombers over that distance. Thus their overconfidence led them to believe that their air fleet was safe. However, an upgraded version of the P-38 gave Kenney the means of carrying out his promise to MacArthur and Nimitz. In February, fifty-eight new P-38s arrived in Australia, equipped with 300-gallon auxiliary gas tanks. These gave them the range to accompany the bombers from Gusap airfield and stay up to one hour over targets at Hollandia. Kenney realized that the number of new planes would not be sufficient if the Japanese had the number of fighters available that photo reconnaissance showed. He ordered that all available facilities begin to fabricate tanks and install them on the older-model P-38s. The deadline he imposed was March 25. Also, as a part of the Allied strategy to fool the Japanese, he ordered that until the order was given for attacking Hollandia, no P-38 was to fly further up the coast than the Tadji airfield. Further, even those were not to remain in the vicinity more than fifteen minutes.

An adjunct order was to have single-plane night raids on the Hollandia area. The pilots were told if possible not to hit anything.[8]

To lull the Japanese further into believing that Hansa Bay was the next target, Whitehead had his bombers strike over and over at targets in that region. Some planes dropped flares at night to simulate night photography missions. Rubber boats were floated onshore to trick the Japanese into believing that reconnaissance patrols had landed. Even parachutes were dropped in the vicinity of Wewak. The Navy also sent destroyers to bombard shore installations at irregular intervals. It is questionable whether all this was necessary since Adachi had already received orders to abandon Wewak, but without a doubt, all this activity in that area underscored the illusion that Hollandia was secure. The Japanese were rudely shaken from this when, on March 30, Kenney sent sixty-five B-24 heavy bombers over the field there. They targeted primarily fuel dumps and antiaircraft positions with more than 14,000 twenty-three-pound fragmentation bombs. An estimated twenty-five planes were destroyed on the ground. The bombers were escorted by eighty P-38s that took on the forty Japanese interceptors and shot down ten with no losses. The next day, a follow-up attack by sixty-eight B-24s with 500-pound bombs struck at the parked planes and the runways. A total of 138 planes were reported as destroyed, and the runways were badly cratered. Thirty Japanese fighters met the accompanying seventy P-38s and, in brief dogfights, lost fourteen planes. On April 3, the bombers returned and completed the destruction of Japanese airpower in western New Guinea. Sixty-three B-24s dropped 100-pound bombs from medium altitude, followed by 171 B-25 and A-20 strafers coming in at low level. Once again the Japanese fighters attempted to challenge the P-38s, only to have twenty-four of the thirty engaged destroyed. The few remaining Japanese aircraft were then withdrawn westward. Thus, by the time Nimitz's carriers arrived to cover the landings, they were needed only for close-in support roles. The feared Japanese airpower at Hollandia had, as Kenney had promised, been annihilated.[9]

Two other major concerns for the planners of Operation Reckless were the terrain features and the potential numbers of defenders at Hollandia and Aitape. The dominant feature in the Hollandia region was the Cyclops Mountains, which ran parallel to the coastline in the immediate interior with peaks as high as 7,000 feet. Another significant feature was Lake Sentani, an irregularly shaped body of water fifteen miles long that covered only a part of the flat plain between the mountains and the coast. It was on this plain that the Japanese had developed their three airfields. The coastline was broken by two large bays, Tanahmerah in the west and Humboldt in the east, separated by twenty-five miles of swamps, mangrove areas, and the Cyclops Mountains. There were many good landing beaches in the Humboldt Bay area but very few at Tanahmerah. All of these, however, were narrow and backed by swamps. There were only trails from both bays leading to the Sentani Plain, located roughly eighteen miles from Humboldt Bay and fourteen from Tanahmerah. Although the worst of the rainy season was finished by April, there was still heavy rainfall expected that would turn the trails into seas of mud and cause severe flooding of the rivers.[10]

The situation at Aitape was quite different. The entire area there was a coastal plain, varying from five to twelve miles in width. The Torricelli Mountains were located far into the interior and would not play a part in the operation. There were no natural barriers to the east and west and only one small hill near where the landing was planned. One potential problem was the many streams that, given the heavy rainfall, might flood and make movement difficult. The most important rivers were the Driniumor, Raihu, Nigia, and Esim. The main Japanese development there was an airfield near Tadji Plantation located eight miles southeast of Aitape. The Japanese had originally planned for three but had completed only one, and this had been used primarily as a staging base for planes in transit to Wewak. Utilizing mainly aerial photos, the planners had selected a landing beach, code-named Blue, near Korako village on the coast near the northwest corner of the airfield. A trail from the village to the airfield could be used by Jeeps and tracked vehicles.[11]

As was true throughout the New Guinea campaign, estimates of the numbers of enemy troops were a major problem. Just before the landings, Ultra reported that there were 8,647 general troops and 7,650 air troops at Hollandia. MacArthur's intelligence chief concluded that this included the forces at Aitape, that there were about 12,000 men at Hollandia, most of whom were service personnel, and that there was only one combat-maneuver battalion available there. In actuality there were 16,000 troops in the area, but Willoughby was correct so far as combat troops available. Later it was determined that only one man in ten of the service and personnel troops carried a rifle and most of the pilots were without planes. Construction and supply troops could not be counted on to defend the area. At Aitape it was estimated that the Japanese had 3,500 troops, of whom only 1,500 were combat troops.[12] However, in planning Reckless, Krueger was always mindful of the possibility that Adachi would move against Aitape and that Hollandia could be threatened by the large Japanese forces believed to be within striking range. This concern explains why almost two divisions were scheduled for Hollandia and a tested regimental combat team would assault Aitape.

The plan for the invasion was to have I Corps, commanded by Eichelberger—who had been involved only in training since the Buna-Sanananda operation—be in overall charge of the Hollandia attack. Eichelberger would have the 24th Division, commanded by Major General Frederick Irving, and the 41st Division (less the 163rd Regimental Combat Team), led by Major General Horace Fuller. The Aitape invasion, code-named Persecution, was considered a separate, although correlate, operation, and was to be carried out by the 163rd, commanded by Brigadier General Jens Doe. The

24th was located on Goodenough Island, where the troops had been undergoing amphibious training for the Hansa Bay operation. The bulk of the 41st, however, was scattered throughout northern Australia and was brought together at Cape Cretin just prior to embarkation. Admiral Kinkaid, in overall command of Task Force 77, had available 215 ships, the largest amphibious force ever in the South Pacific. Admiral Barbey, in charge of the actual landings, had divided his force into three attack groups. The Eastern Group, carrying the 163rd, comprised eleven APDs, seven LSTs, and five destroyers. The Central Group, whose target was Humboldt Bay, was composed of three transports, five destroyer transports, sixteen LCIs, and seven LSTs carrying the 41st Division. There were also seven destroyers for a screen. The Western Group, with I Corps Headquarters and troops of the 24th Division, had four transports, sixteen LCIs, seven LSTs, and a screen of six destroyers. In addition, there were two covering forces of four cruisers and ten destroyers, plus the eight escort carriers and their screen of five destroyers. To the north was the might of Task Force 58 and its fleet carriers, which Nimitz had promised would support the landings for a maximum of two days.[13]

Admiral Barbey, who would accompany the Western Attack Group, laid out a circuitous route that would take the convoy four or five days to arrive before the target beaches. The LCIs left the staging area one day before the transports and spent the night at Seeadler. They made rendezvous with the rest of the convoy on April 20 at a point approximately fifty miles northwest of Seeadler. This included the escort carriers and their destroyer screen. On the evening of the twenty-first, Captain A. G. Noble's Eastern Attack Group, with the escort carriers, broke away and headed for Aitape. They were on station by early morning of D-day. The landing was scheduled for 6:45 A.M. on April 22.[14]

Prior to H-hour, the destroyers slammed the beach area with heavy fire and the two sub chasers in the convoy then gave close-in support for three minutes with rockets prior to the landing scheduled for Blue Beach. The first wave was composed of the 2nd and 3rd Battalions of the 163rd, landing abreast. They were to secure the beachhead, and then the 1st Battalion would push ahead to capture the bomber field. In reserve Krueger had placed the 127th Regiment of the 32nd Division, which was to land the following day. The landing was perfect, against no opposition, except that the troops did not land on Blue Beach. Overcast skies and smoke from fires obscured the area, and therefore the landing was made 1,200 yards east of the scheduled area, near Wapil village. No difficulty was encountered, and the new beach even proved better for landing supplies on than Blue Beach. The few Japanese in the area fled upon the first naval bombardment. After landing, the 2nd Battalion moved west along the beach toward Korako and the trail leading to the airfields. The beachhead was soon extended five hundred yards into the interior. By 10:30, the 1st Battalion had landed and moved quickly toward the southernmost or bomber strip while the 2nd slowly advanced toward the fighter strip. By 12:45, both of the fields had been captured. The perimeter was quickly extended eastward as far as the Nigia River. Meanwhile, the 62nd Works Wing of the RAAF had landed in the morning and immediately begun work on the fighter strip. The Australians worked around the clock for forty-eight hours to prepare the damaged and overgrown field to receive fighters. In the late afternoon of the twenty-fourth, twenty-five P-40s of the 78th Wing of the RAAF landed, followed the next day by the rest of the squadron. However, poor drainage postponed the field's full use until the twenty-eighth, after steel matting had been laid down. Thus, air cover of the Hollandia area from Aitape as envisioned by the planners was not possible. However, this was not crucial, since naval air support of the Hollandia operation and the quick success at the Hollandia and Tanahmerah beaches meant that the RAAF's early support was not needed.[15]

Meanwhile, the Western Attack Group had proceeded to Tanahmerah Bay, and, on schedule, the two Australian cruisers and the destroyers began to lay down a curtain of fire on the proposed

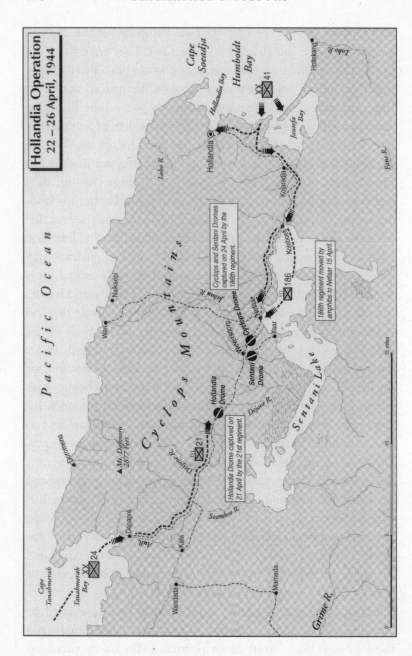

Hollandia Operation
22 – 26 April, 1944

Cyclops and Sentani Dromes captured on 24 April by the 186th regiment.

186th regiment moved by amphibs to Nefaar 15 April.

Hollandia Drome captured on 21 April by the 21st regiment.

landing beaches. In the few minutes before H-hour, of 7 A.M. on the twenty-second, they fired 600 rounds of eight-inch and 1,500 rounds of five-inch shells into suspected Japanese positions. The landings, planned mainly by using aerial photographs, were to take place on two beaches. Red Beach 2, located to the north, was scheduled for the main effort. Although the planners were aware that the beach was only thirty yards deep and there was a swamp adjacent to it, they believed that there was enough dry land for the main supply dumps and bivouac areas. Red Beach 1, located at Dépapré village, was flanked on both sides by hills, and the entrance to the village was partially blocked by a reef. Because of these obvious problems, the proposed landings there had once been canceled. Fortunately, however, Irving convinced Eichelberger to allow the secondary effort to be made. The maps indicated that a good road led from the village to the airfields. The plan was to have the 3rd Battalion of the 21st RCT land first at Red Beach 2, consolidate its position, and, after reinforcements from the 21st and 19th RCTs arrived, take the trail to Red Beach 1, two miles away. Meanwhile, Company A would land at Red Beach 1, quickly secure a beachhead, and move up the road toward the airfields.[16]

The landings were made as planned. The naval covering force, anchored by the cruisers *Australia* and *Shropshire,* took suspected targets under fire, and troops of the 3rd Battalion of the 21st had no opposition when landing at Red Beach 2. However, the troops, on attempting to move into the interior in search of the trail to Red Beach 1, discovered that the swamp was impassable to wheeled vehicles. Only infantry troops could move through the swamp, and only with the greatest difficulty. One soldier recalled:

Someone above us decided that Infantry could solve the problem by wading the swamp on ridge lines, especially those near the base of trees. I was off on another unplanned adventure. The water proved to be about chin

high, if you held your head back and your rifle high over-
head you should be able to make it we were assured. A
number didn't, stepping into holes rather than ridges. For
me, I was miserable with that swamp water streaming
down my front and into my boots; I wondered what kind
of animals might be in the swamp, and I'm not sure if I
found any ridges, and with such a posture, I did veer off to
my right, ending up with a body of troops I had never seen
before.[17]

He also recalled an example of interservice rivalry. Support for the
infantry was to be in part provided by the Marine Corps tank unit.
However:

The tanks went in full bore, but not very far before they
were flooded out, steam streaming from their flooded en-
gines. They had jeered the miserable army as they went in,
now they were sitting on the decks of those tanks waiting
for an Army Engineer unit attempting to fill in a road
through the swamp, to fish their tanks out.[18]

The engineers later attempted to cut a canal to drain a portion
of the swamp to expand the few dry areas. Despite considerable effort, this did not work. They could not build a road into the interior, and they soon discovered that, contrary to the planners' belief,
there was no road connecting to Red Beach 1. Much of the artillery
landed from the LSTs soon became mired in the mud. Supplies
were piled up on the narrow strip of beach, and it became obvious
that supplies and equipment scheduled for D+1 could not be
landed.

Before these problems became serious, the troops were surprised by a visit from MacArthur, who had watched the landings
from the cruiser *Nashville*. After being joined by Barbey and

Krueger, who had been on board the destroyer *Swanson,* the top echelon of the Southwest Pacific Command again took to small boats for the short trip to the beach. MacArthur and his distinguished party had earlier visited the Hollandia landing areas, only four hours after the first assault troops had landed, and they had spent considerable time conferring with Fuller and inspecting the beaches. Shortly afterward, they learned that a Japanese plane had been spotted heading for the beach area. Barbey instructed that the boat be redirected to the relative safety of a nearby destroyer. However, MacArthur overrode this sensible precaution and ordered the boat to proceed directly to the beach. A Japanese plane was spotted soon after, but it continued on toward Hollandia. Once on land, MacArthur, accompanied by Krueger and Eichelberger, spent an hour conferring with Irving and then talking to startled soldiers, ignoring the heat and the mud. MacArthur was impressed with the way the landings at Hollandia and Tanahmerah Bay had been conducted, declaring that it was one of the best operations that he had ever witnessed. After returning to the *Nashville,* still in an optimistic mood, he confided in Eichelberger that if the southwest Pacific were ever authorized another army, he would appoint him to command it.[19]

The secondary landing on Red Beach 1 had also gone as planned. Company A of the 1st Battalion of the 21st landed at 7:45 A.M., encountering no problems with the reefs and quickly secured the beachhead. A few Japanese stragglers were encountered and killed as the troops searched for a route to the airfields. This proved to be a winding trail, so narrow that wheeled vehicles could not use it. Had the Japanese decided to defend the trail, they could have established a series of ambushes at the many hairpin turns. However, as the 1st Battalion troops advanced, they discovered that the Japanese had abandoned a series of half-completed pillboxes. The battalion commander, Lieutenant Colonel Thomas Clifford, sent out search patrols after his men reached Korotome village at noon.

They pushed forward to Jangbena, another village located on a flat plain. Clifford believed that the Japanese had 10,000 men in the airfield area and was sure they would soon counterattack. He therefore pulled back to a more defensible site. His problem was complicated by having lost radio contact with the beachhead at Dépapré. His concern was heightened by an attack by a small group of Japanese during the night.

Meanwhile, most of the 3rd Battalion, having discovered no Japanese in the southern section of Red Beach 2, were ordered to march overland over rugged terrain to Red Beach 1. By midmorning of the twenty-third, Colonel Charles Lyman, commanding the 21st RCT, had most of his troops at Dépapré. Clifford decided to move his 1st Battalion back up the trail past Jangbena. After crossing a small stream a mile beyond the village, one of the companies encountered heavy rifle and machine-gun fire that forced it to retreat. Clifford brought up mortars and requested air support from Task Force 58. Despite the air and mortar attacks, the Japanese could not be dislodged. He therefore pulled back to allow the artillery a better field of fire. By this time the other two battalions had moved up the trail and were close behind the first.

The forward movement toward the airfields was halted not by the Japanese but by nearly insurmountable supply problems. Although the main supply base had been moved from Hollandia to Dépapré, the minimal necessary supplies of food and ammunition to the forward troops could be maintained only with the greatest difficulty. The trail was too narrow for Jeeps or trucks; therefore all supplies had to be hand carried. A battalion of the 19th Infantry that had moved to Dépapré and the cannon companies of both regiments were at first used to carry supplies up the trail. As the situation continued, Irving had three battalions, an antitank company, and the two cannon companies carrying supplies. Bad weather prevented resupply by air. The entire supply system ground to a halt on the twenty-fifth because of the torrential rains. With the clearing of the weather on the twenty-sixth, an airdrop of ammunition from

B-25s that had flown five hundred miles from Saidor allowed for a resumption of the advance. By noon, the Dajaoe River was crossed and it became apparent that the Japanese were evacuating their positions around the airfields as the troops reached Hollandia Drome, the furthest west of the fields. The 1st Battalion completed this phase of the operation by midafternoon, when contact was made with the 186th RCT of the 41st Division, which had been moving west from Humboldt Bay.[20]

That division had been involved in the landings on D-day on four beaches adjacent to the bay and the subsequent movement in the interior toward Hollandia village and Lake Sentani. The 3rd Battalion of the 162nd Regiment, after a preliminary bombardment by the Navy and sweeps by planes from Task Force 58, had landed on White Beach 1 at 7 A.M. on the twenty-second against no opposition. Soon six tanks from the 603rd Tank Company, elements of the 116th Engineers, and the 146th Field Artillery Battalion landed. The troops fanned out and moved to capture the bare Pancake Hill, north of the beach. By noon the 105 mm howitzers were emplaced there. Soon the 1st and 2nd Battalions were on land; the 1st took up defensive duties, while the 2nd moved up the main trail toward Hollandia. General Fuller halted all forward movement after the 3rd Battalion captured the 1,000-foot-high Janemah Hill. This halt indicated the concern that all senior commanders had about the numbers and disposition of the Japanese forces. Although few Japanese had been encountered and the total casualties from the action on D-day amounted to only six killed and sixteen wounded, Fuller was certain that significant enemy forces were concentrated at Hollandia and near the airfields.

The navy and division artillery pounded suspected Japanese concentration areas during the night and early the next morning before the offensive was resumed. There was little opposition to the advance on Hollandia town; the Japanese did not attempt to defend their well-developed defenses. Hollandia was captured by noon, and patrols of the 3rd moved out along the hill lines to secure the coastal areas. At the same time the 1st Battalion made a shore-to-shore movement across the mouth of Imbi Bay to Cape Saedja and then swept up the cape, eliminating scattered groups of Japanese. Portions of the 186th Regiment followed the 162nd on D-day. The 1st and 2nd Battalions marched overland southward, and others concentrated adjacent to the bay to serve as the division reserve. The 3rd Battalion, on D-day, landed on the sand spit to the east and thus secured Cape Tjeweri.[21]

The drive toward the airfields was led by the 1st Battalion of the 186th, which on the twenty-third moved out along the trail toward Leimok Hill. They soon reached Brinkman's Plantation without encountering any opposition. Finally, a mile beyond, scattered Japanese units made a series of uncoordinated attacks in the afternoon that slowed the advance. Ever cautious, the regimental commander, Colonel Oliver Newman, who believed that there were thousands of Japanese near the airfields, halted the advance until he sent out patrols. The forward movement was resumed on the twenty-fourth, and soon they discovered a large, undefended Japanese supply dump. This was only one of many Japanese supply points captured. General Eichelberger recalled:

There were more than six hundred supply dumps. There were clothing dumps as high as houses. There were ammunition dumps everywhere. There were pyramids of canned goods and tarpaulin-covered hills of rice which looked like Ohio haystacks. There were saki and beer. There were tons and tons of quinine and other medical supplies, which, as a result of our landing, never reached the Japanese troops at the front. I believe Hollandia was the richest prize—supplywise—taken during the Pacific War.[22]

Heavy rain on the twenty-fourth made the road to Lake Sentani a series of mud holes that slowed the attack and made the delivery of supplies very difficult. Many LVTs simply bogged down. However, there occurred another event that caused the frontline troops to go on half rations and to conserve their ammunition.

Before D-day, Allied bombers had started a small fire in one Japanese supply dump that the shore party, busy with unloading supplies, had ignored. At 8:45 P.M. on the twenty-third, a single Japanese plane, using the fire as an aiming point, dropped a stick of four bombs. Three fell harmlessly into the water, but the fourth struck a large Japanese ammunition supply dump adjacent to the beach that exploded, sending bombs and debris hundreds of feet into the air and back along the beach, now congested with supplies of all types. The fire spread quickly, causing a number of smaller explosions. The engineering boat crews braved the fire and explosions and brought their small boats in to the beach to evacuate troops caught in the inferno. The fire burned until the twenty-seventh, when engineering troops finally extinguished it. Thus the best beach was effectively closed for three days. More than 60 percent of all division supplies and ammunition on White Beach 1 were destroyed. The casualties of 24 killed and 100 wounded were far more than the division had suffered from Japanese action. Unloading of supplies, equipment, and men from the LSTs was diverted to White Beach 2, where there was even less dry land. It soon became congested, and thus there was little immediate relief for men of the advanced battalions, who were forced onto half rations.[23]

Despite the rain and supply problems, the advance continued on the twenty-fourth, with the 3rd Battalion passing through the 1st. It was halted by a few Japanese, who briefly delayed the attack before retreating. By noon the troops had reached a jetty where the road touched the lake, and by midafternoon the 2nd Battalion, which had been in reserve, joined the other two. That reserve role was assumed by troops of the 34th Infantry of the 24th Division, which had been shifted from Tanahmerah. On the twenty-fifth, the

3rd Battalion moved west along the main road past Koejaboe village toward Nefaar. At the same time, men of the 1st Battalion were loaded onto LVTs at the jetty for transport to a shore point west of Nefaar. By 10 A.M., the village was occupied. Patrols reported considerable Japanese activity near Cyclops Drome, the most easterly of the airfields. However, these reports proved faulty and the airfield was secured after a two-hour march early on the twenty-sixth. By noon, advance elements of the 2nd Battalion secured Sentani Drome, the next airfield, and by midafternoon they made contact with the 21st Infantry, advancing from Tanahmerah Bay, which had captured Hollandia Drome. These actions closed the major phase of the Hollandia operation.[24]

     In the following weeks, the troops' task was to clear the area of scattered enemy troops and try to block the escape routes to the west. The patrolling was continuous in all areas adjacent to the two bays. The 181st Infantry operated along the north shore of the lake and on Polgi and Ase Islands. Northeast of Cyclops Drome, the 1st Battalion encountered approximately four hundred Japanese on Hill 1000, located four thousand yards northeast of the lake. There was little coordinated effort from the Japanese, and many were killed before the majority retreated into the jungle. The 162nd Infantry cleared Cape Saladja before being relieved by elements of the 34th Infantry on May 6. Meanwhile, the Engineer Special Brigade used LVTs and DUKWs to transport troops of the 19th to Demta Bay, west of Tanahmerah Bay. Roadblocks were established on trails from the west end of the lake to Genjeni village, an important inland trail junction fifteen miles away, where the main elements of the surviving Japanese units had earlier congregated before moving farther west, attempting to reach the Sarmi area 125 miles away. By the time most active patrolling ceased in early June, it was estimated that 3,300 Japanese had been killed during the Hollandia campaign. This figure was later updated to 4,478. Surprisingly, given the attitude of individual Japanese toward surrender, 611 of them were captured. The total casualties for U.S. forces were 124 killed, 1,057 wounded, and 28 missing.[25]

The ordeal of the Japanese who had fled the interior was just beginning. General Inada, who had taken command at Hollandia on the eve of the U.S. landings, had had no time to prepare any adequate defense, and the bulk of his force, mostly service troops, had fled into the interior at the first naval bombardment. During the last week of April, the remnants of his command had retired toward the Genjeni area. Inada had no choice but to retreat toward Sarmi. He organized the retreat into nine sections. The first left in early May. The soldiers had, at best, only a week's ration of food, much of this gleaned from the farms in the area. The officers had no maps of the regions ahead. The last of the Japanese were harassed by companies of the 19th Infantry, who patrolled south from Demta village and along all the coastal trails. By early June they had killed 405 Japanese while capturing sixty-four. Many more Japanese were found dead of starvation and disease along the trails. This gave the U.S. troops some idea of what the defeated Japanese were suffering. Japanese postwar estimates placed 7,220 troops at Genjem just before the beginning of the trek and judged that only 7 percent of these had arrived in the Sarmi area. The rest had perished along the way. The few who survived reached the vicinity of Sarmi, only to discover that U.S. forces were attacking Sarmi and Wakde Island. MacArthur's Hollandia campaign not only had secured a major base far beyond the previous areas of control but had also achieved a brilliant tactical victory, destroying more than 11,000 Japanese.[26]

The decision to make Hollandia a major base for future operations in New Guinea and ultimately the Philippines meant that a tremendous amount of construction work had to be undertaken immediately. General Eichelberger continued in charge of preparing the base until the USASOS supply service took over the construction and logistical tasks on June 6. He was aided by the

Netherlands Indies Civil Administration, which handled civil affairs and procured and supervised native labor. Given the tension
between the two, it is doubtful that the presence of General
Krueger, his immediate superior, aided Eichelberger and his subordinates. Krueger had moved his headquarters to Hollekang on the
beach at Humboldt Bay on May 24. Despite the many problems,
the results in construction were amazing. The major task at first
was to improve the road system. This meant the movement of
masses of heavy equipment to improve the main road from Pim village to the lake and at the same time repair and improve the airfields. To reach the airfields, men and equipment bypassed some of
the worst stretches of the main road by taking to boats from the
jetty at Koejaboe. General Whitehead, who had earlier been skepti-
cal about the value of the airstrip, confirmed on a visit that due to
the rain and terrain, B-24 heavy bombers could not be stationed
there. Nevertheless, work to improve the airstrips was accelerated
by army and air force engineering units. Eichelberger would not say
no to any of the requests by Whitehead and his subordinates. Cyclops Drome could be used by fighters and transports by April 29,
and C-47s were using Hollandia by May 2. Dry-weather facilities at
Cyclops were finished by May 15, and the 49th and 475th
Squadrons of P-38s were soon stationed there. They were later
joined by the 3rd Bombardment Group of A-20s and RAAF
Squadrons 98 and 80, flying P-40s. Thus, although the air officers
were not totally satisfied with the fields and pressed for the occupation of Sarmi and Wakde, the Hollandia complex of airfields
served an important role in all upcoming operations.[27]

Looking forward to later operations, the 27th Hospital Center
was constructed. By June 30, the center had four general, two station, and one field hospital with an aggregate of 3,650 beds. This
was continually expanded, so that by the time of the Philippines
campaign, there were almost 9,000 beds available. It would become
the Army's largest overseas general hospital facility. In addition,

there were ambulance boats, LSTs, and transports based there, as were two hospital ships. Ultimately the medical facilities at Port Moresby were reduced in size because of the Hollandia complex.[28]

Later, General Eichelberger recalled with a sense of awe what had been accomplished at Hollandia. He wrote:

Road construction had proceeded simultaneously [with building runways], and this was a gigantic task. Sides of mountains were carved away, bridges and culverts were thrown across rivers and creeks, gravel and stone "fill" was poured into sago swamps to make highways as tall as Mississippi levees. . . .

Hollandia became one of the great bases of the war. In the deep waters of Humboldt Bay a complete fleet could lie at anchor. Tremendous docks were constructed, and one hundred and thirty-five miles of pipeline were led over the hills to feed gasoline to the airfields. Where once I had seen only a few native villages and an expanse of primeval forest, a city of one hundred and forty thousand men took occupancy.[29]

Eleven

THE BOMBER LINE ADVANCES:
WAKDE AND LONE TREE HILL

The quick success of the Hollandia operation against minimal Japanese resistance convinced MacArthur, even before that area had been secured, to move his bomber line farther to the west. His chief air officers, Kenney and Whitehead, after surveying the airfields at Hollandia, had concluded that it would be impossible to develop quickly any of those fields for the heavy bombers needed for later operations. General Headquarters at first believed that the Sarmi area, 140 miles from Hollandia, would be suitable since there was an airfield at Sawat, eight miles southwest of Sarmi. On April 10, MacArthur issued a warning order to alert Alamo Force to the possibility of undertaking a landing there and requested a preliminary plan of operation by the twenty-second. He then discussed the plan with Krueger, Barbey, and Eichelberger while on board the *Nashville*. Barbey reported that his amphibious forces were ready to undertake the new target. Krueger was noncommittal, while Eichelberger, then in charge at Hollandia, opposed the plan partially because he knew that Sarmi was the headquarters of the Japanese 36th Division, with an estimated 6,000 men in the general vicinity. Krueger wanted to use the 32nd Division, then at Saidor. However, the lack of available transport meant that any action using the 32nd against Sarmi could not be undertaken before mid-June. MacArthur was concerned about the central Pacific and what appeared to be crucial time factors in his desire to have his Philippines operation approved. Therefore he overrode Krueger's suggestion and instead decided to use units of the 41st, then at Hollandia. He set May 15 as the date for the operation.[1]

General Whitehead upset this tentative plan when he reported that the area between Sarmi and the mainland opposite Wakde Island was unsuitable for the construction of bomber fields. MacArthur, on the advice of his air officers, then decided to seize Insoemoar Island in the Wakde group, where the Japanese had already constructed an airfield. This island, 110 miles west of Hollandia, referred to in general dispatches as Wakde, was roughly 9,000 feet long and 3,000 feet wide. The airfield had a runway 5,600 feet long built on well-drained coral sand. It was far better than the one at Sawar and could be put into operation quickly to handle the B-24 groups that Kenney wanted to base there. In addition, there were a number of good landing beaches on the south end of the island, opposite the mainland village of Toem. However, the landing areas were too small to accommodate all the necessary supplies. Although MacArthur canceled the Sarmi invasion, there was a need to have a mainland base opposite the island. Thus Operation Tornado was conceived in two parts. The first would be the landing of the 163rd RCT of the 41st Division on the New Guinea coast near the village of Arara on May 17. Once this had been consolidated, a company would be sent to occupy the smaller Insoemanai Island, 3,500 yards offshore, in order to place artillery and mortars to support the operation on Wakde. The following day the 163rd would land on Wakde.[2]

Before the Wakde operation, a series of high-level conferences was held to deal with the suggestion of General Headquarters that Biak Island, 200 miles away, be substituted for the canceled Sarmi

invasion. This came as a surprise to Krueger since the Field Order
to the 41st Division for the Sarmi operation had already been issued. On May 9, a conference attended by Sutherland, Kenney,
Whitehead, and Rear Admiral William Fechtler, who would command the amphibious operations, was held. After considerable debate, the date for the Wakde landings was fixed as May 17, and
Z-day for the invasion of Biak was fixed for ten days later. Biak was
the largest of the Schouten Islands, forty-five miles long and commanding the entrance to Geelvink Bay. Its capture was not essential
to MacArthur's long-range plans. However, the possession of its
airfields would make it possible to strike Palau during Nimitz's
planned Marianas operation, and aircraft from there would provide
cover for the projected invasion of the Vogelkop Peninsula.[3]

Air operations in support of Operation Tornado began on
April 28 with heavy bomber strikes at Wakde and Biak. This was
followed by medium bomber attacks on the island and Sarmi areas
during the next two days. The weather closed in along the coast of
New Guinea on the thirtieth, preventing serious neutralization
until May 13, though a few attacks were made on the Sarmi-Wakde
area during this period. However, B-24s of the Thirteenth Air
Force from the Admiralties continued to bomb Biak as well as
striking northward against Japanese positions in the Caroline Islands. These attacks intensified when the weather cleared. Neither
the Army nor the Navy requested any intense bombing of the landing areas immediately prior to D-day. Nevertheless, RAAF fighters
and fifth Air Force A-20s strafed suspected Japanese positions on
D-day and then maintained air cover until planes could begin to use
the Wakde field.[4]

General Doe's 163rd RCT boarded the APAs at Aitape on May
15 after fears that delays in the loading of supplies might force
postponement of the landing. However, crews working through the
night of the thirteenth had everything ready for the operation. The
naval covering force, divided into three Fire Support contingents,

assembled off the Admiralty Islands on the fifteenth. The growth in Kinkaid's navy can be seen in the numbers of ships committed. Fire Support A had two heavy cruisers and four destroyers, which would target the Sarmi area, while B had three light cruisers and six destroyers, which would bombard Wakde. C was composed of ten destroyers, which would bring the Toem–Maffin Bay area under attack. The naval bombardment was scheduled to begin at H –45 and continue to H –3, when three rocket-firing LCIs would hit the selected beach prior to the landing at Arara, to begin at 7:15 A.M. All went according to plan. After the bombardment, in a cold rain, men of the 3rd Battalion transferred to the first of twenty-four LCVPs. The first wave was followed on schedule by five others. LCMs carried four Sherman tanks. There was no opposition, and the troops fanned out along the shore and quickly secured the beachhead. By 9:30 A.M., the village of Toem, 4,500 yards to the east, had been occupied. An hour later, the troops reached Tementoel Creek, further east, and the Tor River to the west was reached by late morning. Phase two of the operation was begun at 10:45 A.M., when a platoon of Company E was transported to the small, unoccupied island of Isoemanai, where mortars and machine guns were quickly set up. Later the artillery that would support the landings on Wakde was emplaced.[5]

Fire support cruisers bombarded Wakde all afternoon of the seventeenth, and land-based artillery pounded the island during the night. At 8:30 A.M. on the eighteenth, two destroyers moved close and began a fifteen-minute bombardment, and twenty minutes later two rocket-carrying LCMs took the beach under fire. The first of the six waves of the 1st Battalion, commanded by Major Leonard Wing, began the assault on time, only to be met with heavy fire from concealed machine guns and mortars. The assault troops on board the landing craft were relatively safe, but the crews of the 542nd Engineer Boat and Shore Regiment sustained a number of casualties. Eight landing craft were heavily damaged, and the engineers sustained five killed and thirty wounded. The first wave was pinned down on the beach for a half hour before heavy support fire from Isoemanai, combined with that from two Sherman tanks, forced the surviving Japanese in the beach defenses to retreat. As the troops moved inland, they encountered heavy fire from the many bunkers on the island. The tanks' direct fire with their 75 mm guns, combined with strafing attacks by A-20s, systematically destroyed those. Three companies reached the airstrip by 11:30 A.M., and two hours later one had driven to the north shore. The Japanese defenders then became tenacious, preventing the occupation of all of the airfield before the troops dug in for the night short of the eastern end of the island.[6]

Company C was the first to attack across the airfield on the morning of the nineteenth. Supported by three tanks, the troops methodically destroyed each Japanese position, including a number of small coral caves. Company B, moving east along the southern edge of the airstrip, met heavy resistance. Wing then committed Company F and three tanks that destroyed the Japanese defenders, who were firing from wrecked airplanes and brush-covered bunkers. By 2 P.M., with the clearance of the eastern end of the airstrip, the organized Japanese resistance collapsed. By evening, the few remaining Japanese were confined to a small corner in the northeast section of the island. Wing pulled back most of the troops preparatory to turning over the island to the designated Air Force commander on the twentieth.

Repairs to the airfield had begun almost immediately after the arrival of the engineers who had landed under fire on D-day. They survived a banzai charge by thirty-seven Japanese on the twentieth. This desperate action was doomed, and all but one of the attackers were killed. By noon of the twenty-first, the airstrip was operational, and it would soon be extended to both the east and west shores. One company of the 163rd was ordered back to the island on the twenty-second to deal with the few snipers left alive. The entire Wakde Island operation had cost 40 killed and 107 wounded. The Japanese garrison was destroyed, losing 759 killed. Surprisingly, 4 men were taken prisoner. The Wakde exercise justified MacArthur's and Kenney's expectations. Two heavy bomber groups, two fighter groups, a B-25 reconnaissance squadron, and some navy PBYs were located there in time for the Biak operation.[7]

The capture of Wakde ensured the success of Operation Tornado. However, Krueger was apprehensive about the possibility that the Japanese on the mainland to the west of Toem could threaten that base. Doe was also concerned. Patrols had already encountered Japanese units on both sides of the wide Tor River. However, with only one regiment, Doe felt he did not have the force to defend the beachhead and at the same time launch an attack to dislodge the Japanese from the high ground beyond the Tor. He waited for reinforcements, which arrived on the twenty-first. Krueger had ordered the 3,100-man 158th RCT, an Arizona National Guard unit with no prior combat experience, to augment Doe's 103rd at Toem. Immediately after the unit arrived on the twenty-second, Krueger ordered its commander, Brigadier General Edmund Patrick, to take over the forward position held by the 163rd and cross the Tor River with the objective of clearing the Japanese from their dominating position on the heights, especially the one called Lone Tree Hill.

However necessary an offensive against the Japanese was at this juncture, the decision to have a single regiment take the offensive was based on faulty intelligence estimates. Preliminary to Krueger's order, Willoughby had stated that there were very few Japanese holding these positions. Otherwise, he reasoned, they would have attacked Toem earlier. Later, after the offensive began, he revised his estimate upward but still believed that there were only 6,500 troops in the Sarmi area of whom only 4,000 were combat soldiers. The fact was that no one at either General Headquarters or Krueger's command post had any reasonable basis for such estimates. In actuality, Lieutenant General Hachiro Tagami at Sarmi had approximately 11,000 men. The one factor in favor of the attackers was that Imperial Headquarters had written off the entire Eighteenth Army after the failure to bring in reinforcements earlier. It rejected General Anami's more ambitious plan for an attack toward Hollandia. Instead, it drew the line of major resistance between Manokwari and Halmahera. Tagami, commander of the 36th Division, was expected to hold only the Maffin Bay–Sarmi area as long as possible, with no promised aid and scant air support.[8]

Tagami divided the Sarmi region into three defense sectors. The Right Sector force, approximately 1,200 men, was to defend the coast from Tementoe Creek to the Waske River. West of the Waske, the Central Sector troops, in all more than 2,500 men, were responsible for four and a half miles of coast and interior stretches. Finally, the Left Sector, comprising another 2,500 men, was stationed six and a half miles west, from Sawer Creek to Tevar Creek. In addition to the infantry troops, mainly from the 222nd and 224th Infantry, Tagami's force, code-named Yuki Group, had artillery and antiaircraft units and a considerable number of engineering troops. He was also counting on the return of the Matsugama Force, two battalions of the 224th plus an artillery battalion that earlier had been sent forward as a part of Anami's plan to attack Hollandia. Thus, though his situation was desperate, he had far more men than Krueger and Willoughby suspected. By judiciously utilizing the terrain, he could make any attack across the Tor River costly.[9]

Without substantial knowledge of the Japanese positions, in response to Krueger's order, Colonel J. Prugh Herndon, the field commander of the 158th, pushed two battalions across the Tor early on May 23. The 1st Battalion, in the lead, was soon pinned down by heavy machine-gun and rifle fire from the vicinity of three small lakes 1,800 yards west of the Tor. This halted any further movement for the day. On the twenty-fourth, Herndon ordered a heavy artillery bombardment of the area prior to the advance. It was supported by LCVPs along the coast and tanks, which had been brought forward during the night. By noon the troops reached the Tirfoam River, halfway to the hill mass below Maffin Bay, and by early afternoon had crossed to the west. Here they were attacked by a company of the 223rd, led by the commander of the Right Sector Force. This was repulsed, and the attackers retired after suffering heavy losses. However, a Japanese antitank gun disabled three of the tanks, and Herndon ordered a retreat back across the Tirfoam.

The 3rd Battalion resumed the attack on the twenty-fifth after a heavy preliminary artillery concentration that destroyed many of the forward Japanese defenses. This allowed a movement to the Snaky River, just short of Lone Tree Hill. The hill was really a north–south ridge approximately 175 feet high and 1,200 yards long, reaching down to the coast road and the bay. Its name, given to it by aerial reconnaissance interpreters, was misleading. Although they had identified a tall tree, this was only a minor feature. The hill was heavily covered with thick undergrowth that hid the many caves and crevices that the Japanese had improved and were fully manned. Lone Tree Hill was the most heavily defended of the hill area, but there were also Mount Saskin, Hill 225, and Hill 265 to the south, all manned by the Japanese.[10]

Herndon planned to renew the offensive on the twenty-sixth, with destroyers offshore lending their fire support to that of the artillery before the attack would begin. Unfortunately, the navy and artillery fire was not well coordinated with the infantry. The lead battalion, without any good maps of the area showing even approximate Japanese positions, soon got lost. This blunted the offensive, and successive attacks proved fruitless; eventually all units were ordered to halt and wait to resume the attack the next day. After an intense artillery bombardment during the morning of the twenty-seventh, one company of the 1st Battalion reached the top of the eastern ridge, only to discover that the Japanese had allowed them to walk into a trap. Faced with devastating fire from the defenders in their camouflaged caves, the troops fought off a series of small-scale infantry attacks. Convinced of the need for more firepower, Herndon requested tanks. General Patrick agreed and ordered two LCMs to the Tirfoam. However, there was no place to land the tanks, and the engineers, under fire from Lone Tree Hill, had to blast out a landing place in the coral. Herndon then planned a two-pronged attack for the twenty-eighth, with the 1st Battalion advancing forward to the crest of Lone Tree Hill, while the 2nd would move across Hill 225, force the defile between the heights, and strike north along the road to establish contact with the 1st. At first the attack seemed to go well, with Company C of the 1st reaching the crest to join Company A, but soon both were pinned down. Their position during the day grew increasingly desperate as they ran low on ammunition and water. The other movement, through the defile, was stopped by the Japanese. Thus, at the end of the day, the 158th had suffered 300 casualties and, despite heavy firepower, had not been able to make substantial gains against the Japanese defenses. Herndon then informed Patrick that he considered his troops to be exhausted and the units overextended, and he planned to call off the attack. Patrick, who had replaced Doe as Tornado Force commander on the twenty-fifth, reluctantly agreed.[11]

One reason why Patrick, well known for his aggressiveness, agreed to the pullback was the knowledge that Krueger planned to shift the 163rd RCT to Biak. Patrick protested the weakening of his force and wanted a delay until the promised reinforcements of a combat team from the 6th Division arrived. He had every reason for worry, since General Tagami's planned counterattack had been presaged by an attack of an estimated two hundred Japanese of the Matsuyana Force on the night of the twenty-seventh to the twenty-eighth. It had been beaten off by 1st Battalion troops, who had killed approximately thirty of the attackers. This Japanese unit had retired to the west by dawn. Although unsuccessful, the attack had shown how vulnerable Patrick's lines were. Patrick estimated the Japanese strength in the immediate area to be between 2,000 and 3,000 men, with an additional 300 east of Tementoe Creek. In actuality, there were at least twice that number available to Tagami. Krueger was aware of the danger to the 158th if it were left alone. Nevertheless, he notified Patrick on the twenty-ninth that two battalions of the 163rd would be transferred to Biak beginning the next day. Because the one battalion of the 163rd left behind would not be enough to defend Toem, Krueger ordered that one battalion of the 158th be sent back to aid in the defense of the beachhead, thus further weakening the troops that would be needed to continue the assault on Lone Tree Hill.[12] The setting was thus prepared for a potential disaster if the Japanese, who outnumbered the 158th, could coordinate an attack on the beachhead.

Colonel Herndon felt that the position of his forward elements could not be held and decided to withdraw them east across the Tirfoam. General Patrick finally agreed, and the retrograde movement began on the afternoon of the thirtieth. Despite the presence of Japanese forces to the west and south, the withdrawal went smoothly, without the loss of a single man. Just as the new defense line was being established a mile east of the Tirfoam, General Patrick arrived with his chief of staff, Colonel Earle Sandlin. He had changed his mind and claimed that the withdrawal had been unwarranted, as he later reported to Krueger. He informed the shocked Herndon, "I am relieving you of command and am putting Colonel Sandlin in charge. You will report to Finschhafen immediately."[13] As with many other situations where the commander was relieved, the change did not alter the situation. Although Krueger had promised relief, the 6th Division regiments were not scheduled to arrive before June 4.

The reorganization of the beachhead defenses proceeded, with three companies setting up a perimeter along the east bank of the

Tirfoam. The rest of the regiment was spread out along the road to the Tor. Eventually, with the departure of the 163rd, the 158th was stretched out along the coast with twenty-one separate defensive perimeters. The largest of these was in the Arare area, where the 1st Battalion was dug in to protect the original beachhead, headquarters, and most of the supply dumps. Surprisingly, there were no patrols sent southward, and thus the movement of the Japanese toward the coast was not detected.[14]

Tagami's plan was to have the Matsuyama Force attack the eastern sector while the Yoshino Force would attack directly north against the 1st Battalion. However, the Matsuyama Force, exhausted by its long trek eastward and then forced to move back, was in no condition to force the issue with the 158th's defenses. On the night of the twenty-seventh to the twenty-eighth, its premature attack had been beaten off. The remnants then moved away to the southeast, directly away from the Yoshino Force, and was not a factor in the coming assault. This illustrated that one of the main problems of the Japanese was lack of good communications between units. Meanwhile, the Yoshino Force had arrived in its preliminary attack positions. It was then divided into two segments, one led by a Captain Yasuda and the other by a Major Ooki. Yasuda was to attack Arare from the southeast while Ooki struck from the southwest. Yasuda's group got lost in the jungle and undergrowth and was not in contact with other units for two days. Ooki's battalion, however, had no trouble moving to within a few hundred yards from the beach on May 30.[15]

At 6:30 P.M. on May 30, a squad of Japanese attacked an antiaircraft position but was beaten off. Then another antiaircraft site was hit by other Japanese. These attacks continued through the night. Another gun position, with quad 50 machine guns, was also struck at 6:30 P.M. The guns became overheated, and the troops, low on ammunition, abandoned the position and took cover elsewhere. The Japanese captured the guns and soon had them operating against other gun positions, forcing the troops back toward the supply dump. The Japanese launched a suicide attack against this sector but were beaten off in hand-to-hand fighting. Nevertheless the attacks continued until 4:30 A.M., when the Japanese retired to the southwest. For a loss of twelve killed and ten wounded, the main attack by the Ooki force had been repulsed, leaving behind fifty-two dead. The Japanese had lost their best chance of destroying the beachhead.[16]

As the men of the 158th began to take stock of their defenses and improve them, General Patrick was informed that Krueger planned to order the remainder of the 2nd Battalion of the 163rd plus the 167th Field Artillery to Biak to support Fuller's hard-pressed units. Patrick then ordered all troops west of the Tor back across the river to take over the positions held by the 163rd. He also consolidated the various perimeters to eight, and all units were to give up any offensive action and stand on the defense. However, Krueger obviously had second thoughts when confronted with the possibility of losing the beachhead, because he changed his mind about redeploying of the 163rd and other units until the arrival of reinforcements from the 6th Division. For the next few days, all units were ordered to strengthen their positions in expectation of further Japanese assaults. Patrick could not know that General Tagami, in his headquarters on Mount Saksin, had concluded that the heavy combat losses, combined with the exhaustion and near starvation of his forces precluded any further offensives. On June 10, the Yoshino Force began withdrawing southwest across the Tor to new positions in the Maffin Bay area. The remnant of the Matsuyama Force began its withdrawal westward on the twelfth.[17]

Although the number of Japanese in the Sarmi area was unknown, it was believed that fewer than 5,000 were left by the end of May. Once again the estimates were wrong. Japanese records show that there were still 8,000 men, of whom 4,000 were combat troops.[18] Despite the lack of good information, Patrick planned to resume the offensive and bypass Lone Tree Hill by making a shore-to-shore movement to the Sarmi Peninsula. As soon as reinforcements from the 6th Division arrived, he planned to ship two battalions around the heavy defenses and attack the hill mass from the south. This attack would be coordinated with that of the 158th, attacking from the west. However, he was informed that there were not enough landing craft immediately available for the operation. Then Major General Franklin Sibert, commanding the 6th Division, the presumptive commander of Tornado Force, requested that no major offensive action be ordered until he had two RCTs and their supplies in the Arare area. The cancellation of Patrick's excellent plan meant that the 6th Division would be forced to duplicate the head-on, costly attacks on Lone Tree Hill. Patrick canceled the amphibious operation but resumed the offensive on the eighth.

Early in the morning, the 1st Battalion of the 158th, after artillery preparation, moved out along the coast road. The troops ran into a line of bunkers and pillboxes 1,500 yards east of the Tirfoam River. The supporting tanks moved up and by midafternoon had knocked out the defenses. The 2nd Battalion, as part of an enveloping movement, planned to attack the north side of the hill mass, but it met heavy fire and was forced back to the road. The following day, patrols were active as far as the west bank of the Tirfoam, where they discovered that the Japanese had rebuilt and reoccupied the bunkers that had been destroyed during the earlier offensive. Artillery was called in, and fire from the 105 mm and 155 mm guns, in conjunction with tank-infantry teams, destroyed these, and the troops reached the east bank of the river before nightfall. However successful an immediate continuation of these attacks might have been, all further forward movement was canceled by Krueger, who did not want the 158th to sustain more casualties since he planned to use it to invade Noemfoor Island, three hundred miles to the northwest.[19] Therefore only patrolling was done during the following few days.

The 1st RCT of the 6th had landed at Toem on the fifth. The other regiment of the 6th did not arrive until the eleventh and soon relieved the 158th at the forward positions. This latter landing was done hastily, and not all the regiment's equipment was landed. Sibert, who had taken command of Tornado, did not want to resume offensive action until he had all his supplies and equipment. He informed Krueger that he was not prepared to advance until July 1. Krueger, under pressure to end the New Guinea campaign as quickly as possible, was planning to use the 6th Division in an assault on the Vogelkop in September. He wanted to use Maffin Bay as a staging area, and to do this, Lone Tree Hill and the other heights had to be taken as quickly as possible. Therefore, on June 18, he ordered Sibert to begin operations immediately. Sibert would have only his 6th Division, as the 158th had moved back to Tementoe Creek preparatory to the Noemfoor Island operation. It was relieved of all combat responsibility in the Wakde-Sarmi area on the twenty-second. During its combat operations, it had suffered 70 killed and 257 wounded.[20]

The Japanese positions on Lone Tree Hill had not been substantially damaged by the earlier attacks. They still maintained posts in the many caves and crevices, most of which were hidden by the undergrowth. They had artillery pieces both in the beach area and in the deep ravine in the northern sector of the hill. The bunkers on top were constructed of logs and earth and manned by four to eight men. Individually, there were foxholes burrowed out between the roots of the large trees. The Japanese maintained an observation post high up in a tall tree from which they could observe any movement along the eastern slopes or on the road. All attempts to destroy this tree had been unsuccessful. The Japanese had an estimated 2,000 men on the hill complex, and to a certain point reinforcements could be made by shuttling troops from Mt. Saksin. Thus, when Sibert ordered the 1st Battalion of the 20th RCT to begin the offensive early on the morning of June 20, the problem was basically the same as that which had confronted Colonel Herndon. The early attack, along the main road, was a duplicate of the earlier attempts. After advancing to the Snaky River by noon, the troops were halted by sustained Japanese fire. At the same time, the 3rd Battalion, on the eastern slopes of Lone Tree Hill, was also stopped.

For the next few days, the fighting followed a similar pattern. Patrols tried to discover the Japanese positions, and fire by both medium and heavy artillery was called in. On the twenty-second, P-47 fighter-bombers from Wakde raked suspected Japanese positions. All attempts to flank the Japanese in the south failed. However, the 3rd Battalion seemed to make considerable headway, as two of its assault companies reached the crest of Lone Tree by early afternoon of the twenty-second. Later, two companies of the 2nd also reached the crest but could not link up with the 3rd. The Japanese, however, had sprung a trap, and at 5:30 P.M. approximately two companies of Japanese, led by a Colonel Saemon Matsuyama, poured out of the caves and attacked the 3rd's perimeter. In the confused fighting, the Japanese moved to the rear of the 3rd and blocked its line of communication. In this action the 3rd lost 30 killed and 100 wounded. The action continued the next day with a dawn attack from a deep ravine against the perimeter of the 2nd. Despite heavy casualties, the line held and the counterattack pressed the surviving Japanese back to their caves. A linkup was finally made between the two battalions, and hard-pressed supply groups brought up much-needed water and ammunition. They evacuated 300 wounded. Despite this, the two battalions were still cut off and had to fight off a series of attacks during the night of the twenty-third.[21]

General Sibert then planned a shore-to-shore movement similar to that which Patrick had suggested. Two companies of the 1st Regiment were loaded onto ten LVTs on the twenty-fourth and, accompanied by thirteen LVT(A)s with 37 mm guns as escort, landed under fire from a Japanese mountain gun west of Lone Tree Hill.

They were later joined by four tanks. However good the operation looked from a planning position, Sibert had not known of the swampy conditions immediately inland from the landing zone. The tanks could not maneuver, and the infantry could move inland only a few yards. However, the mortar fire from the beach against the Japanese positions on Rocky Point where the cliff overlooked Maffin Bay was extremely effective. The bulk of the fighting was left to the four companies still cut off on the crest. Assault teams with flamethrowers and bazookas cleared the Japanese from a number of caves and secured the supply route up the hill. By the evening of the twenty-fourth, the 2nd Battalion had only 330 effectives and the 3rd only 322. Despite severe losses, the attacks had weakened the Japanese resistance. On the twenty-fifth, two companies of the 1st Battalion and one company of engineers reinforced the battered units on the hill and began to help clear the Japanese from the ravine and Rocky Point. By the close of the day, the Japanese had been cleared from the northern part of the hill. It became apparent to General Tagami and Colonel Matsuyama that the defenses were crumbling, and they decided to pull back to the main defense line west of the Waske River. With that retreat, Sibert's men, after the twenty-fifth, had only to mop up remnants on Lone Tree Hill and clear the adjacent hill areas. An estimated 500 Japanese had been killed and 300 wounded. This count did not include the many sealed in the caves. However, the victory had been costly. By the close of the day on the twenty-fifth, a casualty count indicated that 140 men had been killed and 850 had been evacuated because of wounds and sickness.[22]

The battered battalions of the 20th were relieved by the 3rd Battalion of the 63rd RCT and the 3rd Battalion of the 1st, and these began the task of clearing all Japanese westward to the Waske River. This meant occupying Mount Saksin and the two adjacent hills. Sibert also wanted a secure belt from the Tor River to the Waske for a distance of two miles inland. These operations began on July 1. On the fourth, Hill 225 was occupied, and the following day Mount Saksin was taken with minimal difficulty. Hill 265 proved more difficult, but the Japanese were also cleared from there by July 9. Thus Maffin Bay was secured, as Krueger desired, for staging for future operations. Since he planned to use the 6th Division for action in the Vogelkop, he ordered the 31st Division to Maffin Bay to replace it. The main elements of the 31st, commanded by Major General John Persons, arrived on July 14. The following day, two regiments of the 6th began loading for removal to Hollandia. The 20th RCT remained and was attached to the 31st until late August. General Persons wanted to continue the offensive against the Japanese west of the Weske, but his plans were vetoed by General Headquarters. The offensive against Lone Tree Hill had secured what Krueger needed, and all that the 31st needed to do was to defend the perimeter and offensively patrol the adjacent areas to deal with stragglers. This was no easy task, and by the time the division was relieved by the 33rd Division on September 1, it had lost 39 killed. Its patrols had killed 294 Japanese. The terrible condition of many of the Japanese troops during this period is evidenced by the patrols' discovering 497 dead, ostensibly from sickness and starvation. On September 2, Krueger declared the Wakde-Sarmi operation completed.[23]

The drawn-out conflict, which had surprised General Headquarters by the ferocity of the Japanese defenders on the mainland, produced immediate tangible results. The airfield on Wakde had proven its worth even before the action against Lone Tree Hill had been completed. It became an important factor in all later operations against Biak, Noemfoor, and Halmehera, and in support of Nimitz's operations in the central Pacific. The Thirteenth Air Force, which relieved Kenney's Fifth on Wakde in late August, continued long-range strikes from there against Palau. In terms of control of the Sarmi area, the fighting had for all practical purposes destroyed two Japanese regiments and forced the estimated two thousand survivors into inhospitable areas where they could not be supplied and where sickness and starvation continued to take a heavy toll. The area of Arare-Toem and Maffin Bay became a major staging area for the Biak, Noemfoor, Vogelkop, and later the Philippines operations. Noncombat vessels brought many units to the area, where they would be picked up by assault ships bound for the north and west. The Lone Tree Hill operation was costly, but the possession of Maffin Bay paid both immediate and long-range dividends.

Twelve

BLOODY BIAK

From a theoretical strategic viewpoint, the capture of Biak, the largest of the Shouten group of islands, although not absolutely necessary, appeared to fit well into MacArthur's Reno V plan to advance to the Philippines. The island, located 350 miles northwest of Hollandia and 100 miles east of the Vogelkop Peninsula, had three operational airfields built on the narrow coastal plain inland from the three villages of Sorido, Barokoe, and Mokmer. The fact that Kenney's planes, based there, could dominate Geelvinck Bay and the Vogelkop was the main factor in MacArthur's decision to speed up the operation. The relative ease with which the Wakde-Toem operation had been carried out led him to believe that the airfields on Biak could be quickly seized in time for planes based there to aid in the proposed Marianas operation, scheduled for June.

The chief reason for the problems that developed later was the faulty intelligence reports provided. MacArthur's chief intelligence officer, Major General Charles Willoughby, had assured him that there were only 5,000 to 7,000 Japanese on the island, of whom only 2,300 were combat troops. According to Willoughby, the invasion would encounter "stubborn but not serious resistance."[1] MacArthur also knew that a Japanese convoy bringing an entire division south from Shanghai to reinforce the Vogelkop had been intercepted off Manila Bay by the submarine *Jack,* which had sunk one ship in the convoy. Soon afterward, another submarine, the *Gurnard,* had met the convoy in the Celebes Sea and sunk three more ships. In this latter disaster for the Japanese, thousands of men had drowned.[2] Based on this news as well as intelligence of other successful submarine attacks, MacArthur could thus believe that few reinforcements could have reached Biak.

In contrast to Willoughby's optimism, the estimate of Japanese on Biak given by Ultra far exceeded that of the intelligence chief. Although Ultra missed the fact that there were elements of the Japanese 36th and 14th Divisions and a number of service units on the island, it warned that the Japanese had twice as many troops as Willoughby had projected. In a strange blending, MacArthur accepted Ultra's reports of the location of major Japanese fleet units that could interfere with the invasion, but he chose to agree with Willoughby's conclusion that the only significant resistance the 41st Division would be faced with was the 222nd Infantry Regiment. It is probable that he wanted the operation to go forward quickly and thus was prepared to believe the lower estimate of Japanese strength.[3] Later in the discussions relating to the date of the invasion, Willoughby suggested that Z-day, set for the twenty-seventh, be postponed. This did not indicate a change in his appreciation of the numbers of troops on Biak. Rather, he believed that the landings might cause Admiral Soema Toyoda, commander of the Combined Fleet, to order its main elements southward and thus be in a position to destroy the much weaker Seventh Fleet. MacArthur and the other key members of his staff did not want to wait until a major action by Nimitz's units eliminated this real threat. MacArthur was confident of a quick, favorable conclusion to the Biak operation.[4]

Contrary to MacArthur's information, the Japanese had 11,400 men on Biak, of whom 4,000 were combat-effective. In the months prior to the invasion, Biak had been a source of debate between Japanese army and naval leaders. Not until May 9 did the High Command redefine the southern defense line to exclude Biak. At that time Colonel Naoyuku Kazume was informed that he could expect no substantial reinforcements. He had expected considerable forces from the 3rd Division, located at Geelvinck Bay. He was informed that his initial mission, to deny the Americans the use of the airfields as long as possible, was still in effect. Despite the redrawing of the main defense line in the southwest Pacific, the means available to Kazume to defend the island were considerable. The main combat element was his 222nd Imperial Infantry Regiment, consisting of more than 3,000 men. This was a veteran unit with experience in China that had reached Biak in December 1943. The 222nd was supported by Rear Admiral Sadotoshi Senda's 1,500-man 28th Special Naval Landing Force. There were also a number of specialized units, including heavy artillery units, an antiaircraft battalion, and a battalion of light tanks. He also had available a large number of mortars and many automatic weapons of all calibers. Most important, Kazume and later his senior, Lieutenant General Takezo Numata, were masters of defense. They knew where the landings would probably take place and that the terrain adjacent to that area was perfect for defense.[5]

The beaches along the southern shore of Biak were paralleled by high ridgelines. The first of these was a narrow ridge approximately sixty feet high, a few hundred yards north of Mokmer and Borokoe airfields. Behind this ridge was a series of terraces from which the Japanese could observe any activity on the beaches. Northward there was a series of caves, some of which were large enough to hold a thousand men. In December, Kazume ordered his men to begin construction of a series of interconnecting trenches, tunnels, and fortified positions. He dug in his antiaircraft guns, mortars, and automatic weapons along the ridgelines and positioned his large-caliber guns so that their fire could dominate the beaches. This work was speeded up after the American landings on Wakde. He halted all further work on the airfields to focus all effort on further building up the defenses, and he began deploying his forces for what he intended to be a long battle. There were three strong points in the terraces behind Mokmer airfield. One, the West Caves, was located about fifty yards north of the low ridge and three quarters of a mile from the western end of Mokmer airfield. These were actually three large depressions or sumps connected by tunnels and caverns and surrounded by man-made defenses. These initially sheltered the naval contingent. As long as the Japanese controlled the West Caves, even after Mokmer airfield was captured, Kenney's pilots could not safely use the airfields.

On the main ridge east of the village of Ibdi was another strong point called the Ibdi Pocket. The terrain there was a series of east–west ridges separated by depressions and cross ridges. The area was covered by dense rain forest and undergrowth. The Japanese had constructed pillboxes of coral and logs, as well as small caves, and had dug foxholes at the bases of large trees. North of Mokmer, Kazume had constructed the third strong point, called the East Caves. The steep ridge behind Mokmer airfield, which rose to more than two hundred feet high, could not be climbed without the use of hands. Three fourths of the way to the top was a flat area where there were two large caves. The Japanese had constructed pillboxes below and above the ledge, and in the caves they had sited mortars and machine guns. The East Caves were used mainly as living quarters, supply dumps, and observation posts. However, from there the Japanese could dominate the coast road leading to Mokmer. From each of the strong points Kazume intended to exact a heavy toll on the invaders. He had no intention of wasting troops in futile charges.[6]

Major General Horace Fuller was chosen to lead the Biak invasion, code-named Hurricane. Krueger, who believed that there were a relatively few Japanese on the island, allotted only two of the division's regiments to the action, keeping the 163rd at Hollandia. General Fuller had qualms from the beginning that his 162nd and 186th Regiments would not be sufficient, and he shared his concern with Eichelberger at corps headquarters at Lake Sentani before the operation. His worry did not sway higher headquarters, and the plan for the invasion was not altered to add more troops. After much deliberation, the area chosen for the landing was at Bosnek, once the administrative center, located on the south coast. It had a number of advantages, not the least of which, in contrast to Hollandia, was the considerable solid ground behind the beaches where all the equipment needed could be placed. The main drawback was the fringing coral reef, which blocked free entrance to the beach. The Japanese had converted the village into a main supply base, and there were two stone jetties built over the reef to deep water. The reef ruled out the use of conventional landing craft, and this dictated the way the landing would be carried out by the 542nd Engineer and Boat troops. The Navy committed six LSTs to carry sixty-three LVTs and twenty-five DUKWs to be used in landing the first four waves of the 162nd. The bulk of the troops would follow in fifteen LCIs, which could use the jetties. Tanks and the artillery would be landed later from LCTs, towed by the LSTs. The Navy also provided overwhelming firepower, with three light cruisers and twenty-one destroyers to cover the landing.[7]

The convoy arrived off Biak on schedule, and the cruisers and destroyers began their preinvasion bombardment. The three cruisers concentrated on the airfields and in forty-five minutes sent 1,000 rounds of six-inch shells at various suspected concentrations. Meanwhile, the destroyers were firing at targets adjacent to the landing beaches. At first light, twelve B-24s of the Thirteenth Air Force hit the airfield area. Later, at 7 A.M., twenty-five more B-24s dropped their bombs in the same areas. Just before noon, seventy-seven B-24s of the Fifth Air Force bombed targets in the airdrome area.[8] These initial air strikes were followed by others, by both heavy and medium bombers. The men of the 186th Regiment could certainly believe that with all that firepower, the Japanese resistance would be slight. However, the plan began to unravel as the 2nd Battalion of the 186th, in sixteen LVTs, approached the beach. Eight of these were to land the men between the jetties at Bosnek, while the remainder was supposed to land on either flank. However, the poor visibility caused by the smoke from the naval and air attacks combined with a six-mile-per-hour westerly current caused the landing of the first three waves to be put ashore just west of Mandon village, two miles west of the proposed site. Nevertheless, the 2nd Battalion moved inland to the Bosnek–Mokmer road and the 3rd to a position at the west end of the beach. The 162nd, assigned the task of seizing Mokmer field, landed behind the 186th, and its 3rd Battalion passed through the lines and began moving toward Parai town, closely followed by the 2nd. By then much of the two battalions' direct support artillery and the division's 155 guns had been landed and were in position at Bosnek. One company of the 2nd had gone inland across the main ridge preparatory to moving parallel to the coast to provide flank protection. It found a series of ridges covered with heavy vegetation that blocked its advance and was forced to rejoin the main body. Despite the foul-ups, Fuller could be satisfied that all was going well and his troops were not behind schedule. By the end of the day, the 3rd Battalion was approximately midway between Parai and Mokmer village and the 2nd was at Parai jetty. Although the Japanese kept up harassing fire during the night, casualties were light and there was a general feeling of optimism at higher headquarters.[9]

This was clearly demonstrated by MacArthur, who on the day after the invasion announced the impending capture of the island and noted that it would represent "the practical end of the New Guinea campaign."[10] On the same day he radioed Krueger, "My heartiest congratulations to you, General Fuller, General Doe and all officers and men under your command concerned upon the brilliant success attained at Wakde and Biak."[11] Located far away in Brisbane, out of touch with the reality of the fighting on Biak, he announced on June 1 that the Japanese resistance was "collapsing" and two days later that "mopping up" was "proceeding." The tendency to claim premature victory was a problem at MacArthur's headquarters. Eagerness for victory and ignorance of the situation had earlier caused MacArthur to relieve General Edwin Harding at Buna. He was now displaying the same attitude toward Fuller at Biak. Contrary to the optimistic view of the success of Operation Hurricane, the Japanese resistance was just beginning.

East of Mokmer village, the coral heights turned north and widened out to a coastal plain. A coral cliff twenty feet high ran diagonally across this, forming a terrace and the Parai defile. The Japanese controlled the high ground, and on the twenty-eighth they attacked and drove a wedge between units, cutting off elements of the 3rd Battalion. They also pinned down the 2nd with devastating fire. All wires were cut, isolating units from one another. Further advance was impossible, and in the afternoon surveying his mounting casualties, Colonel Harold Haney, commanding the 162nd, ordered a withdrawal. This became very difficult; supplies were running short and the men of the cut-off units had to repulse several Japanese attacks. Finally, the LVTs ran a gauntlet of fire to bring in supplies and evacuate the wounded. Heavy artillery fire, air support, and tanks enabled the 3rd Battalion to escape and move back beyond the 2nd Battalion. Meanwhile, the 182nd had made probing attacks north and east of Bosnek. Later in the afternoon of the twenty-eighth, Fuller reported to Krueger that the situation was grave and requested that the third of his regiments, the 163rd, then at Hollandia, be sent at once. Krueger alerted the 163rd, and it was embarked immediately, arriving on May 31. He also moved the 503rd Parachute Regiment from Oro Bay to Hollandia to act as a reserve force.[12]

The situation on Biak did not improve much on the third day, though there were a few successes. The 2nd Battalion sustained three separate counterattacks from the west. In one of these the Japanese committed most of their tanks. Though good enough for crowd control or against troops without armor, the Japanese tanks were woefully inadequate in a confrontation with the heavier Shermans, which were brought into action in the first tank battle of the Pacific war. The Japanese tanks, attacking in a column, were systematically blown to pieces by the Shermans' 75 mm guns. Seven of the Japanese tanks were destroyed, and others were badly damaged. Led by tanks, 162nd troops then moved through a narrow defile eastward toward Mandon to make contact with troops of the 186th, which had basically been involved in patrolling where they had discovered a road connecting the village of Opiaref with the airfield under construction north of Bosnek. By the end of the day, it was apparent that no successful move could be made along the coast toward Mokmer airfield as long as the Japanese held the high ground.[13]

By this time, Fuller had developed a new plan. He ordered the newly arrived 163rd to relieve the 186th, which was to concentrate near the uncompleted airfield and then move westward along the high ground north of the coral ridges in order to assault Mokmer airfield from the north. At the same time, the 162nd was to repeat its attempt to advance along the narrow coastal corridor. The concentration of troops near the airfield was completed by June 1. The next day, the 2nd and 3rd Battalions, accompanied by tanks and road-building equipment, began the advance. In addition to problems of terrain, the troops of both regiments suffered from the heat and particularly from lack of water. Water supply became crucial for any significant advance, and the men of the 116th Engineers worked desperately to improve the road system to supply the advancing 186th. Despite stubborn resistance, they had advanced 4,600 yards by nightfall. To the south the 162nd had made less progress, but troops of its 2nd Battalion made contact with the 186th northwest of Ibdi and then came under the command of Colonel Oliver Newman, commander of the 186th. Because of the difficult terrain, the advance north of the ridgeline continued slowly during June 3, moving 3,500 yards westward. The 162nd was once again halted by the Japanese at the narrow Parai Defile. The following day, patrols attempted to find other trails to the airfield in order to bypass the blockage at the Defile. An attempt to envelop the Japanese on the ridges northwest of Ibdi failed. However, success came on the seventh as the 2nd Battalion of the 186th, having moved to the eastern ridges dominating the Mokmer airfield, launched an early-morning attack; by 8:50 A.M., they had captured the airfield. They then had to suffer heavy artillery bombardment from the sump area on the left. Another victory had been achieved without opposition on June 2, when a company of the 163rd, in an amphibious operation, had occupied Woendi and Owi Islands. Heavy equipment was immediately brought in, and an airstrip on Owi was ready for fighter planes on the seventeenth. The Navy began to use Woendi as a PT base on the third.[14]

Even after the arrival of the 163rd, General Fuller was concerned that he did not have enough force to dislodge the Japanese from their well-fortified positions. His frontline troops were tired—many had been constantly in combat in the hot, humid weather, and casualties from the Japanese, sickness, and exhaustion had reduced the effectiveness of his units. This led him, on June 13, to request another regiment. Krueger, by then plagued by MacArthur's demands, only reluctantly agreed and ordered the 34th Infantry Regiment of the 24th Division to Biak. It did not arrive until the eighteenth. Krueger also discounted Fuller's reports of Japanese reinforcements. Later it was discovered that Kazume had received more than 1,000 troops, barged from the mainland and Noemfoor Island. These were only a partial commitment by the Japanese High Command to reinforce Biak. Long before Fuller made his request for more troops, the Japanese had planned to give General Numata, who had assumed command, the necessary force to hold the island and perhaps destroy Kinkaid's small Seventh Fleet units.

The Japanese naval command had never fully agreed with the Army's decision to abandon Biak. They considered the island vital to the success of Operation A-Go, the plan to force the U.S. Navy into a final, decisive battle. On May 28, Admiral Toyoda, commander of the Combined Fleet, ordered Rear Admiral Yoshioka Ito's 23rd Air Flotilla at Sorong, strengthened by fifty fighters from Japan and forty planes from the Mariana Islands. Later, seventy-six additional planes were shifted from the Philippines to Sorong and Halmahera. The greatly strengthened Japanese naval air force was thus very active on Z-day, boldly striking the beachhead during the day. On June 2, surprising the air defense in the beach area, they attacked it for more than an hour; the next day, they attacked destroyers and LSTs. In these the Japanese sustained heavy losses from ground fire and U.S. fighters. However, on the night of June 5–6, two bombers scored a major victory by attacking the crowded airfield at Wakde. Although the exact number of planes put out of action is in dispute, there were at least ninety aircraft either destroyed or damaged. The destruction of so many planes parked wing to wing seriously damaged the Fifth Air Force's ability to support Fuller's troops.[15]

All these air attacks were merely adjuncts to the proposed main effort of the Japanese navy to relieve Biak. Its Operation Kon was planned to transport 2,500 troops from Mindanao in warships. Rear Admiral Naomasa Sakonju was to command the landing and covering force with one battleship, three heavy cruisers, and eight destroyers. At the same time, barges would bring in troops from Manokwari. The concentration of heavy ships also indicated the secondary objective of destroying as much of the Allied naval force as possible. The convoy sortied from Zamboanga on May 31 with a target of June 3 for the landings. The hoped-for surprise ended when a B-24 reconnaissance plane discovered the task force. Surprisingly, Admiral Toyoda, presumably fearing a large U.S. naval force including an aircraft carrier, decided not to risk his ships and called off the attack before the proposed landings. A new plan was then developed wherein 600 troops from Sorong would be loaded into barges, which would be towed to Biak by destroyers. Sakonju committed two cruisers and six destroyers to the operation, which was to be protected by planes from the 23rd Air Flotilla. This plan also failed as the convoy was discovered on June 7, and subsequently planes from Wakde sank one destroyer and damaged three others. The fleeing Japanese ships were chased back to their base by Admiral Crutchley's destroyer divisions.

A more serious threat to Fuller's forces came when Admiral Jisaburo Ozawa commanding the Japanese Mobile Fleet, which was committed to the A-Go operation, nevertheless released the super-battleships *Yamato* and *Musashi,* one light cruiser, and six destroyers to be attached to Vice Admiral Matoma Ugaki's new Kon force at Batjan. Thus there was available a covering force of two battleships, two heavy and three light cruisers, and seven destroyers to attack Biak. Kinkaid's naval force in the area would be heavily outnumbered, and Fuller's troops would be subject to the same type of heavy bombardment that the Japanese had launched at Guadalcanal. Fortunately for MacArthur's plans, this attack, scheduled for June 15, never happened because on that date Nimitz's central Pacific campaign invaded the key island of Saipan in the Marianas. Admiral Toyoda, realizing that Japan could not afford to lose Saipan and sensing a chance to bring on A-Go to finally destroy the main U.S. fleet elements, canceled Kon. All available Japanese fleet elements were then concentrated on Saipan, and the commander of the 23rd Air Flotilla was ordered to release all naval aircraft to Palau. Three days later, Ozawa's fleet was nearly destroyed in the Battle of the Philippine Sea. Japan's naval airpower never recovered from the "Marianas Turkey Shoot."[16]

Meanwhile, on Biak, the offensive was resumed on June 9, with the 2nd Battalion of the 162nd moving east from Mokmer airfield to establish contact with the rest of the regiment and open up a much-needed supply route. Much of the 162nd was still held up at the Parai Defile, and the entire coastal corridor was still under fire. The 2nd and 3rd Battalions finally bypassed the defile by wading through waist-high surf. In the sector of the 186th, harassed by enemy patrols and mortar fire, the units were organizing better beach defenses. There was a heavy attack on the evening of the eighth that was beaten off, causing the attackers forty-two dead. Colonel Newman sent out patrols that used hand grenades and flamethrowers to clear the Japanese from a number of caves in the vicinity of Mokmer and north of the beachhead. Two companies attempted to advance west along the ridge but were met with heavy fire from concealed positions. The use of rocket launchers and 75 mm tank fire had little effect. Bringing in more tanks, Fuller launched a coordinated attack with both regiments against the ridges north and northwest of Mokmer airfield on the eleventh. The lead battalion of the 162nd met sustained fire from Japanese pillboxes, which were later flanked and neutralized. By the next day, most of the initial objectives had been reached. A continuation of these attacks on the thirteenth against heavy resistance, despite considerable losses, reached the main Japanese defenses of the West Caves. Elsewhere, Japanese positions in the defile area between the Parai jetty and Ibdi had been destroyed. By June 15, Fuller had both of his regiments deployed abreast, north and northeast of Mokmer airfield. Even before this, one of Fuller's main goals had been achieved. Repeated attacks by troops of the 162nd and 163rd had cut off all reinforcements to the Japanese isolated in the Ibdi Pocket. It appeared only a matter of time before the final stages of the battle could be launched.[17]

Far away in Brisbane, MacArthur, after having issued his premature victory statement and concerned that the "mopping up" would not be quick enough to allow assistance to Nimitz's campaign, began pressuring Krueger. On June 5, he radioed Krueger, "I am becoming concerned at the failure to secure the Biak airfields.... Is the advance being pushed with sufficient determination? Our negligible ground losses would seem to indicate a failure to do so."[18] Krueger's reply indicated that he, too, was dissatisfied, and he directed Fuller "to push his attack with utmost vigor." He reported that he had considered removing Fuller but delayed until he had the report of his chief of staff, Brigadier General George Decker, who had been sent to Biak to report on the situation there.[19]

On June 8, with the positive evidence from his subordinates, Krueger sent a long communiqué to MacArthur, explaining in detail the situation on Biak. This recapitulation was a masterpiece of brevity and accuracy in which he defended Fuller. He pointed out that Fuller had been faced with a difficult task and that a possible alternate plan for the capture of the airfields was "judgement after the event and presupposes that there were enough troops on the spot to permit it, which is debatable since the 163rd RCT (less 1 Bn.) did not arrive until 31 May." He pointed out that he had considered removing Fuller but that Fuller now had his full confidence. He noted, "I am glad I did not do so then, and feel that it would be unwarranted now when, I am sure, he is about to accomplish his mission successfully."[20] Although at this juncture Krueger was concerned about Fuller's inability to beat down the Japanese resistance, he understood the problems of reducing the main defenses, without which the airfields could not be used. Within a week he had altered this glowing support and removed Fuller from command of the Hurricane operation.

The reason for this turnabout was due to the pressure from MacArthur, who wanted at least one of the airfields to be operational by June 15. MacArthur did not appreciate the many problems facing Fuller, and on June 14, in an eyes-only dispatch to Krueger, he stated, "The strategic purpose of the operation is being jeopardized by the failure to establish without delay an operating field for aircraft."[21] After receiving this message, Krueger decided that he had to give in to MacArthur, and he ordered Eichelberger and his entire I Corps staff, then at Hollandia, to Biak to take command of the operation. Fuller would revert to being only the 41st Division commander.

Eichelberger later reported that he had been surprised and shocked by Krueger's decision. He had been busy supervising the various construction projects that were needed to make Hollandia a major Allied base. He claimed that at the time he was ordered to meet with Krueger before leaving for Biak he

> had received no information of the progress of the fighting at Biak. . . . General Byers [I Corps chief of staff] and I were old hands at this game and particularly remembered the time we were ordered to Buna with no warning of any kind . . . working as we were at Hollandia we received absolutely no reports from Sixth Army or GHG about how things were going at Biak. This would seem unbelievable that a force in the field wouldn't be kept informed about what was going on in adjacent combat units but it was typical, even into Japan.[22]

Such a situation might have been typical, but I Corps was not totally unaware of the situation on Biak. Byers did not want a repeat of the Buna situation, when Eichelberger had been ordered to relieve General Edwin Harding and take control of the offensive. Byers ordered the corps signal officer to intercept messages between Alamo Force and General Headquarters. Later, Byers recalled that he had caught "the dickens from Mac's Chief Signal Officer for this but it was the only way we could keep aware of the trouble on Biak."[23]

The breach of protocol certainly aided Eichelberger in understanding his new task, since he recalled that his staff had had, on arrival at Biak on the fifteenth, "only a few maps with us but almost no knowledge of what we would find at Biak."[24] One of the first things he discovered was an angry General Fuller, who resented his demotion and believed it was Krueger who had been unjustly critical of his handling of the campaign. Eichelberger's assumption of command only confirmed his belief that Krueger had concluded that he had failed. Fuller had already decided before Eichelberger arrived that Krueger was responsible and had sent a letter to Alamo Force requesting to be relieved of command and reassigned outside the Southwest Pacific Theater.

Eichelberger and Fuller were friends and had been classmates at West Point, and once again Eichelberger was placed in the embarrassing role of taking command from a friend. He tried to convince Fuller not to pursue the resignation but to stay on in command of the 41st Division. Friendship aside, this was practical since Fuller knew much about the situation on Biak that even under the best of circumstances Eichelberger would have to master quickly. Fuller remained adamant despite Eichelberger's arguments and the reiteration of MacArthur's promise that Fuller would soon be awarded command of a corps. He considered Krueger a villain and simply refused to serve under him any longer. He insisted that a radio message be sent immediately to Alamo Force headquarters to speed up his relief. Krueger approved the request and appointed Jens Doe to take over as acting divisional commander.[25]

Before leaving the island, Fuller addressed a letter to the men of the 41st, congratulating them on their performance and exonerating them of any part in any failure to live up to higher headquarters' expectations. Fuller's overreaction and his assumption of Krueger's prime responsibility may have been incorrect, but his belief that he had not been treated fairly was accurate. Two of the 41st regimental commanders agreed with their commander that the Biak operation was well in hand. The airfields had been captured, and it was only a matter of time before the low ridgeline and the West Caves would be secured. Colonel Oliver Newman, commanding the 186th, recalled that he had not been aware of a time factor. He wrote:

I was never informed that there had been a deadline set for the capture of the Biak Airfields, nor that there was any pressure being applied on General Fuller from higher headquarters. I only learned that after his relief. As far as I knew the operation was proceeding with fairly satisfactory speed. Had I known of the need for speed in supporting the Marianas attack I might have acted differently on several occasions.[26]

Fuller left Biak on the eighteenth and later was received cordially by MacArthur, who praised him for not complaining about his treatment. Fuller was awarded the Distinguished Service Medal by MacArthur for his actions at Hollandia and Biak.[27] His desire to serve outside the Southwest Pacific was honored, and he would later serve as deputy chief of staff to Lord Louis Mountbatten in the Southeast Area Command. A question about this affair lingers: Would Fuller have been so well disposed toward MacArthur had he known that it was MacArthur and not Krueger who had caused his demotion?

Eichelberger, MacArthur's fireman, was later supportive of Fuller's handling of the operation. He pointed out that the invasion had been begun with only two regiments, which meant only a rough parity with Kazume's forces. Military textbooks stated that an invader should have a three-to-one advantage. Two days before the offensive was renewed, Eichelberger, after personally surveying the front line, wrote, "This is the toughest terrain I have seen yet to fight in except at Buna. The interior is a series of coral cliffs with numerous natural caves. It has been and will continue to be a rough fight." He also admitted that the "Japanese defense of Biak was based on brilliant appreciation and use of terrain." Considering all the facts, he concluded that the 41st Division had not done badly.[28] Such statements by the I Corps commander pose the question: Did Fuller's relief hasten the collapse of the Japanese resistance and the use of the airfields?

As was the case in many instances where a commander was removed, there was no appreciable gain on Biak. After studying the situation for three days, Eichelberger ordered an offensive, to begin on June 19. He brought nothing tactically new to the offensive; rather his attack plans were roughly the same as Fuller's had been. The major difference was that he could attack with four regiments, supported by a larger force of tanks and tank destroyers. During the period when Eichelberger was planning his offensive, aggressive patrolling was continued, with the 186th units moving toward Borokoe, closing a gap that had separated the 2nd Battalion from the rest of the regiment. Troops of the 163rd that had taken over areas occupied by the 186th eliminated pockets of resistance east of Bosnek and later moved west as far as Parai town. Its 3rd Battalion pushed overland northeast, surprising the Japanese by capturing Hill 320, which provided an excellent observation point. The plan that Eichelberger finalized was not especially ingenious but rather dictated by the situation he had inherited from Fuller. The main area of Japanese resistance was in the West Caves area, where a number of caves or sumps contained hundreds of defenders. There were three major sumps. The first two, in the east, were approximately 75 feet in diameter. The third, with a much wider opening, was 300 feet to the west. These were connected by galleries, the main one being forty feet high. The entrances to the sumps were shielded by stalagmites and stalactites.[29]

Eichelberger's plan was to launch a coordinated effort to envelop the Japanese right flank, seize the high ground north of Mokmer airfield, and occupy one ridgeline 1,000 yards east of Boroke airfield. The 2nd Battalion of the 186th was to be the main assault unit. It was to move north and east from positions above Mokmer. Units of the 163rd held positions in the eastern area of the sumps, and the 162nd was to attack frontally. Before the assault the Japanese positions were pounded by artillery and mortar fire. The attack was a success, two companies of the 2nd Battalion reaching their objectives by 11:30, overrunning the Japanese north of the West Caves. These became the objective for the 20th. Men of the 1st Battalion of the 162nd, using drums of gasoline that they dropped into the entrances to the sumps and then ignited, killed a large number of Japanese, but they were unsuccessful in reducing the opposition from the caves. The following day, the caves were once again attacked by troops with flamethrowers supported by tanks. Once again gasoline was poured into the openings of the westernmost cave and then ignited, causing tremendous explosions. The desperate situation for the defenders was shown when Colonel Kazume, who had resumed command after General Numata had left the island, held a ceremony in the officers' cave at approximately 3 A.M. on the twenty-second. The regimental colors were burned, and he urged all present to lead attempts to break out to the north to continue the struggle. These actions were a clear indication that the Japanese knew the battle was lost. In accordance with his wishes, the troops in the West Cave, on the night of the twenty-second, attempted to break through the ring imposed by the 186th. Three separate attacks were contained, and a total of 115 Japanese were killed.[30] This marked the last organized resistance in the vicinity of Mokmer airfield. However, reduction of the caves continued until June 27, when the last Japanese were cleared out. Even before this the air corps engineers, who had been landed on June 9 but could do little work until the West Caves had been cleared, began to clean up Mokmer airfield, and on the twenty-first fighter aircraft began to use the field. Soon B-25s staging there could be used to support the infantry in the attacks against the East Caves. The improvement in the general situation on Biak was clearly shown when Eichelberger and his I Corps staff returned to Hollandia on the twenty-ninth, leaving Doe in command of the operation.

Elsewhere the systematic destruction of the Japanese defenses continued. The 34th Infantry Regiment, which had landed to the west on June 18, occupied Borokoe and Sorido airfields two days later. It then moved north and was assigned the task of securing the area northwest of Mokmer airfield. In conjunction with elements of the 186th, they took a long, fingerlike ridge in two days of fighting and afterward counted 135 dead Japanese. Once these initial objectives had been obtained, the regiment was withdrawn back to Hollandia to be in reserve for the Noemfoor operation. Meanwhile, on the 25th, troops of the 186th had overrun a cul-de-sac three hundred yards long called the Teardrop. Later it was discovered that the commander of the Japanese second Area Army had issued orders for a mass withdrawal to the interior whenever possible to begin guerrilla action.

With the capture of the three airfields and the West Caves, Eichelberger's attention had shifted to the East Caves. These were two large depressions not unlike the sumps of the West Caves. Located on a ledge north of Mokmer village, they were more than fifty feet wide. Each of them was honeycombed with tunnels. On the upward slope above the cave entrance were five pillboxes, and in the sump itself the Japanese had sited 81 mm and 90 mm mortars and heavy machine guns. The caves were defended by approximately 1,000 troops, most of whom were technicians and laborers. The most experienced were 300 naval troops. The Japanese in this vicinity had been generally ignored as the main effort had been directed toward the west. The Japanese in the East Caves had proved a nuisance since they had good observation of the coast road and from time to time fired on truck traffic there. This eventually brought on air strikes. On the twenty-fourth, B-25s based at Mokmer airfield, in one of the shortest missions on record, skip bombed the area. Most of their bombs missed the main sump holes, but the explosions caused the Japanese to stop the harassing fire for a few days.[31] Harassing fire from the East Caves became more than a nuisance on the twenty-seventh, with the shelling of a company of the 542nd Engineer Boat Regiment working at a gravel pit northwest of Mokmer. Two days later, 4.2-inch mortars were brought up to silence the Japanese fire. Over the next three days, more than eight hundred rounds were pumped into the cave area. On June 30, the mortar fire was joined by direct fire from a 105 mm howitzer. Elements of the engineer regiment moved into the caves under cover of tank fire. A few Japanese were killed, and the engineers sealed some of the tunnels. At the same time, a company of the 163rd entered the caves from Mokmer village against little opposition. On July 6, the main part of the caves was occupied; only ten Japanese were found in the area. The Japanese had begun evacuation of the caves on the twenty-eighth, when Colonel Minami, commanding the forces in the area, committed suicide. Small groups of Japanese afterward slipped out onto the flats north of the main ridge.[32]

After the East Caves were neutralized and the Parai Defile was cleared, the main coast road was finally relatively safe. However, the Japanese in the hill area known as the Ibdi Pocket were still in a position to harass traffic from Bosnek to the airfields. Here the Japanese 3rd Battalion of the 222nd Infantry, over eight hundred strong and with many service troops, manned the most formidable defenses on the island. After the capture of the defense complex, it was discovered that the central portion of the pocket, an area 400 yards long and 600 yards wide, contained seventy-five four-man pillboxes constructed of logs, coral, or concrete. One pillbox was constructed with nine layers of logs. There were twenty-one major natural formations. Most of these caves had been enlarged and deepened. The entire area was covered with heavy growth. Although much of the Japanese equipment had been destroyed, eight 90 mm mortars, three 75 mm mountain guns, and two 20 mm weapons were discovered.[33] The Japanese had not taken full advantage of the Ibdi position. Had they done so, traffic along the coast road could have been totally disrupted. This lack, however, meant that they had been virtually ignored as the assaults on the West and

East Caves developed. Fuller, and later Eichelberger, realized that the Japanese there could no longer affect the outcome of the main offensives, and after June 7 the Ibdi Pocket was simply contained.

After the Mokmer area and the Parai area had been relatively neutralized, Doe turned his attention to the pocket. Beginning on the twenty-first, the 146th Field Artillery Battalion, the 163rd's cannon company, along with mortars and guns from tank destroyers, began a systematic shelling of the area. At first only two companies were brought into the area, but later most of the 1st and 2nd Battalions began to move through the undergrowth to isolate the main center of resistance. By the twenty-seventh, that was reduced to only about 600 yards square. The decision was then made to use the superior firepower to reduce the pocket. By July 9, more than 20,000 artillery shells and 2,000 mortar rounds had been fired into the complex. Two days later, troops of the 3rd Battalion moved with flamethrowers and bazookas to reduce many of the pillboxes and caves. On the twelfth, approximately two hundred Japanese sneaked out, leaving behind only the dead and a few defenders. Nevertheless, the positions held by the Japanese were considered too strong for more direct assaults, and the tactics reverted to using artillery. By the twenty-second, an additional 1,000 rounds of 105 mm and 275 rounds of 155 mm shells were poured into the Japanese defenses. Finally, eight B-24s dropped 1,000-pound bombs; these seemingly paralyzed the remaining defenders, and the 3rd Battalion troops, moving in, reported only slight resistance.

The neutralization of the Ibdi Pocket meant an end to organized resistance on Biak. However, there were still an estimated four thousand Japanese on the island. It would take the bulk of three infantry regiments involved in pacification of the interior until mid-August to end the active operations. The Japanese High Command, still believing that an offensive could be launched, ordered a concentration of available troops near Wardo Bay. Any hope that the Japanese there posed a threat was ended when the 1st

Battalion of the 186th, in an amphibious operation, landed there on August 17. This broke up the Japanese forces into small groups whose main goal was to find food. Constant combat patrolling for more than a month quickly reduced the numbers of Japanese survivors.[34] On August 20, Krueger was satisfied that active resistance had ended and officially declared Hurricane finished. Contrary to the optimistic expectations at General Headquarters in May, the main Biak operation had taken more than a month to secure the airfields. It had cost 400 dead and 2,000 wounded, most from the 41st Division. In addition, 7,234 men had reported sick due to malaria, skin diseases, dengue, and typhoid. Almost the entire Japanese garrison had been killed. The best estimate of their losses was 4,700 killed and 220 captured. More than 600 Javanese and Indian slave laborers were liberated.[35]

The possession of Biak and Owi Island gave Kenney and Whitehead advanced bases for their heavy bombers, which would be invaluable in later actions in the Vogelkop and to MacArthur's plan to invade the southern Philippines. The prolonged struggle for Biak had convinced Whitehead that work should begin immediately on a heavy bomber field at Owi. General Headquarters agreed, and on June 9 aviation engineers began work on an airfield. Enough work had been completed for P-38s to begin using the field by the seventeenth. Within a week, two squadrons of the 8th Fighter Group were based there, later to be joined by a night fighter squadron. The plan for Biak's airfields approved by General Headquarters on June 23 was to construct heavy bomber fields at Mokmer and Sorido and a fighter strip at Borokoe. Although the ground at Sorido proved not to be adequate and the construction there was halted by mid-June, the other fields were accommodating B-24 squadrons of the Fifth Air Force as well as the 78th Wing of the RAAF. The Fifth Air Force forward command post was then moved to Biak from Nadzab.[36] At the same time, construction crews were busy building roads and repairing and building jetties and storage buildings. A four-hundred-bed hospital was in operation by the end of September. By mid-August, eight LST slots were under construction, as well as two floating docks for Liberty ships. Eventually, Biak would be capable of full logistical support for 70,000 air and ground troops that were needed to support the operations against Noemfoor Island, Sansopor-Mar, and eventually Leyte.[37]

Thirteen

FINAL CONQUESTS: DRINIUMOR RIVER, NOEMFOOR, AND SANSAPOR

After the successful conclusion of the Hollandia and Aitape operation, General MacArthur and his staff focused upon securing air bases and staging areas at Biak, on Noemfoor Island, and in the Vogelkop region of extreme western New Guinea. They were aware that General Adachi still had a significant force of his battered Eighteenth Army in the Wewak area, but they believed that the distance of his main force at Wewak from the nearest U.S. force at Aitape would mitigate against any significant threat. MacArthur was content to allow Adachi's force to "wither on the vine" while Alamo Force captured the areas to the west so vital to his overall plan of returning to the Philippines. In this he was supported by General Marshall, who noted, "So long as the 18th Jap army remains physically isolated and in radio communication with other Jap units it will continue to afford us valuable source for cryptoanalytic assistance. To the extent that it will not interfere with your present operations it is highly desirable that this situation be preserved and fully exploited."[1] MacArthur's G-2, General

Willoughby, had confidentially predicted that if Adachi had meant to attack the Aitape area, he would have done so before the Wakde operation.

Willoughby would soon change his appreciation of the situation as more information on the movement of the Eighteenth Army became available, because by mid-May it was obvious that Adachi had moved considerable forces westward. Adachi had earlier received orders from Anami to move his army west to defend Wewak and ultimately Aitape and Hollandia. This meant that he had to move his battered army from the Ramu River region to Wewak and, if he were to defend Aitape, a further 350 miles westward. By mid-April his 51st Division had just reached Wewak, the 20th was still in the Ramu region, and the 41st stretched between Madang and Hansa. It was projected that it would take fifty days to move to the Aitape area. At the time of the Hollandia invasion, Adachi's army was scattered along a three-hundred-mile stretch of northern New Guinea and it was in short supply of almost everything, particularly trucks and artillery, and was operating over poor native trails without air cover. After the Hollandia invasion, his superiors in the Southern Army Command, without specifically canceling the earlier order, informed him that he was to conduct delaying actions. They assumed that Adachi would understand that there was no longer any need to attack Aitape. Adachi disagreed. He believed that instead of resting in the Wewak area and allowing his force to disintegrate, he could drive the U.S. force from Aitape and at worst force a shift of units away from other objectives.[2]

In May, at Aitape, General Gill, commanding the 32nd Division, organized his defenses, centered on Tadji airfield. He divided the area into two sectors. The 126th RCT was given the West Sector, while the 127th was posted to the East Sector. When the reserve unit, the 128th, was released by Krueger on June 10, he then created a Central Sector. As a part of his defense, he established an outpost line and a main line of resistance and had patrols probing for the Japanese as far as ten miles inland. The East Sector was the most active, as Lieutenant Colonel Merle Howe, commanding the 127th, pushed his patrols further eastward. The point unit for this was a composite group, the Nyaparake Force, built up around C Company, led by Captain Tally Fulmer. On May 13, the leading elements of his patrols encountered a significant Japanese force. That night the Japanese made three separate attacks and surrounded the company, forcing the evacuation of Company C as well as Company A, which was also threatened. On May 19, Gill made further changes. He put the assistant division commander, Brigadier General Clarence Martin, in charge of the East Sector and placed Captain Herman Bottcher, of Buna fame, in charge of a reinforced Nyaparake Force.[3]

Further advance eastward by the Nyaparake Force was blocked by a significant number of Japanese. It was nearly surrounded, and on the twenty-second Bottcher ordered a fighting retreat to avoid encirclement. Gill, increasingly concerned about the Japanese presence, ordered the 126th east to stem any further Japanese advances. On May 31, Lieutenant Colonel Cladie Bailey, commanding the 126th, began an offensive to drive the Japanese back. After at first making good progress, the 1st Battalion met heavy resistance east of Yakamul and was forced back to a defensive line at that village. Bailey was then ordered to leave two companies, approximately 350 men, to hold Yakamul; he named this unit Herrick Force as it was commanded by Captain Gile Herrick. He then took the rest of his command, code-named Bailey Force, to probe inland along the Harech River as far as the foothills of the Torricelli Mountains, approximately five miles inland. The Japanese artillery struck the Yakamul command post during the night of June 1–2 and two days later the Japanese mounted a major attack on the village. One group swung inland to attack from the south, threatening to isolate the defenders. On the fourth, in company strength, they forced a retreat across a small stream that had been one of the eastern defense lines. Bailey was ordered to halt his patrol into the interior and rejoin those defending the village. Moving as rapidly as possible through the heavy jungle, the men of Bailey Force straggled into the village area just before noon on the fifth. Martin decided to cut his losses and ordered Bailey Force to fall back to the Driniumor River, leaving Herrick to cover the retreat. Soon he dispatched a number of small boats to evacuate the rest of the troops. Covered by rocket and machine-gun fire from an LCM, the men had to run to the boats while under Japanese fire. Eventually they joined the rest of the battalion on the Driniumor line. The two weeks of firefights had cost eighteen men killed and seventy-five wounded.[4]

The increasing action near Aitape alerted General Headquarters to the danger. Willoughby had changed his mind about the possibility of a major Japanese attack. By June 1, Ultra provided information about a potential attack at Aitape. Then intercepts from Japanese transmissions allowed the G-2 section to predict that Adachi would probably launch an offensive in late June or early July. MacArthur wanted the Eighteenth Army eliminated as a threat to future operations but did not want to divert troops from other planned operations to the west. Krueger was already coping with this problem. He was moving the 43rd Division from New Zealand, but it would not arrive until mid-July. Until then he sent the 112th Cavalry Regiment and the 124th RCT of the 31st Division to Aitape to reinforce the Driniumor line, which had been greatly strengthened since the early clashes with the Japanese. Finally, he sent Major General Charles Hall and his XI Corps staff to take over the defenses, and he visited Aitape on June 27. In conference with Hall and Gill, he rejected Gill's arguments to continue the static defense centered on the airfield. He and Hall preferred a more active role for the planned-for eight RCTs that Hall would have. After the arrival of the 43rd Division, Hall planned for a dual defense line, with that division and the 124th RCT echeloned around the airfield while the rest of his force would be aligned along the Driniumor. He positioned General Cunningham's 112th Cavalry Regiment around Afua village in the south while two regiments of the 32nd Division, the 128th RCT in the center and the 124th RCT, were in the north. General Martin remained in tactical charge of what was called the covering force while Gill commanded the larger part of Corps troops guarding the airfield.

Krueger was receiving pressure from MacArthur to clean up the problem in the Aitape area, no doubt because he feared any possible adverse publicity would endanger his Philippines plans. Krueger therefore ordered two separate reconnaissances to ascertain, if possible, the Japanese positions and the size of the forces east of the Driniumor. For these Hall selected the 1st Battalion of the 128th to move eastward along the coast, while the 2nd Squadron of the 112th Cavalry, on the south end of the line, would search to the southeast. He did not feel it necessary to replace these along the main river line, thus necessitating a repositioning of units and thinning out of the defense capability. The reconnaissance units moved out on the morning of July 10. The coastal force met no resistance to its actions. The cavalry also penetrated southeastward without encountering any significant Japanese presence. However, they had to cut their way through heavy jungle undergrowth before reaching a defensible position in the foothills. To compound their problems, communication with the main area was lost. Surprisingly, neither patrol force encountered the Japanese in the final stages of their buildup for the attack. Neither unit was in any position to assist in defending the Driniumor line.[5]

The situation of the Japanese Eighteenth Army, based solely on numbers, did not appear as bad as the reality. Adachi had approximately 55,000 men under his command, of whom 15,000 were in the forward areas. However, more than 3,000 men were hospitalized, and at the end of June he could command only 5,000 frontline troops. These were tired, hungry men who had marched hundreds of miles over wretched native trails. Their meager rations at the time of Adachi's proposed offensive was 330 grams per man per day. Many of the Japanese survived by eating sago palm leaves. There were shortages of all necessary supplies, particularly medicine.[6] Common sense should have dictated a policy of standing on the defense, since Adachi knew that the focus of U.S. attention was removed far to the west. Adachi had dispatched a staff officer to the Driniumor area in late June to assess the U.S. position. His appreciation of the situation, which he presented to Adachi when he arrived at Charon, closer to the front, was negative. He recommended that the attack on Aitape be canceled, as it showed little sign of success.

Adachi rejected all negative arguments, and on July 3 he issued his attack plan, which was fundamentally simple, depending on surprise and a breakthrough in the center of the U.S. line along a 300-yard front approximately five miles inland from the coast. It would be a frontal attack by the 20th and 41st Divisions. One reason for this was that Major General Miyake Sadehiko, commanding the 20th, reported that his men were too exhausted for a flank attack. In addition to surprise, Adachi depended upon the spirit of his troops. He showed this clearly in the address to his forces on July 6 when he said:

> I cannot find any means nor method which will solve this situation strategically or tactically. Therefore, I intend to overcome this by relying on our Japanese *Bushido*. I am determined to destroy the enemy in Aitape by attacking him ruthlessly with the concentration of our entire force in that area. This will be our final opportunity to employ our entire strength to annihilate the enemy. Make the supreme sacrifice, display the spirit of the Imperial Army.[7]

The Japanese timetable was upset by delay in moving the attack forces into position. Not until midafternoon of the tenth were the spearheads on line. The attack began at 11:30 P.M. when Major

Kawahigashi Moritoski led his 1st Battalion of the 78th Regiment into the river, expecting that the entire central line would be held by only three U.S. battalions. His aim was directed at two companies of the 1st Battalion of the 128th. Once aware of the attack, the U.S. artillery, which had been preregistered, opened up to join the concentrated mortar fire from closer in. The Japanese massed in midstream were also struck by rifle and machine-gun fire from the west bank. The surviving Japanese soon broke off the attack. Only an estimated 90 Japanese of the 400 who had begun the crossing survived. Major Koike Masao had also led his 3rd Battalion into the river, and most of his men suffered the same fate as they were slaughtered by the massed artillery and mortar fire. However, some Japanese managed to reach the west bank and passed through gaps in Company E's lines, and these later caused considerable problems.

Further to the north, three companies of the Japanese 1st Battalion of the 237th attacked on a 75-yard front against Company E. Flares illuminated the attackers, and U.S. artillery once again began its devastating fire. One Japanese company, caught on a small island, was almost totally destroyed. Nevertheless, pushed by the rest of the 237th, the Japanese reached the west bank. The distance between Company E's strong points was too great. The Japanese could not be halted, and the company was overrun and scattered. The attackers then regrouped to move northwest of the main area of combat while the 78th's battered force drove southwest to flank the U.S. forces around Afua. To the south, Company G, with its flank exposed, pulled back to the vicinity of the mortars. Communications with higher headquarters, which had been lost, was finally restored and Martin ordered Company G and some members of Company H to fall back 3,000 yards, to River X-Ray. This withdrawal, undertaken under continuous pressure, took three days. The breakthrough, though successful, cost the Japanese dearly. The 78th Regiment had lost an estimated 600 men, and the 237th had also suffered heavy casualties. However, by early morning of the

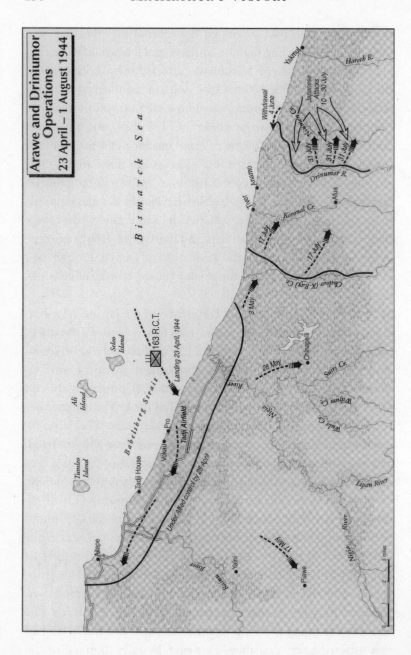

Arawe and Driniumor
Operations
23 April – 1 August 1944

eleventh, the Japanese had punched a 1,300-yard-wide hole in the Driniumor defense line.[8]

The most vulnerable of the U.S. force was the 112th, since half of its men were east of the river and out of contact with the rest of the unit. This caused some delay in getting the order to the 2nd Squadron to pull back to the Afua area. By that time Martin had ordered Cunningham to move back 1,500 yards to River X-Ray. This was accomplished in heavy rain by midnight of the eleventh, soon after the 2nd reached Afua totally exhausted after their hurried march. With his command once again intact, Cunningham established a 4,500-yard defensive front. The Japanese need to reorganize delayed the southward movement of the 78th and 80th Regiments, and thus they could not prevent the retreat of the 112th. At the same time, the 1st Battalion of the 128th and the 3rd Battalion of the 127th fell back to more defensible positions along X-Ray.[9]

On the eleventh, General Krueger flew into Tadji to confer with Hall. Neither knew much about the situation along the Driniumor. However, Krueger ordered a halt to any further retreat. He reorganized the command, removing Martin from command of the Covering Force and replacing him with Gill. Due largely to the gap in the line caused by the breakthrough, there were created North Force and South Force. Krueger expected Hall to take the offensive to restore the original line. More artillery, much of which had been preregistered, was brought forward to cover all areas. Martin had already ordered the 112th to move back to its abandoned positions around Afua. Aside from a brief flurry of action against an advance guard from the Japanese 20th Regiment, this was accomplished by late afternoon of the twelfth. At the same time, the 1st Battalion of the 128th had begun a forward movement along the coast.

The bulk of the fighting for the next two weeks centered on Afua in a series of desperate, confused actions. On the fourteenth, Cunningham initiated action by attacking north with the objective of meeting the 124th, which was to attack southward, thus closing the gap. The 1st Squadron advanced almost a mile without encountering any Japanese. However, troops of the 124th got lost in the jungle, and the linkup was not achieved. By nightfall, Cunningham was informed that two Japanese regiments were only two miles northwest, preparing to attack. Although this did not materialize, the presence of this significant Japanese force caused Cunningham to request another regiment to bolster South Force. Once again Gill, out of touch with the reality of the situation, denied the request. For all practical purposes, the gap was closed by a delayed linkup on the fifteenth.

The Japanese were also regrouping. The battered 78th and 80th Regiments were combined into a single command led by Major General Miyake Sadahiko. The goal of this Miyake Force was Afua. On the sixteenth, Adachi also ordered the 66th Regiment of the 51st Division to the area to expand the Japanese control west of the Driniumor. Miyake's screening patrols were in position for an all-out attack on South Force by the eighteenth, and the 3rd Battalion of the 78th attacked from the south while the 2nd Battalion of the 80th struck from the west. In a two-hour battle Troop A was forced back three hundred yards. The fighting became confused as the Japanese and cavalrymen blundered into one another in grim man-to-man action. By evening, however, South Force was back to its original positions. The Japanese renewed the attack the next day, with little success. By the twentieth, Miyake Force was almost destroyed. Miyake then received reinforcements of 700 men from the 79th Regiment, and on the twenty-first he ordered an all-out attack with the entire 79th. It struck Troop C, whose members soon found themselves surrounded. U.S. artillery finally broke up the attack, causing heavy casualties. However, Troop C was still surrounded. Cunningham sent A and B Troops and part of the 127th to break through and rescue the trapped cavalrymen. It was finally successful on the twenty-third, when men of the 127th reached the perimeter by evening. They then found they could not immediately break out. The ensuing battle of attrition, though costly to the cavalrymen, ground down the Japanese attackers, and Troop C managed to pull back to the command post by the twenty-seventh.[10]

Both sides continued to be in the dark as to the exact nature of the situation near Afua. Gill did not believe that Cunningham was facing more than a shattered 78th. He rejected Cunningham's assessment of the size of the attacking force and could not understand why it was taking so long to clear the Japanese from the area. Despite his losses, Adachi decided to commit all of the 20th Division, augmented by the 41st Division, which he had pulled back from a proposed assault on Kwamakajima to the north. On the twenty-fifth, Cunningham began a cautious attack south to break the Japanese defense line. In so doing his troops ran into remnants of the Japanese 79th Division. The rain, which had been continuous for days, became even worse as the Japanese and cavalrymen struggled in the jungle in a series of small-unit actions that continued through the rest of the month. The 2nd Battalion of the 127th, in redeploying, came up against the Japanese 66th Regiment on the twenty-ninth, also beginning a number of small-unit actions. On August 1, two battalions of Japanese launched separate attacks on Sagi Point, north of Afua. One was a mass assault against Troop C by two hundred to three hundred troops. Artillery was called in, and, in combination with small-arms fire, the Japanese were slaughtered. After this action, Cunningham canceled his planned southward attack.

General Hall decided to go on the offensive on the thirty-first and ordered three battalions of the 124th RCT of North Force to cross the Driniumor near the mouth of the river. This composite unit, code-named Ted Force, moved south along Niumen Creek against minimal opposition by Japanese service and support troops and by August 5 turned southwest toward Afua in an attempt to envelop the Japanese. This proved unnecessary. On the afternoon of the second, Adachi had ordered an attack northwest of Sagi Point by the pitiful remnants of his point regiments. In their typical mass formation, they were cut to pieces by artillery and mortar fire. At the same time he ordered the 41st Division troops to cross the river and attack the by now well entrenched 1st Squadron. Like most of the attacks, it was destroyed by massed fires. More than 100 were killed, their corpses stacked like cordwood in front of the cavalrymen. The final assault on the 112th positions was when troops of the 41st, in a two-hour attack, tried to overrun the dug-in troopers. Approximately 175 were killed, the bodies choking the river.[11]

These latter attacks were even more unnecessary than the earlier ones since Adachi had decided to break off all attacks on the third and began retreating toward the southeast. The following week was spent by U.S. long-range patrols, mainly from the newly arrived 43d Division, pursuing the retreating Japanese and engaging in dangerous small unit actions against the rear guard and stragglers. The 112th, which had borne the brunt of the fighting, was relieved on August 10. In its forty-five days on the line, it had sustained 317 casualties, 21 percent of its strength. By the time Krueger declared the campaign over on August 25, the entire U.S. force had lost 597 killed, 169 wounded, and 85 missing. It is impossible to know the exact number of casualties suffered by the Japanese in Adachi's failed offensive. It was estimated that the 20th and 41st Divisions, by the time they straggled back toward Wewak, had lost more than 8,800 men. This included almost all the battalion and company-grade officers.[12] The battle had stripped the Eighteenth Army of any real offensive potential and thus made secure the Aitape and Hollandia areas from future threats from Wewak.[13] Adachi had not even slowed MacArthur's westward drive, since the units necessary to halt the Japanese were either already at Aitape or deployed from bases farther east. The planned attack to seize Noemfoor Island for advance air bases was not impeded in any way by the deadly Driniumor action.

The delay in capturing the airfields on Biak had led Kenney, now commanding the newly formed Far Eastern Air Force—also comprising the Thirteenth Air Force—and Whitehead, the new commander of the Fifth, to suggest to MacArthur that the island of Noemfoor be seized in order to provide immediate air support to isolate the Japanese in the Manokwari area and on Halmahera. Specifically, they hoped to repair the existing airfields to accommodate both bombers and fighters. MacArthur agreed. On June 5, he informed Krueger of his intentions, and on the fourteenth he instructed him to prepare plans for a joint occupation of the island. Krueger was to coordinate the efforts of the three services. Most of the planning was done at Alamo Force headquarters at Cape Cretin. There was much discussion of the date for the invasion. MacArthur wanted it done as quickly as possible, but the demands of simultaneous operations at Biak and Sarmi placed a great strain on Kinkaid's naval forces. Finally it was agreed that Operation Cyclone would take place on June 30.

Noemfoor, located seventy-five nautical miles due west from Biak, was almost a circle approximately fifteen miles long from north to south and twelve miles wide. The northern part was low and flat, while the south was more rugged. Most of the interior was covered by heavy rain forest, and there were only two hills of any consequence. The bulk of the small native population after the Japanese occupation had simply fled into the interior. The highest point, only 670 feet high, was near the center of the island. The island was surrounded by a wide reef, and there were few beaches suitable for landings. The best, according to aerial photographs, was in the northwest, near Kamiri village. The Japanese, not being able to count on the natives for work, had brought out approximately three thousand Indonesians to build the airfields. In typical Japanese fashion, overwork, starvation, and disease reduced this workforce to only 403 survivors, to be rescued by U.S. forces. By mid-1944, they had nearly finished three airfields. The one nearest completion was at Kamiri and had a main runway 5,000 feet long, complete with dispersal areas. The others, one at Kornasoren in the north and Namber near the coast on the southeast, were not as developed but could quickly be repaired to accept fighter aircraft.[14]

Once again estimating the numbers and dispositions of the Japanese worried the planners. The estimates given by Ultra and MacArthur's headquarters of approximately 1,750 men, of whom only 700 were combat troops, did not satisfy Krueger and Kenney. Despite evidence of the inability of the Japanese to supply reinforcements, Kenney believed that this was taking place and that the U.S. invasion force might confront much larger numbers than estimated. Other sources placed the number of Japanese on the island at between 2,850 and 3,250, men of whom 1,600 to 2,000 were combat troops, mainly of the 3rd Battalion of the 219th Infantry Regiment, commanded by Colonel Suesada Shimizu.[15] Krueger therefore sent a reconnaissance group on PT boats to the island on June 21. Landing on the east coast, they stayed for two days. They did not find evidence of large numbers of Japanese and were able to pinpoint the main Japanese defenses near Kamiri. They discovered that the trail from the Kamiri area could not immediately be used by heavy vehicles. More important, they found a four-hundred-foot break in the reef near Kamiri. This confirmed what the planners had concluded, that despite the Japanese defenses being concentrated near Kamiri airfield, the landings should be made there. Once the landings had been made, the airfield could be seized quickly, allowing construction crews to begin repairing the field in preparation to receive an Australian fighter squadron. In addition, a landing there would isolate the Japanese defenders further down the coast.[16]

MacArthur had suggested that elements of the 6th Division, then still fighting in the Sarmi area, be withdrawn to conduct the Cyclone operation. Krueger disagreed and convinced General Headquarters instead to use the 158th RCT, comprising the 158th

Infantry and the 147th Field Artillery Battalion, commanded by Brigadier General Patrick. This comprised a total of 7,415 combat troops but also had more than 6,000 service and construction personnel. The fears of a large Japanese contingent on the island led Krueger to alert the 503rd Parachute Infantry Regiment, then at Hollandia, to stand by as the main reserve force, as well as the 34th Regiment, at Biak.[17] The caution as to the numbers of the enemy was in direct contrast to the underestimation of Japanese forces elsewhere in New Guinea and would result in bringing in the paratroops early, with near-disastrous results. However, these fears led to the heaviest preinvasion air and naval bombardment in the Southwest Pacific Theater at that time.

Much of the aerial preparation for the Noemfoor operation had already been done in support of Biak. Throughout June, the 3rd Bombardment Group had struck at targets at the Manokwari, Jeymon, and Samate airfields near the tip of the Vogelkop Peninsula as well as Noemfoor. On June 16, forty-five B-25s, followed by another flight escorted by P-38s, destroyed most of the remaining Japanese planes at Manokwari airfield. The raids on targets in the Vogelkop continued throughout the last week of June. No Japanese fighter aircraft were reported after June 22. On June 31, A-20 pilots from the 3rd Bombardment Wing claimed to have destroyed 107 small Japanese oceangoing craft, mostly luggers used to transport troops. For the immediate preinvasion attack, planes from the Fifth were joined by heavy bombers from the Thirteenth Air Force, then in the process of deploying the bulk of its operations west from the Solomon Islands. On July 1, eighty-four B-24s and forty-eight medium bombers struck Kamiri airfield and the adjacent defenses. On D-day, in support of the landings, thirty-three B-24s and twenty-one medium bombers targeted the beach and adjacent ridgelines with 500-pound bombs.[18]

The naval force to support the landing was equally impressive. There were no serious concerns that the Japanese navy might intervene in any way. The failure of the Kon operation and more recently, in the central Pacific, the disaster in the Philippine Sea had driven the remnants of the Combined Fleet to harbor either in the Philippines or in Japan. Kinkaid had designated Rear Admiral William Fechtler as operations commander of Task Force 77. He divided his force into three groups. Admiral Russell Berkey, in general support, had one heavy cruiser, two light cruisers, and ten destroyers. Fechtler commanded the main force comprising fifteen destroyers, eight LSTs, eight LCTs, and fourteen LCIs. The third group was an LCT-LCM unit with three APCs, five LCTs, and forty LCMs manned by the 543rd Engineer Boat and Shore Regiment personnel. Later they would be joined by Commodore J. A. Collins's (RAN) Task Force 74–75, which had been active off Biak, and this would add the firepower of three more cruisers. The main body and support ships began deploying at 5 A.M. on D-day, and at H-hour −80 began a systematic bombardment of the Kamiri beach region. The Australian heavy cruiser *Australia* fired 288 rounds of eight-inch shells while the three light cruisers pumped 1,500 rounds of 4.7-inch and five-inch shells in the restricted beach region. Naval gunfire was suspended at H −15, allowing the air force to bomb the beach and ridgelines.[19]

There was no opposition to the 5 A.M. landing by the 1st and 2nd Battalions. The greatest difficulty was presented by the reef, which caused a number of landing craft to hang up. Amphtracs proved valuable during the landing and immediately afterward, giving armored support to the troops and carrying supplies forward. The tremendous aerial and naval bombardment had destroyed the bulk of the Japanese defenses, and many of the defenders were obviously shell-shocked by it. The 2nd Battalion, advancing to the east, encountered approximately forty Japanese, who fled from a cave. They were so disoriented that they milled around with little awareness of what was happening and were easy targets for the advancing troops. Tanks were landed at 8:50 A.M. and added their firepower to the infantry's. The 3rd Battalion landed and took up the responsibility of securing the beachhead while the two assault units moved east and south toward the Kamiri River. By late afternoon the airfield was secured and the perimeter had been expanded to 3,000 yards wide and 800 yards deep. LCMs began unloading trucks and bulldozers, although many of them had to be towed in after being off-loaded at the reef. Soon temporary causeways were constructed, and by the end of the day most of the heavy equipment had been landed. Despite the fear of snipers, engineers of the 543rd began repairing the airfield even before the arrival of Australian and U.S. engineering battalions. At the end of July 2, Patrick had 7,000 men on shore. There had been little resistance, the most serious being artillery attacks during the morning. The casualties were amazingly light—only 3 men killed and 19 wounded. A total of 115 Japanese had been killed and 3 prisoners taken.[20]

One of the prisoners under interrogation told of three thousand men who had arrived on the twenty-fifth to reinforce the garrison. Although this later proved untrue, it confirmed for Patrick that he still had at least four thousand Japanese in the interior to deal with. He therefore requested that Krueger bring in the reserves immediately, thus contributing, though not intentionally, to the tragedy of the 503rd airdrop. Krueger responded by ordering the paratroops to prepare for the assault. The 1st Battalion, led by Colonel George Jones, was loaded onto forty-one C-47s of the 317th Troop Carrier Group early on the morning of the third. Patrick sent messages to Alamo Force headquarters recommending that the transport planes fly over the field in single file in order to avoid casualties from the troopers' dropping onto obstacles along the narrow airstrip. This suggestion was never relayed to Jones or the pilots. Apparently no one at higher headquarters believed the suggestion to be important. The leading planes, flying two abreast, arrived over the field at approximately 10 A.M. Amazingly, the first two planes came in at only 175 feet. The next eight pulled up to the planned 400 feet. Many of the paratroops landed on vehicles parked along the runway, while others landed on tree stumps. By the time all the planes had finished dropping the 739 men of the 1st Battalion, the unit had suffered 72 casualties. Thirty-one of the paratroops suffered severe fractures. Upon being advised of this, Krueger ordered all vehicles cleared from the drop zone and the next day planes in single file should line up on the runway and the troops should jump at 400 feet. Even with these precautions, there were still many casualties on the fourth. The reinforcement by air caused a total of 128 casualties, of which 59 were serious. This represented a rate of almost 9 percent. Viewing this, Jones convinced Patrick to bring in the rest of the regiment by water. Bad weather prevented the 2nd Battalion from joining up until July 11.[21]

The 1st Battalion of the 523rd immediately took over responsibility for the defenses around Kamiri airfield, allowing the 2nd and 3rd Battalions of the 158th to extend the perimeter eastward. On the fourth, Kornasoren airfield was occupied without opposition. The 1st Battalion of the 158th pushed south, crossing the Kamiri River and occupying the village before moving on to a large Japanese garden area. The trail southwest from there joined the main road from Kamiri to Namber and passed along the southern slope of Hill 201. Fear that the Japanese might have occupied the hill in force caused the battalion commander to halt the forward movement on the fourth. He prepared a double envelopment, routing a Japanese platoon in the swampy area of the garden. He brought up heavy mortars and had the 105 mm guns of the 147th Battalion register in on the hill. Early in the morning of the fifth, the Japanese attacked along the southern and southeastern perimeter. Mortar and artillery fire was called down, and the attackers were cut to pieces. Those who did get through the barrage were trapped behind a long log fence. The fighting soon became a series of small-scale Japanese suicide attacks. In an hour the attack was over. Immediately patrols were sent out and found that the attacking force had amounted to 350 to 400 men of the Japanese 219th Infantry and 150 armed Formosan workers. There were 200 dead Japanese in the vicinity of the perimeter. Later discovery of further dead and wounded and those captured indicated that almost all the attackers had become casualties.[22]

This was the last serious coordinated offensive undertaken by the Japanese. However, the action against the large remnant of Colonel Shimizu's forces was no mere mopping-up detail and would last for almost two months. On July 6, the 3rd Battalion of the 158th was transported in a shore-to-shore operation landing on the north side of the bay at the lower end of Namber airfield. The field was quickly secured. For purposes of pursuit, the island was divided into two sectors. The 158th remained in the north, while the 503rd dealt with the major Japanese resistance in the central and southern part. By mid-July, it was estimated that Shimizu had at least 500 men concentrated near Hill 670. Contact was made with this group on the thirteenth, but by the time the 1st Battalion reorganized to attack the hill three days later, the Japanese had retreated into the heavily forested regions. Contact was lost until the twenty-third, when patrols found them four miles northwest of Inasi village, on the shore of the east lagoon. After skirmishing, the Japanese once again slipped away, and most retreated toward Hill 308. However, they were not discovered near there until August 10. The 3rd Battalion, supported by artillery, then advanced on the hill, while the 1st Battalion moved south to block any escape. Nevertheless, Shimizu once again led his followers, now reduced to 200 men, around the block to move toward Pakriki on the south coast. Two heavy firefights on the seventeenth broke the resistance of the main group. Forty-three prisoners were taken after these engagements. Patrols continued throughout the rest of the month, killing and capturing a few more stragglers. Krueger then declared the operation over on August 31. The entire campaign had cost 67 killed and 43 wounded, mostly during the patrols of late July and August. The Japanese lost an estimated 1,730 men killed, and 186 had been captured. Five hundred fifty-two Korean prisoners were released, and 403 Japanese slaves, the pitiful remnant of those earlier brought to the island, were freed.[23]

The immediate results of Operation Cyclone were disappointing. The reef line presented an ongoing supply problem, and even after naval demolition teams blasted a slot in the reef off Kamiri and built an LST jetty, there was a shipping backlog that delayed the off-loading of equipment and personnel. The Japanese airstrips at first proved of little use. The Kamiri airfield was poorly surfaced with sand and clay. Work on the field began on D-day and on the fifth the 1874th Engineer Aviation Battalion began a twenty-four-hour-a-day schedule to make it usable. The coral resurfacing was completed in ten days, and the airfield was ready for C-47s by July 16. On the twenty-first, P-40s of the 78th RAAF Wing flew in, to be joined by ground elements of the 77th Wing after the twenty-fourth. Eventually, in August, RAAF Bostons and Beaufighters were stationed there. Namber could handle transports, but to use it would require a difficult supply trip from Kamiri. Whitehead decided against trying to make it into a fully functioning fighter-bomber field. Kornasoren airfield, according to one observer, "was only a location," and bringing it up to standards would normally have taken weeks. However, General Headquarters notified the island command of the need to station fifty P-38s there by July 25 so they could support operations against Halmahera. The RAAF 6th Construction Wing and combat troops pressed into service met the deadline. The 55th U.S. Air Group was flown in to Kornasoren in time for the Sansapor operation.[24]

At the same time as planning for the Noemfoor operation was under way, MacArthur and his staff were looking ahead to the seizure of territory for airfields in the Vogelkop Peninsula as a preliminary to an invasion of Halmahera. A further reason for interest in the Vogelkop was the presence there of petroleum. Before the war, the Dutch, and later the Japanese, had done little to exploit the reserves. However, as early as 1942 planners in Washington had looked at the region and projected production of as much as 16,000 barrels a day if construction crews could be brought into the Klamono District. If the oil field could be brought into production, it would save much time and effort needed to bring oil over the long supply route to Australia. The project had progressed by early 1944 to the creation of the Engineering Petroleum Production Depot, located in California. By then it had 3,300 engineering and construction workers with experience in oil production. In February, MacArthur requested that the unit be transferred to the southwest Pacific by November since at that time he projected an invasion of the Vogelkop by October. Nothing came of these plans since a restudy indicated that even with a maximum commitment of men and resources, the field could not be put into operation until mid-1946. In July, the Joint Chiefs canceled the oil project.[25]

The speed of the occupation of Japanese positions along the northwest coast caused General Headquarters to advance the assault on the Vogelkop. On June 6 General Headquarters ordered Alamo Force to begin planning for operations against a main Japanese base at Sorong and also against Weigo Island, sixty miles northwest of Sorong. The target date suggested was July 25. Krueger's staff had completed preliminary plans for the operation that would use most of the 6th Division when, on the twentieth, General Headquarters reversed the order. Photo reconnaissance had indicated that these areas left much to be desired for the construction of airfields. Instead, it was decided that the area between Cape Sansapor and the village of Mar, approximately seventy miles east of Sorong, would be more appropriate. Krueger objected that those areas, according to the Air Force, also did not have good locations for the airfields that had to be constructed. MacArthur, who wanted the operation to begin as soon as possible, nevertheless authorized a reconnaissance of the area by a scouting party. It was landed near Mar and spent the next week investigating the area. The party found a number of places suitable for airfields and sub-

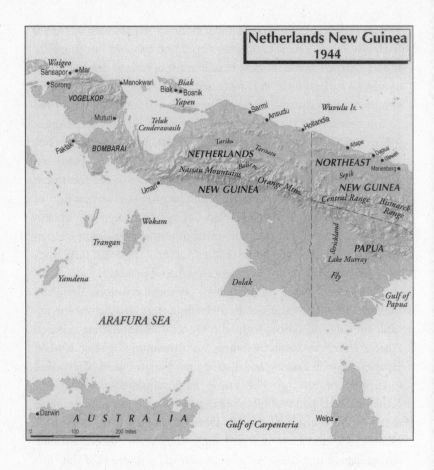

Netherlands New Guinea
1944

mitted its report.[26] By that time General Headquarters, without seeing the report, had already decided to occupy the area. Plans were hastily made at Alamo Force headquarters at Hollekang to use only one RCT of the 6th Division. Representatives of the three services met on July 8 to finalize the details, and the date of Operation Typhoon was set for the thirtieth.

There were several reasons for Krueger's initial reluctance to mount an attack on the Vogelkop. The area was rugged and, as he noted, "poorly adapted for military purposes." The coastal plain in the north was limited in size. The Tamrau mountain range was at most only twenty miles inland, and in some places the hills came down almost to the sea. Dense rain forest covered most of the region, though in places there were swamps and areas of high kunai grass. There were few villages, the most important being Sorong, at the northwest tip of the bird's head, and Manokwari, located on the northeast corner, which had been the principal government and trade centers for the Dutch prior to the war. The only good roads were in the vicinity of these towns. Most of the villages were linked only by native trails. Sorong and Manokwari had become major centers for the Japanese soon after the beginning of the war. Manokwari was the headquarters of the Second Area Army as well as its major component, the 35th Division. Before the abortive Kon operation, General Anami, commanding the Second Area Army, had planned to send the 35th Division from Sorong and Halmahera to Biak. The failure of that operation combined with that of the A-Go plan meant that the Japanese did not have a sufficient naval force to cover such a movement. It was then decided to concentrate the division at Manokwari, and much of the division was transported there by barge. This was hardly a wise move, since the area there did not have a large supply of natural food and the 12,000 to 15,000 men there had soon all but exhausted the warehoused supplies. The dominance of the air and sea lanes by the Allies meant that little could be expected from Halmahera or Sorong. Thus, just before the beginning of Operation Typhoon, the 35th Division was ordered, beginning on July 1, to move back to Sorong over native trails. The task was expected to take forty days, but the available food supplies meant that there were rations for only half that period. As they approached Kor village, they found their way blocked by the Typhoon troops, and they were forced inland to try to avoid the perimeter by then established by the U.S. 6th Division. A new organization, the 1st Independent Brigade, was created mainly of service troops to protect Manokwari and the adjacent coastal areas as the headquarters and covering troops of the Second Area Army left on July 3 to move 150 miles overland to Windehsi village on the narrow neck of land separating Vogelkop from the rest of New Guinea. There the Japanese could hope for more food from native plants. Despite the movement of the Japanese toward both the east and west, Krueger believed that there were an estimated 15,000 troops in the Vogelkop, some of which, he believed, could be used to oppose any landing.[27]

During the week prior to the landing at Mar, the Fifth Air Force avoided making large-scale attacks on the beach and inland areas near there. Rather, Whitehead concentrated on shipping and land targets on Halmahera. The 498th Bombardment Squadron flew two missions a day, targeting shipping around Halmahera, and other squadrons struck at Amboina and the area from Cape Sansapor to Sorong. The result was one small freighter sunk, two others set on fire, nine luggers and six barges destroyed, and a host of small vessels strafed. The Fifth also made several attacks against the airfields in the vicinity of Manokwari. RAAF P-40s, flying from Biak, also struck targets of opportunity in the Vogelkop. On D-day, B-25s were on station to provide air cover for the attacking forces. However, General Sibert determined that heavy bombardment of the beach was not necessary.

The Typhoon attack force, made up of two RCTs of the 6th Division plus the 6th Cavalry Reconnaissance Troop, was loaded on ships of Task Force 77, commanded by Fechtler. These included twenty-four LSTs, fifteen LCIs, five APDs, and nineteen destroyers. A covering force of three cruisers and nine destroyers accompanied the main body. The fleet took a circuitous route, hoping to lull the Japanese into believing that Sorong was the target. This show of might, while impressive, was not necessary since it was determined that a preliminary bombardment was not needed. The landing, begun at 7 A.M. on July 30, was uneventful, as the lead elements of the 1st Regiment met no opposition. The 2nd Battalion landed on the west of Red Beach, while the 1st was on the left. Troops of both pushed inland immediately. The terrain in front of the 1st proved difficult, but elsewhere the movement inland was rapid. The only Japanese encountered were three unarmed Japanese, who were killed by a 2nd Battalion patrol. The 3rd Battalion, landing later, quickly moved west along the coast to the Wewe River, one and a half miles away. The artillery was onshore by noon, as was the 836th Engineer Battalion, which immediately began building roads and a bivouac area. The major problem was supply, as the loose sand made the use of wheeled vehicles difficult. A planned adjunct to the main landing was the occupation of two off-shore islands. The 6th Cavalry Reconnaissance Troop and some men from the 1st Battalion of the 63rd RCT effected a landing on Middleburg Island, and later a small group occupied Amsterdam Island. On the thirty-first, troops of the 1st Battalion of the 1st left the mouth of the Wewe for Green Beach at Cape Sansapor, five miles away, in a shore-to-shore operation. There was no opposition. The natives who had been interviewed earlier had been correct: the small Japanese garrison there had been withdrawn.[28]

Patrolling began immediately, and finally some Japanese were found. On August 3, 92 Japanese and Formosan wounded were captured in a hospital near Cape Opmarai. Elsewhere, 23 more Japanese were captured and 4 were killed. Patrols of the 63rd ranged as far east as Kor village, eleven miles to the east, and those of the 1st reached the Mega River, thirty miles from Red Beach. By mid-August, large numbers of Japanese were reported moving toward Kor from the east. Although the Japanese tried to avoid combat, the various clashes in the area resulted in 156 Japanese killed and 42 captured. Elsewhere, by the end of the month, the 1st Battalion killed 197 and captured 154 and the Reconnaissance Troop killed 42. The loss of more than 500 men had for all practical purposes destroyed what remained of the Japanese 35th Division.[29]

Losses by the 6th Division during Typhoon had been minimal. However, this would change as scrub typhus was diagnosed early in August. By the end of the month, 9 soldiers had died and 121 men were hospitalized. Strict antityphus measures were established, and regularized evacuation by air and sea took the most serious cases to base hospitals at Hollandia and Australia. Nevertheless, a total of 275 persons were diagnosed definitively with typhus, and 530 with high fever were suspected of having the disease. Despite the epidemic, work on building the airfields continued with hardly any interruption.[30]

Brigadier General Earl Barnes of the Thirteenth Air Force arrived at Mar on D-day and surveyed the area for an airfield site. Despite much of the area being forested and swampy in places, he finally selected a position just west of Red Beach. The 836th Aviation Engineer Battalion and later the 617th Engineer Base Company began work on the field. By mid-August, most of a 5,000-foot runway was completed. A crippled B-24 made an emergency landing there on the fourteenth. Later the runway was extended by an additional thousand feet. Middleburg Island was considered a better locale for a fighter strip, and that field was ready for use by the end of the month. The first part of August witnessed the mass movement of 6,500 men of the Thirteenth Air Force, many from as far away as New Caledonia, to the Sansapor area. The 347th Fighter Group, the 419th Night Fighter Squadron, and the ground echelon were in place at Mar by the nineteenth. In early September, the 18th Fighter Group and the 418th Night Fighter Squadron arrived at Middleburg.[31]

The final offensive of the long New Guinea campaign was highly productive. The bases at Mar and Sansapor and on the offshore islands had been secured with minimal losses. With the completion of the two airfields and the movement of planes to them, combined with the airfields on Biak and Noemfoor, the Japanese ground forces at Sorong and Manokweri were surrounded. The considerable garrisons of the Second Area Army were effectively isolated. Some Japanese escaped to Ambon, Ceram, and the Celebes, and a few made the difficult overland trek across the Vogelkop to minor bases on the Bomberai Peninsula. Most, however, as with their counterparts on New Britain, remained quiescent until the end of the war.

EPILOGUE

The occupation of Sansapor-Mar, which secured the isolation of the Japanese in the Vogelkop Peninsula, marked the end of active offensive operations by MacArthur in New Guinea. He had come to Australia in March 1942 hoping to find enough men and matériel that would enable a quick offensive against the Japanese. Instead he found a shattered small air force, inadequate naval units, and a tiny Australian army made up almost entirely of untried reservists. The bulk of the regular Australian army was still in North Africa, where it was acting as a bulwark against German advances in the desert. MacArthur faced a foe that had in a few short months captured Malaya, Burma, the Philippines, and the Dutch East Indies, and from their base at Rabaul in New Britain was threatening Australia. His major task from the beginning was to convince his superiors in the United States and Britain to provide him with an adequate force, first to defend Australia and then to take the offensive. He was hampered in this by the Europe-centered policy of the United States, which would continue to shift the bulk of supplies and men across the Atlantic. He also faced the active opposition of the Navy, whose chief wanted to relegate his theater of operations to a secondary role, placing the main emphasis upon Admiral Nimitz's central Pacific operations. This opposition would continue until July 1944 and meant that MacArthur would not receive the kind of naval support he not only wanted but at first needed.

Despite these problems, MacArthur succeeded far beyond the expectations of his many critics. From the earliest months he maintained that the first line of defense for Australia was New Guinea. This proved extraordinarily difficult, since in 1942 the Japanese had aerial superiority and the initiative, even threatening to seize Port Moresby, the major Allied base in New Guinea. The Australians bought time with their heroic defense of the Kokoda Trail. The first offensive against the Japanese at Buna showed clearly the inadequacies of the Allied forces. Without a significant naval presence or even adequate artillery support, they were forced to fight a grinding battle of attrition before securing that vital area on the north coast of New Guinea. MacArthur, who by then had been receiving driblets of supplies and men, could say with reasonable conviction that he would fight no more Bunas.

One key to his success was his selection of senior officers. When he arrived in Australia, he inherited many with whom he ultimately disagreed. He could not replace them immediately, but eventually he had competent subordinates whom he trusted implicitly. Some of these, "the Bataan Gang," he brought with him in his escape from the Philippines. Chief among these were his chief of staff, the acerbic Richard Sutherland, and his G-2, Charles Willoughby. A continuing problem at first was the commanders of the Allied naval forces. MacArthur and Admirals Leary and Carpender did not mesh well, partly as a result of the long-simmering disagreement with Admiral Ernest King, the Chief of Naval Operations. However, when Thomas Kinkaid was appointed to head the Seventh Fleet, most of the friction disappeared, though MacArthur could never obtain the naval support he felt he should have. More important, with the assignment of Daniel Barbey to command the amphibious operations, he obtained one of the most innovative and supportive commanders. MacArthur's brilliant strategy of bypassing Japanese strong points would not have been possible without the near genius of Barbey and later William Fechtler.

One command problem MacArthur never fully solved, although he created a system that modified it, was the position of General Blamey, who was in charge of the Allied land forces. It is obvious that from the beginning MacArthur did not want an Australian to command U.S. troops. However, at first he could do nothing about it. He had to depend largely upon Australian troops for the first year, although he did not fully appreciate their value. In this he did them a great disservice, since fighting normally in the rough, heavily forested interior, they had done everything he asked of them. The Australian leaders, such as Generals Savige, Vasey, and Wootten, were superior to most of the U.S. commanders. MacArthur's nativism can be seen in the fact that no Australian was given a high position on his general staff. As more U.S. troops arrived, MacArthur partially solved his problem by creating another organization called Alamo Force, which contained the bulk of the U.S. Sixth Army which operated directly under his command, thus bypassing Blamey. After mid-1943, the Australian troops were given secondary roles and Alamo Force became responsible for the many amphibious operations. A combination of factors, not just MacArthur's opinion, reduced the contributions of the Australian troops during the latter stages of the campaign. A need to reduce the cost of the war led the Australian political leaders to cut the size of the army. Thus the war under any circumstances would devolve onto the growing U.S. force. As MacArthur's attention became more concentrated on the Philippines, he allowed Blamey and his subordinates latitude to attack the remaining concentrations of Japanese on New Guinea, New Britain, and Bougainville. These were not essential to ultimate victory, but they allowed the Australians to feel themselves a valued part of the war effort.

To command Alamo Force, MacArthur chose a sixty-two-year-old who, prior to the war, had been one of the senior army generals. At the time of his appointment, General Krueger commanded the Third Army and had resigned himself to never commanding an army in the field. Krueger proved to be a staunch supporter of MacArthur and one of the best U.S. Army commanders. MacArthur and his staff would work out the overall strategy and issue general orders to Krueger, who would then, in consultation with the Navy and Air Force, work out the general tactical plans. He, like Sutherland, was not universally liked by his subordinates, but both performed fully to MacArthur's expectations. Another senior commander was Robert Eichelberger, considered by MacArthur to be the commander who could rescue what he believed to be faltering offensives. Eichelberger replaced General Harding at Buna and General Fuller at Biak. Each of these affairs was partially caused by a major problem that was never solved during the campaigns: faulty intelligence. Although neither relief was probably justified, Eichelberger carried out his assignment fully. He was rewarded in September 1944 by being given command of the newly formed Eighth Army, which would be fleshed out in time for the Philippines campaign.

The greatest change in MacArthur's attitude was in his relations with and appreciation of the Air Force. He was vocal in his criticism of its early performance, overlooking its lack of planes and equipment. He also did not like its first commander, George Brett. All this changed with the arrival of Kenney to take over the Fifth Air Force. Kenney became one of MacArthur's closest confidants and taught him that, given the proper equipment, he could destroy Japanese airpower and also support any planned offensive. Although perhaps exaggerating what airpower could accomplish, he largely lived up to his boasts. As soon as MacArthur's command began to receive more and better planes, the Japanese, at their great forward base of

Rabaul, were systematically attacked and ultimately isolated without air or naval protection. Each of the advances up the coast of New Guinea was planned largely to provide airfields to support further amphibious operations. In one of the most significant air operations of the Pacific war, in the Battle of the Bismarck Sea, an entire invasion flotilla was annihilated by Fifth Air Force planes. The Fifth Air Force, with more advanced planes, destroyed Japanese navy and army airpower at Lae, Wewak, Biak, and Manokweri.

In the year following Buna, where the 32nd Division had to fight through swamps without adequate air or naval support, MacArthur received considerable amounts of supplies and equipment of all types. Although he and Barbey never believed they had enough landing craft, they had available increasing numbers of all types, which enabled MacArthur to plan and execute his long-range bypass operations. The Seventh Fleet, although small by comparison to Nimitz's blue-water fleet, was more than adequate to support the landing operations. By early 1944, each of the major landings had the support of a number of destroyers and many U.S. and Australian cruisers. By the time of the Vogelkop operation, Krueger had available nine U.S. and four Australian infantry divisions and a host of supporting air, engineering, and land elements.

As the Allies' power increased, that of the Japanese suffered a succession of major losses, both in the central Pacific and in MacArthur's theater. Chief among the former were the Solomon's land and sea battles and the advance of Nimitz's forces across Micronesia, culminating for the Japanese in the disastrous Philippine Sea engagement. In the southwest Pacific, the attacks on Rabaul had rendered that once great base impotent. Without naval or air support, Japanese Generals Imamura and Anami became powerless to halt MacArthur's various offensives. Japanese total battle casualties can only be guessed at but probably exceeded 50,000 killed during the campaign. Those who were wounded or who died of sickness and starvation cannot even be estimated. With each succeeding landing the Japanese garrisons in New Guinea became even more isolated. The nearly 95,000 Japanese on New Britain, concentrated mainly near Rabaul, became a nonfactor in the war. General Adachi could not defend Aitape and Hollandia even though he had almost 55,000 men. His late attack on the U.S. forces along the Driniumor River was an exercise in futility that lost him most of the men in his best divisions. With the occupation of Biak and Sansapor, a further estimated 25,000 Japanese were rendered ineffective in the Manokwari region of the Vogelkop Peninsula.

Even MacArthur's harshest critics will grant that his overall strategy in the two-year campaign to secure the 1,500-mile move up the coast of New Guinea was successful, at a cost of fewer men killed than were lost in the one central Pacific battle for Iwo Jima. The 500-mile move up the coast to secure Hollandia was a particularly brilliant idea, well executed by Alamo Force. MacArthur had begun his operations to secure Australia in 1942, and as his means of confronting the Japanese improved, he moved quickly from one victory to another. From the beginning his ultimate goal was to return to the Philippines, which he considered absolutely necessary to achieve final victory over the Japanese. Despite the strenuous opposition of the Navy and his political detractors, MacArthur, after a face-to-face meeting with President Roosevelt and Admiral Nimitz on July 26–27, 1944, in Hawaii, left the meeting convinced that he had received permission to invade not only the southern Philippine Islands but also Luzon. He had already instructed his and Krueger's staff to prepare plans for this. The long-drawn-out campaign for New Guinea was finished by August 1944. The axis of the attack for the Sixth and the newly formed Eighth Army was now shifted toward the north to carry out MacArthur's promise, made in the dark days of March 1942, that he would return to the Philippines.

NOTES

CHAPTER 1: OFFENSIVE PREPARATIONS

1. Harry A. Gailey, *MacArthur Strikes Back, Decision at Buna: New Guinea 1942–1943* (Novato, Calif.: Presidio Press, 2000), Chapter 4.

2. Samuel Milner, *The United States Army in World War II, the War in the Pacific: Victory in Papua* (Washington, D.C.: Office of the Chief of Military History, 1957), p. 370.

3. Cited in D. Clayton James, *The Years of MacArthur*, vol. 2, *1941–1945* (Boston: Houghton Mifflin Co., 1975), p. 218.

4. Cited in ibid., p. 219.

5. Ibid; Gailey, *MacArthur*, pp. 20–21.

6. Ibid., p. 311.

7. Ibid., p. 307.

8. Thomas B. Buell, *Master of Sea Power, A Biography of Fleet Admiral Ernest J. King* (Boston: Little, Brown & Co., 1980), pp. 197 and 300–301; Douglas MacArthur, *Reminiscences* (Greenwich, Conn.: Crest Books, 1965), p. 172; ibid., p. 284.

9. James, *The Years of MacArthur*, pp. 226–227.

10. Blamey to MacArthur, November 19, 1942, USAFPAC Correspondence, Allied Landing Forces, MacArthur Memorial Archives (MMA), Norfolk, Va., Box 6, Folder 1.

11. James, *The Years of MacArthur*, p. 239.

12. Ibid., p. 311.

13. Gailey, *MacArthur*, pp. 42–43.

14. Quoted in Samuel Eliot Morison, *History of United States Naval Operations in World War II,* vol. 6, *Breaking the Bismarcks Barrier, 22 July 1942–1 May 1944* (Boston: Little, Brown & Co., 1950), p. 96.

15. Paolo E. Coletta, "Daniel Barbey: Amphibious Warfare Expert," in *We Shall Return! MacArthur's Commanders and the Defeat of Japan, 1942–1945,* ed. William M. Leary (Lexington, Ky.: University Press of Kentucky, 1988), pp. 214–215.

16. Ibid., p. 215; James, *The Years of MacArthur,* p. 311.

17. Gailey, *MacArthur,* p. 191.

18. Wesley F. Craven and James L. Cate, *The Army Air Forces in World War II,* vol. 4, *The Pacific: Guadalcanal to Saipan* (Chicago: University of Chicago Press, 1950), pp. 114–115; Gailey, pp. 105–106.

19. Gailey, *MacArthur,* p. 19.

20. Walter Krueger, *From Down Under to Nippon: The Story of the Sixth Army in World War II* (Washington, D.C.; Zenger Publishing Co., 1979), pp. 5–6.

21. Ibid., p. 10.

22. D. M. Horner, "Blamey and MacArthur, The Problem of Coalition Warfare," in *We Shall Return! MacArthur's Commanders and the Defeat of Japan,* ed. William M. Leary (Lexington, Ky.: University Press of Kentucky, 1988).

23. Jay Luvaas, *Dear Miss Em: General Eichelberger's War in the Pacific, 1942–1945* (Westport, Conn.: Greenward Press, 1972), p. 30.

24. Horner, "Blamey and MacArthur," p. 41.

25. Gailey, *MacArthur,* p. 77.

26. Horner, "Blamey and MacArthur," p. 41.

CHAPTER 2: THE AUSTRALIANS DEFEND WAU

1. Peter Ryan, *Fear Drive My Feet* (Melbourne, Australia: Melbourne University Press, 1959), p. viii.

2. Allan Walker, *Australia in the War of 1939–1945,* ser. 5, vol. 3, *The Island Campaigns* (Canberra, Australia: Australian War Memorial, 1962), p. 144.

3. Ryan, *Fear,* p. viii.

4. Walker, *Australia,* p. 131.

5. Ibid., p. 137.

6. Ibid., p. 133.

7. Ibid., p. 126.

8. Dudley McCarthy, *Australia in the War of 1939–1945,* ser. 1, vol. 5, *South-West Pacific Area—First Year, Kokoda to Wau* (Canberra, Australia, Australian War Memorial, 1959), pp. 534–536.

9. Ibid., p. 538.

10. Ibid., pp. 540–544.

11. Author's interview with John Donegan, Palo Alto, Calif., December 2002.

12. Craven and Cate, *The Army Air Forces,* p. 141.

13. Ibid., pp. 136–137.

14. Ibid., p. 137.
15. Gailey, *MacArthur,* p. 232; Henry I. Shaw, Jr., and Douglas Kane, *History of U.S. Marine Corps Operations in World War II,* vol. 2, *Isolation of Rabaul* (Washington, D.C.: Historical Branch, U.S. Marine Corps, 1963), p. 10.
16. Craven and Cate, *The Army Air Forces,* p. 136.
17. Cited in McCarthy, *Australia,* p. 575.
18. Ibid., p. 545.
19. Ibid., pp. 546–547.
20. Ibid., p. 546.
21. Walker, *Australia,* pp. 132–133.
22. Hugh Buggy, *Pacific Victory: A Short History of Australia's Part in the War Against Japan* (Canberra, Australia, Ministry of Information, n.d.), pp. 217–220.
23. McCarthy, *Australia,* p. 576.
24. Ibid., p. 556.
25. Ibid., p. 563.
26. Craven and Cate, *The Army Air Forces,* p. 137.
27. McCarthy, *Australia,* p. 568.
28. Walker, *Australia,* p. 134.
29. Buggy, *Pacific Victory,* pp. 220–221.
30. McCarthy, *Australia,* p. 581.
31. Ibid., pp. 579–581; Ryan, *Fear Drive My Feet,* p. viii.
32. McCarthy, *Australia,* pp. 586–587.

CHAPTER 3: THE BISMARCK SEA BATTLE AND CARTWHEEL PRELIMINARIES

1. United States Strategic Bombing Survey (Pacific), *The Allied Campaign Against Rabaul* (Washington, D.C.: Naval Analysis Division, 1946), pp. 10–11.
2. Louis Morton, *The U.S. Army in World War II, Strategy and Command: The First Two Years* (Washington, D.C.: Office of the Chief of Military History, 1962), p. 542.
3. James, *The Years of MacArthur,* p. 864.
4. Craven and Cate, *The Army Air Forces,* pp. 138–139.
5. Morison, *Bismarcks Barrier,* p. 55.
6. Paul S. Dull, *A Battle History of the Imperial Japanese Navy (1941–1945)* (Annapolis, Md.: Naval Institute Press, 1978), pp. 279–280; ibid.
7. Morison, *Bismarcks Barrier,* pp. 56–58; and Craven and Cate, *The Army Air Force,* p. 145.
8. Craven and Cate, *The Army Air Forces,* pp. 148–149.
9. Cited in Morison, *Bismarcks Barrier,* p. 60.
10. Author's interview with John Donegan, December 2002.
11. Garrett Middlebrook, *Air Combat at 20 Feet* (Fort Worth, Tex.: Global Group, 1989), p. 113.
12. Morison, *Bismarcks Barrier,* p. 62.

13. Craven and Cate, *The Army Air Forces,* p. 149.

14. James, *The Years of MacArthur,* p. 297; Douglas MacArthur, *Reminiscences* (Greenwich, Conn.: Crest Books, 1965), p. 185.

15. D. M. Horner, *Blamey, The Commander in Chief* (St. Leonards, Australia: Allen and Unwin, 1998), pp. 409–414.

16. Ibid., p. 417.

17. McCarthy, *Australia,* p. 577.

18. Gailey, *MacArthur,* pp. 137–139.

19. Coletta, "Daniel Barbey," pp. 214–215.

20. Cited in Horner, *Blamey,* p. 413.

21. William F. McCartney, *The Jungleers: A History of the 41st Infantry Division* (Washington, D.C.: Infantry Journal Press, 1948), p. 51.

22. David Dexter, *Australia in the War of 1939–1945, the New Guinea Offensives* (Canberra, Australia, Australian War Memorial, 1961), p. 97.

23. Ibid.; Walker, *Australia,* p. 146.

24. Buggy, *Pacific Victory,* p. 232; Dexter, *Australia,* p. 125.

25. Dexter, *Australia,* pp. 99–106, 138–139.

26. Buggy, *Pacific Victory,* p. 233.

CHAPTER 4: SALAMAUA-LAE OPERATIONS

1. Francis T. Miller, *History of World War II* (Philadelphia: Universal Book and Bible House, 1945), p. 190.

2. U.S. Strategic Bombing Survey (Pacific), p. 11.

3. George C. Kenney, *General Kenney Reports* (Washington, D.C.: Office of Air Force History, 1987), p. 274.

4. Miller, *History of World War II,* p. 190.

5. Craven and Cate, *The Army Air Forces,* p. 176.

6. Ryan, *Fear Drive My Feet,* p. 241.

7. Craven and Cate, *The Army Air Forces,* pp. 177–178.

8. Ibid., pp. 178–179.

9. Morison, *Bismarcks Barrier,* p. 262.

10. Ibid., p. 259.

11. Craven and Cate, *The Army Air Forces,* p. 185; Kenney, *General Kenney Reports,* pp. 293–294.

12. MacArthur, *Reminiscences,* p. 194.

13. E. F. Aitken, *The Story of the 2/2nd Australian Pioneer Battalion* (Melbourne: 2/2nd Pioneer Battalion Association, 1953), pp. 198–203; Miller, pp. 207–210.

14. Cited in Morison, *Bismarcks Barrier,* p. 260.

15. G. Hermon Gill, *Australia in the War of 1939–1945: Royal Australian Navy, 1942–1945* (Canberra, Australia: Australian War Memorial, 1968), p. 327.

16. Ibid., pp. 328–329; Morison, *Bismarcks Barrier,* pp. 261–264.

17. Morison, *Bismarcks Barrier,* pp. 261–265.

18. R. P. Serle, *The Second Twenty Fourth Australian Infantry Battalion* (Brisbane, Australia: Jacaranda Press, 1963), pp. 253–255; Miller, p. 206.

19. Dexter, *Australia,* p. 354; Walker, *Australia,* p. 275.

20. Dexter, *Australia,* p. 362.

21. Cited in Miller, *History of World War II,* p. 211.

22. Dexter, *Australia,* p. 391.

23. Miller, *History of World War II,* p. 211.

24. Dexter, *Australia,* pp. 350–354.

25. Ibid., pp. 364–368.

26. Buggy, *Pacific Victory,* pp. 234–235.

27. Dexter, *Australia,* p. 325.

28. McCartney, *The Jungleers,* pp. 61–66; Dexter, *Australia,* pp. 316–321.

29. Dexter, *Australia,* p. 324.

30. Ibid., p. 358.

31. Aitken, *2/2nd,* pp. 204–209; Dexter, *Australia,* pp. 377–378.

32. Dexter, *Australia,* p. 372.

33. Ibid., pp. 384–389.

34. Aitken, *2/2nd,* p. 213.

35. Dexter, *Australia,* p. 392.

36. Ibid., p. 401.

CHAPTER 5: THE OCCUPATION OF FINSCHHAFEN

1. James, *The Years of MacArthur,* pp. 328–329.

2. Ryan, *Fear Drive My Feet,* pp. 247–248.

3. Dexter, *Australia,* p. 392.

4. Cited in ibid., p. 405.

5. Serle, *Second Twenty-fourth,* pp. 269–270; ibid., pp. 407–409.

6. Dexter, *Australia,* pp. 414–415.

7. Ibid., pp. 418–423.

8. Ibid., pp. 428–430.

9. Ibid., pp. 437–443.

10. Morison, *Bismarcks Barrier,* p. 270.

11. Cited in Dexter, *Australia,* p. 455.

12. Morison, *Bismarcks Barrier,* pp. 270–271.

13. Dexter, *Australia,* pp. 480–483.

14. Miller, *History of World War II,* pp. 217–218; Buggy, *Pacific Victory,* pp. 251–252.

15. Serle, *Second Twenty-fourth,* pp. 274–275.

16. Dexter, *Australia,* pp. 498–499.

17. Cited in ibid., p. 523.

18. Ibid., pp. 524–525.

19. Ibid., p. 526.

20. Morison, *Bismarcks Barrier,* p. 274.

21. Ibid., pp. 274–275.

22. Buggy, *Pacific Victory,* pp. 254–255.

23. Serle, *Second Twenty-fourth,* p. 276.

24. Ibid., pp. 279–281.

25. Cited in ibid., p. 282.

26. Buggy, *Pacific Victory,* p. 257.

27. Serle, *Second Twenty-fourth,* pp. 285–287.

28. Walker, *Australia,* pp. 193–194.

29. Craven and Cate, *The Army Air Forces,* pp. 190–192.

30. Cited in Dexter, *Australia,* p. 402.

CHAPTER 6: COMMAND RELATIONS

1. James, *The Years of MacArthur,* pp. 331–333.

2. E. B. Potter, *Bull Halsey* (Annapolis, Md.: Naval Institute Press, 1985), pp. 238–239.

3. Harry A. Gailey, *Bougainville, The Forgotten Campaign, 1943–1945* (Lexington, Ky.: The University Press of Kentucky, 1991), p. 42.

4. For the New Georgia operation, see Eric Hammel, *Munda Trail, Turning the Tide Against Japan* (New York: Orion Books, 1989).

5. Gailey, *Bougainville,* pp. 184–185.

6. Bombing Survey, pp. 10–12.

7. Gailey, *MacArthur,* p. 21.

8. James, *The Years of MacArthur,* pp. 330–332.

9. Kenney, *General Kenney Reports,* pp. 312–324; and Craven and Cate, *The Army Air Forces,* pp. 318–321.

10. MacArthur, *Reminiscences,* p. 195.

11. Craven and Cate, *The Army Air Forces,* pp. 324–328; Kenney, pp. 316–323.

12. Harry A. Gailey, *The War in the Pacific: From Pearl Harbor to Tokyo Bay* (Novato, Calif.: Presidio Press, 1995), p. 270.

13. Gerald Wheeler, *Kinkaid of the Seventh Fleet* (Washington, D.C.: Naval Historical Center, 1995), pp. 343–344.

14. Ibid., pp. 344–346.

15. D. M. Horner, *Blamey, the Commander in Chief* (St. Leonards, Australia: Allen and Unwin, 1998) pp. 425–428.

CHAPTER 7: ARAWE AND CAPE GLOUCESTER

1. Henry I. Shaw, Jr., and Douglas T. Kane, *History of U.S. Marine Corps Operations in World War II: Isolation of Rabaul,* vol. 2 (Washington, D.C.: Historical Branch, U.S. Marine Corps, 1963), pp. 300–305.

2. James, *The Years of MacArthur,* pp. 342–343.

3. Morison, *Bismarcks Barrier,* p. 372.

4. Kenney, *General Kenney Reports,* pp. 326–327.

5. Miller, *History of World War II,* pp. 284–285.

6. Ibid., pp. 286–287.

7. Ibid., p. 287.

8. Ibid., p. 288.

9. Shaw and Kane, *Rabaul,* p. 393.

10. Ibid., p. 393.

11. Ibid., p. 394.

12. Ibid., p. 329.

13. Ibid., p. 332.

14. As cited in ibid., p. 322.

15. Shaw and Kane, *Rabaul,* p. 392.

16. Morison, *Bismarcks Barrier,* p. 382.

17. Shaw and Kane, *Rabaul,* pp. 370–373.

18. Miller, *History of World War II,* p. 200.

19. Morison, *Bismarcks Barrier,* p. 386; Craven and Cate, *The Army Air Forces,* pp. 340–341.

20. Cited in Richard Wheeler, *A Special Valor* (New York: Harper & Row, 1983), p. 212.

21. Krueger, *From Down Under,* p. 34.

22. Richard Wheeler, *A Special Valor,* p. 212.

23. Author's interview with Charles Clay, Mission Viejo, Calif., June 23, 2001.

24. Author's interview with Brigadier General Harold Deakin (ret.), Los Altos, Calif., August 25, 1982.

25. Richard Wheeler, *A Special Valor,* p. 214.

26. Burke Davis, *Marine: The Life of Chesty Puller* (New York: Bantam Books, 1962), pp. 175–176.

27. Richard Wheeler, *A Special Valor,* p. 219.

28. Shaw and Kane, *Rabaul,* pp. 388–389.

29. Davis, *Marine,* pp. 180–183.

30. Shaw and Kane, *Rabaul,* pp. 420–423.

31. Richard Wheeler, *A Special Valor,* p. 223.

32. Quoted in ibid., p. 224.

33. Krueger, *From Down Under,* p. 36.

34. Shaw and Kane, *Rabaul,* pp. 430–431.

CHAPTER 8: SAIDOR AND SHAGGY RIDGE

1. Serle, *Second Twenty-fourth,* p. 293.

2. Buggy, *Pacific Victory,* pp. 259–260; Walker, *Australia,* pp. 196–197.

3. Miller, *History of World War II,* pp. 297–298.

4. Eric Bergerud, *Touched with Fire: The Land War in the South Pacific* (New York: Penguin Books, 1997), p. 508.

5. Morison, *Bismarcks Barrier,* pp. 390–391.

6. Krueger, *From Down Under,* p. 40.

7. Miller, *History of World War II,* pp. 299–300.

8. Ibid., pp. 299–300.

9. Walker, *Australia,* pp. 204–205.

10. Craven and Cate, *Army Air Forces,* p. 349.

11. Walker, *Australia,* p. 208.

12. Aitken, *2/2nd,* p. 229.

13. Buggy, *Pacific Victory,* pp. 262–263.

14. Walker, *Australia,* pp. 228–229.

15. Ibid., p. 239.

16. Ibid., p. 213.

17. Ibid., p. 224.

CHAPTER 9: THE ADMIRALTY ISLANDS GAMBIT

1. MacArthur, *Reminiscences,* pp. 203–204.

2. Ibid., p. 203.

3. Edward J. Drea, *MacArthur's Ultra* (Lawrence, Kans.: University Press of Kansas, 1992), p. 101.

4. Ibid., p. 102.

5. Ibid., p. 103.

6. James, *The Years of MacArthur,* p. 381.

7. Morison, *Bismarcks Barrier,* pp. 436–437.

8. Cited in Stephen R. Taaffe, *MacArthur's Jungle War: The 1944 New Guinea Campaign,* (Lawrence, Kan: University Press of Kansas, 1998), p. 61.

9. Miller, *History of World War II,* p. 325.

10. Cited in B. C. Wright, *The 1st Cavalry Division in World War II* (Tokyo: Tappan Printers, 1947), p. 19.

11. Miller, *History of World War II,* p. 331.

12. Ibid.

13. Craven and Cate, *The Army Air Forces,* p. 567.

14. Morison, *Bismarcks Barrier,* p. 442.

15. Wright, *1st Cavalry Division,* pp. 20–22.

16. Taaffe, *MacArthur's Jungle War,* p. 66.

17. Krueger, *From Down Under,* p. 51.

18. Wright, *1st Cavalry Division,* p. 23.

19. Morison, *Bismarcks Barrier,* p. 441

20. Taaffe, *MacArthur's Jungle War,* p. 69.

21. Craven and Cate, *The Army Air Forces,* pp. 567–569.

22. Wright, *1st Cavalry Division,* p. 27.

23. Miller, *History of World War II,* pp. 340–343.

24. Ibid., pp. 347–348.

25. Taaffe, *MacArthur's Jungle War,* pp. 72–73.

26. James, *Years of MacArthur,* pp. 387–389.

27. Potter, *Bull Halsey,* p. 294.

28. Krueger, *From Down Under,* pp. 54–55.

CHAPTER 10: HOLLANDIA: THE GREAT LEAP
FORWARD

1. Robert Ross Smith, *United States Army in World War II: The Approach to the Philippines* (Washington: Center of Military History, 1996), p. 16.

2. Samuel Eliot Morison, *History of United States Naval Operations in World War II,* vol. 8, *New Guinea and the Marianas* (Boston: Little, Brown & Co., 1962), p. 67.

3. Drea, *Ultra,* pp. 106–107.

4. Taaffe, *MacArthur's Jungle War,* p. 78.

5. MacArthur, *Reminiscences,* p. 205.

6. Kenney, *General Kenney Reports,* pp. 376–377.

7. Drea, *Ultra,* p. 109.

8. Kenney, *General Kenney Reports,* pp. 374–375.

9. Ibid., pp. 380–381.

10. Smith, *Philippines,* pp. 16–17.

11. Krueger, *From Down Under,* p. 59.

12. Drea, *Ultra,* p. 113.

13. Morison, *New Guinea,* Appendix I, pp. 404–406.

14. Ibid., pp. 68–69.

15. Smith, *Philippines,* pp. 107–109.

16. Ibid., pp. 53–55.

17. Memoir of Lieutenant Colonel Roger Heller, Oakland, Calif., p. 12.

18. Ibid., p. 11.

19. Robert Eichelberger, *Our Jungle Road to Tokyo* (New York: Viking, 1950), p. 107; James, p. 452.

20. Smith, *Philippines,* pp. 64–68.

21. Ibid., pp. 70–72; and McCartney, *The Jungleers,* pp. 78–80.

22. Eichelberger, *Jungle Road,* p. 114.

23. Morison, *New Guinea,* p. 85.

24. Smith, *Philippines,* pp. 73–76.

25. Ibid., pp. 83, 76–77.

26. Ibid., pp. 101–102.

27. Craven and Cate, *The Army Air Forces,* p. 610.

28. Mary E. Condon-Rall and Albert Cowdrey, *United States Army in World War II, Medical Service in the War Against Japan* (Washington, D.C.: Center of Military History, 1998), pp. 258–259.

29. Eichelberger, *Jungle Road,* pp. 113–114.

CHAPTER 11: THE BOMBER LINE ADVANCES:
WAKDE AND LONE TREE HILL

1. James, *Years of MacArthur,* pp. 455–456.

2. Krueger, *From Down Under,* pp. 81–82.

3. Ibid., pp. 82–84.

4. Craven and Cate, *The Army Air Forces,* pp. 625–626.

5. Smith, *Philippines,* pp. 219–220.

6. Morison, *New Guinea,* pp. 99–101.

7. Smith, *Philippines,* pp. 224–231.

8. Ibid., p. 232.

9. Anthony Arthur, *Bushmasters: America's Jungle Warriors of World War II* (New York: St. Martin's Press, 1987), p. 103.

10. Smith, *Philippines,* p. 244.

11. Ibid., pp. 247–249.

12. Krueger, *From Down Under,* p. 89.

13. Arthur, *Bushmasters,* p. 127.

14. Smith, *Philippines,* pp. 254–255.

15. Arthur, *Bushmasters,* pp. 132–133.

16. Ibid., pp. 142–146; Smith, *Philippines,* pp. 257–258.

17. Smith, *Philippines,* p. 259.

18. Ibid.

19. Krueger, *From Down Under,* p. 90.

20. Smith, *Philippines,* p. 262.

21. Ibid., pp. 267–271.

22. Ibid., p. 275.

23. Ibid., pp. 275–277.

CHAPTER 12: BLOODY BIAK

1. Drea, *Ultra,* pp. 135–136.

2. Ibid., p. 135.

3. Ibid.

4. Ibid., p. 136.

5. Ibid.

6. Details of the Biak operation are in Alamo Force Operations Report, and Hurricane Task Force Operations Report, National Archives, College Park, Md. For a short account, particularly on the relief of General Fuller, see Harry Gailey, "MacArthur, Fuller and the Biak Episode" in Judith Bellafaire (ed.), *The U.S. Army in World War II* (Washington, D.C.: Center of Military History, 1998), pp. 303–315.

7. Morison, *New Guinea,* p. 110.

8. Craven and Cate, *The Army Air Forces,* p. 634.

9. McCartney, *The Jungleers,* pp. 103–106.

10. James, *Years of MacArthur,* p. 459.

11. Radio message, MacArthur to Krueger, May 28, 1944, MMA, Box 14, Folder 3, RG 4.

12. Krueger, *From Down Under,* p. 95.

13. McCartney, *The Jungleers,* p. 107.

14. Ibid., pp. 107–112; Krueger, *From Down Under,* p. 99.

15. Craven and Cate, *The Army Air Forces,* p. 630.

16. Morison, *New Guinea,* pp. 119–133.

17. McCartney, *The Jungleers,* pp. 114–116.

18. MacArthur to Comdr. of Alamo Force, June 5, 1944, MMA, Box 14, Folder 3, RG 4.

19. CG Alamo Force to CNC SWPA, June 5, 1944, MMA, Box 14, Folder 3, RG 4.

20. Letter, Krueger to MacArthur, June 8, 1944, Box 14, Folder 3, RG 4.

21. Eyes alone dispatch, MacArthur to CG Alamo Force, June 14, 1944, Box 14, Folder 3, RG 4.

22. Cited in Luvaas, *Dear Miss Em,* p. 126.

23. Ibid., p. 143.

24. Eichelberger, *Jungle Road,* p. 138.

25. CG Alamo Force to GHQ, June 16, 1944, and MacArthur to CG Alamo Force, June 16, 1944, MMA, Box 14, Folder 3, RG 4.

26. Cited in Smith, *Philippines,* p. 345.

27. Taaffe, p. 168; *MacArthur's Jungle War,* Smith, *Philippines,* p. 344.

28. Eichelberger, *Jungle Road,* p. 144.

29. Profile drawings of sumps are in McCartney, *The Jungleers,* p. 122.

30. Smith, *Philippines,* p. 374.

31. Ibid., p. 382.

32. Ibid., pp. 382–383.

33. Ibid., p. 389.

34. Ibid., pp. 389–391.

35. Ibid., p. 392.

36. Craven and Cate, *The Army Air Forces,* pp. 642–645.

37. Smith, *Philippines,* pp. 93–95.

CHAPTER 13: FINAL CONQUESTS: DRINIUMOR RIVER, NOEMFOOR, AND SANSAPOR

1. Marshall to MacArthur, June 11, 1944, MMA, RG 4, Box 17, Folder 1, p. II.

2. Edward J. Drea, *Leavenworth Papers No. 9, Defending the Driniumor: Covering Force Operations in New Guinea, 1944* (Fort Leavenworth, Kans.: Combat Studies Institute, 1984), pp. 17–18.

3. H. W. Blakeley, *The 32d Infantry Division in World War II* (Madison, Wis.: 32d Infantry Division History Commission, n.d.), p. 154.

4. Ibid., pp. 155–157.

5. Smith, *Philippines,* pp. 138–140.

6. Drea, *Driniumor,* pp. 26–28.

7. MacArthur, *Reminiscences,* p. 211.

8. Drea, *Driniumor,* pp. 74–79.

9. Smith, *Philippines,* pp. 155–158.

10. Drea, *Driniumor,* pp. 105–109.

11. Smith, *Philippines,* pp. 188–205.

12. Drea, *Driniumor,* pp. 122–132.

13. Taaffe, *MacArthur's Jungle War,* p. 208.

14. Krueger, *From Down Under,* pp. 106–107.

15. Smith, *Philippines,* p. 398.

16. Krueger, *From Down Under,* p. 108.

17. Ibid., p. 109.

18. Craven and Cate, *The Army Air Forces,* p. 657.

19. Smith, *Philippines,* pp. 403, 406–407.

20. Ibid., pp. 408–411.

21. Craven and Cate, *The Army Air Forces,* p. 659; ibid., pp. 415–416.

22. Smith, *Philippines,* pp. 417–418.

23. Ibid., pp. 419–421.

24. Craven and Cate, *The Army Air Forces,* pp. 660–661.

25. Smith, *Philippines,* pp. 427–428.

26. Morison, *New Guinea,* p. 141.

27. Smith, *Philippines,* p. 444.

28. Morison, *New Guinea,* pp. 142–144; ibid., pp. 440–442.

29. Smith, *Philippines,* pp. 443–445.

30. Condon-Rall, *Medical Service,* p. 217.

31. Craven and Cate, *The Army Air Forces,* p. 669.

BIBLIOGRAPHY

ARCHIVES

The major archives for the New Guinea Campaign are the Australian War Memorial, Canberra, Australia; National Archives, College Park, Maryland; Marine Corps and Naval Archives, Washington, D. C.; and MacArthur Memorial Archives, Norfolk, Virginia.

OFFICIAL HISTORIES, INTERVIEWS, AND SECONDARY ACCOUNTS

Aitken, E. F. *The Story of the 2/2nd Australian Pioneer Battalion.* Melbourne, Australia: 2/2nd Pioneer Battalion Association, 1953.

Arthur, Anthony. *Bushmasters: America's Jungle Warriors of World War II.* New York: St. Martin's Press, 1987.

Barbey, Daniel. *MacArthur's Amphibious Navy: Seventh Amphibious Force Operations, 1943–1945.* Annapolis, Md.: U.S. Naval Institute, 1969.

Bergerud, Eric. *Touched with Fire: The Land War in the South Pacific.* New York: Penguin Books, 1997.

Blakeley, H. W. *The 32d Infantry Division in World War II.* Madison, Wis.: History Commission, 1945.

Buell, Thomas B. *Master of Sea Power: A Biography of Fleet Admiral Ernest J. King.* Boston: Little, Brown & Co., 1980.

Buggy, Hugh. *Pacific Victory: A Short History of Australia's Part in the War Against Japan.* Canberra, Australia: Ministry of Information, n.d.

Churchill, Winston. *The Second World War.* Vol. 4, *The Hinge of Fate.* New York: Houghton Mifflin & Co., 1950.

Coletta, Paolo E. "Daniel Barbey: Amphibious Warfare Expert." In *We Shall Return! MacArthur's Commanders and the Defeat of Japan, 1942–1945,* ed. by William Leary. Lexington, Ky.: University Press of Kentucky, 1988.

Condon-Rall, Mary Ellen and Albert Cowdrey. *United States Army in World War II. The Medical Department: Medical Service in the War Against Japan.* Washington, D.C.: Center of Military History, 1998.

Connaughton, Richard. *Shrouded Secrets: Japan's War on Mainland Australia, 1942–1944.* London: Brassey's, 1994.

Craven, Wesley Frank, and James Lea Cate. *The Army Air Forces in World War II.* Vol. 4, *The Pacific: Guadalcanal to Saipan.* Chicago: University of Chicago Press, 1964.

Davis, Burke. *Marine, The Life of Chesty Puller.* New York: Bantam Books, 1962.

Dexter, David. *Australia in the War of 1939–1945 (Army Series).* Vol. 5, *The New Guinea Offensives.* Canberra, Australia: Australian War Memorial, 1961.

Drea, Edward J. *Leavenworth Papers, Defending the Driniumor: Covering Force Operations in New Guinea, 1944.* Fort Leavenworth, Kans.: Combat Studies Institute, 1984.

———. *MacArthur's Ultra: Codebreaking and the War Against Japan, 1942–1945.* Lawrence, Kans.: University Press of Kansas, 1992.

Dull, Paul S. *A Battle History of the Imperial Japanese Navy (1941–1945).* Annapolis, Md.: Naval Institute Press, 1978.

Eichelberger, Robert L. *Our Jungle Road to Tokyo.* New York: Viking Press, 1950.

Gailey, Harry A. *Bougainville, 1943–1945.* Lexington, Ky.: University Press of Kentucky, 1991.

———. "MacArthur, Fuller and the Biak Episode." In *The U.S. Army in World War II,* ed. by Judith Bellafaire. Washington, D.C.: Center of Military History, 1998.

———. *MacArthur Strikes Back, Decision at Buna: New Guinea, 1942–1943.* Novato, Calif.: Presidio Press, 2000.

———. *The War in the Pacific: From Pearl Harbor to Tokyo Bay.* Novato, Calif.: Presidio Press, 1995.

Gill, G. Hermon. *Australia in the War of 1939–1945 (Navy Series): Royal Australian Navy, 1942–1945.* Canberra, Australia: Australian War Memorial, 1968.

Gillison, Douglas. *Australia in the War of 1939–1945 (Air Series): Royal Australian Air Force, 1939–1942.* Canberra, Australia: Australian War Memorial, 1962.

Goldstein, Donald M. "Ennis Whitehead: Aerial Tactician." In *We Shall Return! MacArthur's Commanders and the Defeat of Japan, 1942–1945,* ed. by William Leary. Lexington, Ky.: University Press of Kentucky, 1988.

Griffith, Thomas E., Jr. *MacArthur's Airman: General George C. Kenney and the War in the Southwest Pacific.* Lawrence, Kans.: University Press of Kansas, 1998.

Hammel, Eric. *Munda Trail: Turning the Tide Against Japan.* New York: Orion Books, 1989.

Hasluck, Paul. *Australia in the War of 1939–1945: The Government and the People.* Canberra, Australia: Australian War Memorial, 1970.

Hayashi, Saburo, and Aluin Cook. *Kogun: The Japanese Army in the Pacific War.* Quantico, Va.: Marine Corps Association, 1959.

Hetherington, John. *Blamey: The Biography of Field-Marshal Sir Thomas Blamey.* Melbourne, Australia: F. W. Cheshire, 1954.

Horner, D. M. *Australia in the War of 1939–1945: High Command, Australia and Allied Strategy.* Sydney: George Allen and Unwin, 1982.

———. "Blamey and MacArthur: The Problem of Coalition Warfare." In *We Shall Return! MacArthur's Commanders and the Defeat of Japan, 1942–1945,* ed. by William Leary. Lexington, Ky.: University Press of Kentucky, 1988.

———. *Blamey, The Commander in Chief.* St. Leonards, Australia: Allen and Unwin, 1998.

———. *Working Paper 28, Australia and Allied Intelligence in the Pacific in the Second World War.* Canberra, Australia: Australian National University, 1980.

James, D. Clayton. *The Years of MacArthur.* Vol. 2, *1941–1945.* Boston: Houghton Mifflin, 1975.

Kenney, George C. *General Kenney Reports.* Washington, D.C.: Office of Air Force History, 1987.

Krueger, Walter. *From Down Under to Nippon.* Washington, D.C.: Zenger Publishing Co., 1979.

Larrabee, Eric. *Commander in Chief.* New York: Harper & Row, 1987.

Leary, William M. (ed.). *We Shall Return! MacArthur's Commanders and the Defeat of Japan, 1942–1945.* Lexington, Ky.: University Press of Kentucky, 1988.

———. "Walter Krueger: MacArthur's Fighting General." In ibid.

Long, Gavin. *MacArthur as a Military Commander.* London: B. T. Batsford, 1969.

Luvaas, Jay (ed.). *Dear Miss Em: General Eichelberger's War in the Pacific, 1942–1945.* Westport, Conn.: Greenwood Press, 1972.

MacArthur, Douglas. *Reminiscences.* Greenwich, Conn.: Crest Books, 1965.

Manchester, William. *American Caesar: Douglas MacArthur, 1880–1964.* New York: Dell Books, 1978.

McCarthy, Dudley. *Australia in the War of 1939–1945 (Army Series): South-West Pacific Area—First Year, Kokoda to Wau.* Canberra, Australia: Australian War Memorial, 1959.

McCartney, William F. *The Jungleers: A History of the 41st Infantry Division.* Washington, D.C.: Infantry Journal Press, 1948.

Middlebrook, Garrett. *Air Combat at 20 Feet.* Fort Worth, Tex.: Global Group, 1989.

Miller, Francis T. *History of World War II.* Philadelphia: Universal Book and Bible House, 1945.

Milner, Samuel. *The United States Army in World War II, the War in the Pacific: Victory in Papua.* Washington, D.C.: Office of the Chief of Military History, 1957.

Morison, Samuel Eliot. *History of United States Naval Operations in World War II.* Vol. 6, *Breaking the Bismarcks Barrier, 22 July 1942–1 May 1944.* Boston: Little, Brown & Co., 1950.

————. *History of United States Naval Operations in World War II,* Vol. 7, *New Guinea and the Marianas, March 1944–August 1944.* Boston: Little, Brown & Co., 1962.

Morton, Louis. *The U.S. Army in World War II, Strategy & Command: The First Two Years.* Washington, D.C.: Office of the Chief of Military History, 1962.

Odgers, George. *Australia in the War of 1939–1945 (Air Series): Air War Against Japan, 1943–1945.* Canberra, Australia: Australian War Memorial, 1963.

Pogue, Forrest C. *George C. Marshall: Organizer of Victory.* New York: Viking Press, 1973.

Potter, E. B. *Bull Halsey.* Annapolis, Md.: Naval Institute Press, 1985.

————. *Nimitz.* Annapolis, Md.: Naval Institute Press, 1976.

Rettell, Paul. *A Soldier's True Story.* Bradenton, Fla.: privately printed, 1995.

Robertson, John, and John McCarthy. *Australian War Strategy, 1939–1945: A Documentary History.* St. Lucia, Australia: University of Queensland Press, 1985.

Rogers, Paul P. *The Bitter Years, MacArthur and Sutherland.* New York: Praeger, 1990.

Rottman, Gordon L. *World War II, Pacific Island Guide: A Geo-Military Study.* Westport, Conn.: Greenwood Press, 2002.

Ryan, Peter. *Fear Drive My Feet.* Melbourne, Australia: Melbourne University Press, 1959.

Serle, R. P. (ed.). *The Second Twenty-fourth Australian Infantry Battalion of the 9th Australian Division.* Brisbane, Australia: Jacaranda Press, 1963.

Shaw, Henry I., Jr., and Douglas Kane. *History of U.S. Marine Corps Operations in World War II.* Vol. 2, *Isolation of Rabaul.* Washington, D.C.: Historical Branch, U.S. Marine Corps, 1963.

Smith, Robert Ross. *The United States Army in World War II, The War in the Pacific: The Approach to the Philippines.* Washington, D.C.: Center of Military History, 1996.

Spector, Ronald. *Eagle Against the Sun.* New York: Free Press, 1985.

Stanton, Shelby L. *World War II Order of Battle.* New York: Galahad Books, 1991.

Taaffe, Stephen R. *MacArthur's Jungle War: The 1944 New Guinea Campaign.* Lawrence, Kans.: University Press of Kansas, 1998.

Taylor, Michael J. H. (ed.). *Jane's American Fighting Aircraft of the 20th Century.* New York: Modern Publishing, 1995.

United States Strategic Bombing Survey (Pacific). *The Allied Campaign Against Rabaul.* Washington, D.C.: Naval Analysis Division, 1946.

Walker, Allan S. *Australia in the War of 1939–1945: The Island Campaigns.* Canberra, Australia: Australian War Memorial, 1962.

Wheeler, Gerald. *Kinkaid of the Seventh Fleet.* Washington, D.C.: Naval Historical Center, 1995.

Wheeler, Richard. *A Special Valor*. New York: Harper and Row, 1983.

Whitney, Courtney. *MacArthur: His Rendezvous with History*. New York: Knopf, 1964.

Willoughby, Charles A., and John Chamberlain. *MacArthur: 1941–1951*. New York: McGraw-Hill, 1954.

Wright, B. C. *The 1st Cavalry Division in World War II*. Tokyo: Tappan Printers, 1947.

INDEX

ABOUT THE AUTHOR

The late HARRY A. GAILEY was an emeritus professor of history at San Jose State University and the author of twenty books, the most recent of which include *MacArthur Strikes Back, The War in the Pacific,* and *The Liberation of Guam.*